A More Beautiful and Terrible History

A More Beautiful and Terrible History

THE USES AND MISUSES OF CIVIL RIGHTS HISTORY

JEANNE THEOHARIS

BEACON PRESS
BOSTON

BEACON PRESS
Boston, Massachusetts
www.beacon.org

Beacon Press books
are published under the auspices of
the Unitarian Universalist Association of Congregations.

21 20 19   8 7 6 5 4

This book is printed on acid-free paper that meets the uncoated paper
ANSI/NISO specifications for permanence as revised in 1992.

Text design and composition by Kim Arney

Excerpts from the poem "A Dead Man's Dream,"
by Carl Wendell Hines Jr., are reprinted here by permission.

Library of Congress Cataloging-in-Publication Data

Names: Theoharis, Jeanne, author.
Title: A more beautiful and terrible history : the uses and misuses
of civil rights history / Jeanne Theoharis.
Description: Boston : Beacon Press, 2018. | Includes
bibliographical references and index.
Identifiers: LCCN 2017030979 (print) | LCCN 2017052365 (ebook) |
ISBN 9780807075883 (e-book) | ISBN 9780807075876 (hardcover : alk. paper)
Subjects: LCSH: African Americans—Civil rights—History—20th century. |
African Americans—Civil rights—Historiography. | Civil rights movements—
United States—History—20th century. | Civil rights movements—United States—
Historiography. | United States—Race relations—History—20th century. |
United States—Race relations—Historiography.
Classification: LCC E185.61 (ebook) | LCC E185.61 .T44 2018 (print) |
DDC 323.1196/0730904—dc23
LC record available at https://lccn.loc.gov/2017030979

*To Julian Bond, who taught me how to tell
this story and carry this history forward*

*And to my parents, Nancy and Athan Theoharis,
for their commitment to and insistence on
justice, truth-telling, and perseverance*

Contents

A Dream Diluted and Distorted

It's a system of power that is always deciding in the name of humanity who deserves to be remembered and who deserves to be forgotten. . . . We are much more than we are told. We are much more beautiful.

—Eduardo Galeano[1]

American history is longer, larger, more various, more beautiful, and more terrible than anything anyone has ever said about it.

—James Baldwin, "A Talk to Teachers"[2]

BY THE TURN OF THE MILLENNIUM, the history of the civil rights movement had become a national story. When asked to name a "most famous American" other than a president "from Columbus to today," high school students most often chose Martin Luther King Jr. and Rosa Parks.[3] Students chose two freedom fighters who in life had challenged the racial injustice at the heart of American society and who had often been treated as "un-American" for doing so. Now the civil rights movement had come to embody American grit, courage, and resolve, and these two activists could be invoked as the country's most famous emblems.

Arguably beginning when President Ronald Reagan signed the bill in 1983 to make the third Monday of January a federal holiday for Martin Luther King Jr., the political uses of memorializing the movement took on heightened possibility as a national narrative. Fifteen years of opposition to the holiday gave way to recognizing its political utility. The civil rights movement became a way for the nation to feel good about its progress— and King's legacy became enshrined in his "dream speech." His popularity expanded. By 1987, 76 percent of Americans held a favorable opinion of the civil rights leader, almost the reverse of his popularity at the end of his life (only 28 percent of Americans had a favorable opinion of him in 1966).[4] President after president, from Reagan to Bush to Clinton to Obama, hailed King's "dream" in their tributes to him. With these national stamps of approval, the civil rights leader's broader commitments to challenging the "giant triplets of racism, extreme materialism, and militarism" and his legacy of sustained struggle shrank further into the background.[5]

At the same time, memorials to the civil rights movement became national events—from President Bill Clinton's trip to Little Rock for the fortieth anniversary of the Little Rock Nine's desegregation of Central High School, to Congress's decision to have Rosa Parks's coffin lie in honor in the Capitol, to the First Family's trip to Selma, Alabama, on the fiftieth anniversary of the Selma-to-Montgomery march. These national events honored not just the work of the civil rights activists but the advancement of the nation itself. They marked the Americanness of the civil rights struggle, and held up the power of US democracy and progress to the world.

Political leaders, pundits, and citizens came to see and tell the story of the modern civil rights movement as one of progress and national redemption.[6] Jim Crow was framed as a horrible Southern relic, and the movement to unseat it became a powerful tale of courageous Americans defeating a long-ago evil. Activists from Paul Robeson to Malcolm X—who had once been deemed national security threats—showed up on postage stamps. A movement that had challenged the very fabric of US politics and society was turned into one that demonstrated how great and expansive the country was—a story of individual bravery, natural evolution, and the long march to "a more perfect union."

A story that should have reflected the immense injustices at the nation's core and the enormous lengths people had gone to attack them had become a flattering mirror. The popular history of the civil rights movement now served as testament to the power of American democracy. This framing was appealing—simultaneously sober about the history of racism, lionizing of Black courage, celebratory of American progress, and strategic in masking (and at times justifying) current inequities. This history as national progress naturalized the civil rights movement as an almost inevitable aspect of American democracy rather than as the outcome of

Black organization and intrepid witness. It suggested racism derived from individual sin rather than from national structure—and that the strength of American values, rather than the staggering challenge of a portion of its citizens, led to its change.[7] The movement had largely washed away the sins of the nation, and America's race problem could be laid to rest with a statue in the Capitol.

In the process, politicians and others shrank the progressive, expansive, challenging vision of the modern Black freedom struggle into something more passive, individualistic, and privatized—a dream diluted and distorted. The celebration of the movement became a way to avoid acknowledging the "enormous gap between [America's] practices and its professions," as historian John Hope Franklin had explained.[8] And it became a way to take the beauty and power away from one of the most successful social movements of the twentieth century and the vision it offers us for today.

The recounting of national histories is never separate from present-day politics. What of the past is remembered, celebrated, and mourned is at the core of national identity—and the process of what is told and not told is often a function of power. The act of making an historical tribute necessarily resolves it and fixes it in time and place. As anthropologist Michel-Rolph Trouillot observes, the task of commemoration "help[s] to create, modify or sanction the public meanings attached to historical events deemed worthy of mass celebration . . . to create a past that seems both more real and more elementary."[9] The use of the word "history" itself is slippery, Trouillot reminds us: "In vernacular use, history means both the facts of the matter and a narrative of those facts, both 'what happened' and 'that which is said to have happened.'"[10] Thus, reflection on popular uses of history is crucial as "we move closer to an era when professional historians will have to position themselves more clearly within the present, lest politicians, magnates, or ethnic leaders alone write history for them."[11] Memorials in their essence are for the dead, for events long since over. And the task of honoring can also be a form of stripping and silencing.[12]

Racial injustice is America's original sin and deepest silence.[13] The ways the country came to honor the civil rights movement were not simply about paying tribute to these courageous acts and individuals in the past but also about sanctioning what will—and will not be—faced about the nation's history and present. Explained former Birmingham mayor David Vann: "The best way to put your bad images to rest is to declare them history and put them in a museum."[14] So, paradoxically, the ways the nation has memorialized the civil rights movement has become a way to maintain such silences. The history of American racism had become just that . . . history. While these tributes honored the movement, they simultaneously depoliticized the scope of the struggle, distorted the work of the activists honored, demonized Black anger, and obscured ongoing calls for racial justice through a celebration of a nearly postracial, self-correcting America.

No better proof of the country's progress was the election and presidency of Barack Obama. Movement symbolism was highlighted throughout the 2008 election, both by the Obama campaign itself and by others. Candidate Obama accepted the Democratic nomination for president on August 28, 2008—the forty-fourth anniversary of the March on Washington.[15] Posters decorated churches and community centers, telephone poles and schools, delineating this historical progression: "Rosa sat so Martin could walk. Martin walked so Obama could run. Obama ran so our children could fly." By voting for him, individuals could help realize the dream. Many trumpeted Obama's victory as the culmination of the civil rights movement and a testament to a "postracial America"—an America that had largely moved past its history of racism. Even those who did not share such a rosy view of American progress were awed by the immensity of seeing the election of a Black man to the presidency of the United States. Given the momentous nature of his victory, referencing the history of the movement became more central to the presidency of Barack Obama than that of any of his predecessors—and the president himself, his supporters, and many commentators regularly appealed to its legacy.

And the public who elected him rejoiced in it. Used as a way to bask in our own association with this grand historical line, the civil rights movement had become our national redemption song. The election of President Obama made many of his supporters feel like *we had overcome*. It had delivered us. And therein lay the danger—rather than a rung on a steep ladder, the election became the zenith, the top of that climb, where all who wished could take credit for the triumph.

Many people, President Obama included, didn't subscribe to this postracial idea. Indeed, he explicitly said that the United States was *not* a postracial society. But he did subscribe to the idea that we were almost there. At the historic Brown Chapel in Selma, Alabama, during the campaign in 2007, he said the civil rights generation "took us 90 percent of the way there, but we still got that 10 percent in order to cross over to the other side."[16] Just 10 percent—not a fundamental, woven-into-our-institutions racism requiring policy and institutional transformation but a remnant racism. And therein lay the seduction of the almost-there.

To support this almost-there, 10-percent-to-go idea, the version of the movement promoted in these memorials and public tributes distorted and diminished the history of the period. The genius of this almost-there frame was that it acknowledged the history of racism but then simultaneously claimed that America had now largely moved past it. It honored the role of courageous struggle but then asserted that we didn't necessarily need such civil disobedience anymore (and, in fact, contemporary protesters were often treated as an affront to King's legacy).

A narrative of dreamy heroes and accidental heroines, the story was narrowed to buses and lunch counters and Southern redneck violence. It became a key way that Americans publicly acknowledged the country's legacy of racial injustice—in the past—where the death-defying courage and sacrifices of these heroes and heroines vanquished it, as opposed to in the present, where our own resolve might be needed as well. And it became a way the nation celebrated its own identity; President Obama at the fiftieth anniversary of the Selma-to-Montgomery march characterized the civil rights movement as a "manifestation of a creed written into our founding documents."[17]

This frame was advanced not just by liberals; conservatives joined in. In the second Republican presidential debate in 2015, contenders Marco Rubio, Ted Cruz, and Donald Trump all named Rosa Parks as *the* woman they would chose for the ten-dollar bill. Weeks before the 2016 election, Trump lawyer Michael Cohen tweeted a photo of Trump, Muhammad Ali, and Rosa Parks to demonstrate that candidate Trump was "a man for ALL people!" When controversy over President Trump's nomination of Jeff Sessions for attorney general sparked massive controversy, supporters of Sessions detailed his long embrace of Rosa Parks. And when he met with the pope on his first foreign trip, in May 2017, Trump gave him a first-edition set of Martin Luther King Jr.'s writings and a piece of granite from the King memorial sculpture in Washington, DC.[18]

Invoking the civil rights movement had become a clever suit to assert one's enlightened bona fides. It crossed party and ideology. Simply everyone was doing it. In the process, these inspirational stories, with their distortions, embellishments, and omissions, had taken on the power of a national fable. This fable became a new way to paper over the long history of struggle and enduring racial injustice in the United States today. With their element of self-congratulation, these often bipartisan acts of memorialization whitewashed the history of the movement, becoming a veil to obscure enduring racial inequality, a tool to chastise contemporary protest, and a shield to charges of indifference and inaction.

While seemingly bestowing great honor on freedom fighters of old, this national mythologizing of the civil rights movement also took the movement away from everyday people, from community leaders and young activists and elder freedom fighters seeking to understand where the country was and how to build movements today. It turned it into scratchy church clothes, admirable but uncomfortable, and not meant for daily use but appreciation from afar. The iconization of King and Parks and the erasure of many other leaders and participants seemed to suggest that Americans, particularly young people of color today, could not do what these civil rights heroes and heroines did. At a time when new movements for racial and economic justice have emerged on the national scene, this fable of the movement became a potent obstacle and bludgeon used to diminish contemporary efforts, making today's activists seem inappropriate troublemakers who lacked the gravitas of yesterday's activists and who just weren't going about it the right way.

The public spectacle of these memorials at times provides a shield for present-day action and inaction, a live-action "split screen": a coterie of political leaders dedicating the Rosa Parks statue on the day the Supreme Court heard arguments in *Shelby County v. Holder* (the suit that successfully challenged part of the Voting Rights Act); President Trump taking Martin Luther King's writings as a gift to Pope Francis in the same week he introduced a budget that gutted many of the social programs these freedom fighters had won. The "split screen" was not simply ironic; it was useful in rendering contemporary issues and injustices as far different from the ones these movements fought against.

During President Obama's second term, a new movement brewing over years blossomed onto the national scene. Growing outrage over the "new Jim Crow,"[19] the execution of Troy Davis, the killing of Trayvon Martin and subsequent acquittal of George Zimmerman, the incarceration of Marissa Alexander, the police killing of Michael Brown and the movement on the streets of Ferguson that subsequently erupted, and the death in custody of Sandra Bland and the "Say Her Name" campaign galvanized into what has become known as Black Lives Matter (BLM). Alongside these were courageous struggles for immigrant and indigenous rights, in which new generations of Latinx and Native Americans joined elders to carry the fight in new directions, from United We Dream, undocumented student organizing, and #Not1More (opposing deportations) movements to Standing Rock and #NoDAPL (No Dakota Access Pipeline).

For many participants and longtime activists, including Harry Belafonte and many former members of the Student Nonviolent Coordinating Committee, the continuities of struggle were readily apparent. But this national fable of the civil rights movement became a weapon some used against these new movements for justice, as comparison after comparison was made to the civil rights movement to find BLM wanting. Across the political spectrum, from presidential candidate Mike Huckabee to Reverend Barbara Reynolds to Atlanta mayor Kasim Reed, many made comparisons with the civil rights movement to critique and chastise new movements for justice, holding up the civil rights movement as the "right" way to do it and Black Lives Matter as the wrong way. In advance of the grand jury verdict in Ferguson, former Republican presidential candidate and Arkansas governor Huckabee wrote a blog post instructing the protesters in Ferguson to be more like Martin Luther King Jr. The Reverend Barbara Reynolds, herself part of the civil rights movement, took to the pages of the *Washington Post* to draw a deep distinction:

> Many in my crowd admire the cause and courage of these young activists but fundamentally disagree with their approach. Trained in the tradition of Martin Luther King Jr., we were nonviolent activists who won hearts by conveying respectability and changed laws by delivering a message of love and unity. BLM seems intent on rejecting our proven methods.[20]

In July 2016, Atlanta mayor Kasim Reed invoked King's spirit and the power of free speech but then explained to reporters the large police presence at demonstrations following police killings of Alton Sterling and Philando Castile: "Dr. King would never take a highway."[21] There is something deeply ahistorical and ironic to call for voices muted, tactics softened, disruption avoided, and more honorable spokesmen located, when these very criticisms were lobbed at the civil rights movement as well. And there is something convenient, too—a way of justifying re-move, by making it seem as if people would join movements such as BLM if the upstanding likes of Rosa Parks and Martin Luther King were part of it, but these new movements were just going about it the wrong way. Looking more deeply into the Black freedom struggle challenges such misuses of civil rights history and reveals the politics behind this mythmaking.

Public tributes and invocations of the movement provide lessons on the past to secure our national identity in the present.[22] The fable of the civil rights movement traffics in an "epistemology of ignorance," as phi-losopher Charles Mills has explained it, selective and distorted in what is seen and remembered. *"White misunderstanding, misrepresentation, evasion and self deception on matters of race* are among the most perva-sive mental phenomena of the past few hundred years," Mills writes. "And these phenomena are in no way *accidental,* but *prescribed* . . . which re-quires a certain schedule of structured blindnesses and opacities in order to establish and maintain the white polity."[23] These stories flatter us as a country, minimizing our failings and marking our progress as inexorable, as opposed to deeply contested and often eroded.

This book thus takes up the political uses and radical possibilities of civil rights history in twenty-first-century America. Given the centrality and misuse of civil rights history in current American politics, a consid-ered analysis is urgently needed to grapple with the "structured blind-nesses" in this national fable—to see the ways the stories they tell and the elements they leave out and distort are perilous for our present. These civil rights mis-histories befuddle us. Inspiring and powerful, they leave us in our feelings of sadness, surprise, awe, and guilt, and in doing so, help to obscure what the movement entailed, how it happened, what it stood for, and how it challenges us today. By diminishing the substance and scope of American racism and what the movement actually involved, these render-ings work to maintain current injustice, at times chastising contemporary protesters in ways similar to the ways civil rights activists were demonized, and blind us to how we might do it again.

They are not the histories we need. As a nation, we need fuller histories—uncomfortable, sobering histories—that hold a mirror to the nation's past and offer far-reaching lessons for seeing the injustices of our current moment and the task of justice today. "The historian's task," as British historian Tony Judt reminds, "is to tell what is almost always an uncomfortable story and explain why the discomfort is part of the truth we need to live well and live properly. A well-organized society is one in which we know the truth about ourselves collectively, not one in which we tell pleasant lies about ourselves."[24] To know the truth about ourselves collectively reveals the immensity and ongoing nature of the modern Black freedom struggle, the injustices that continue in many of our current policies, and the problematic assumptions that support them.

The modern Black freedom struggle remains one of the most important examples of the power of ordinary people to change the course of the nation. But the popular stories we get impoverish our ability to see how change happens. A more expansive history transforms how we imagine what a movement looks like, sounds like, and pushes for, and understand how it is received and often reviled. It shows us that leadership, vision, steadfastness, and courage came in many forms, as did the opposition to it. Giving us necessary tools for understanding the past, it suggests lessons for long-distance runners in the struggle for racial and social justice today.

This book, in certain ways, expands on my last. *The Rebellious Life of Mrs. Rosa Parks* opened with an analysis of Rosa Parks's funeral. In October 2005, Parks became the first woman and second African American to lie in honor at the US Capitol.[25] But, as I argued in the book's introduction, the congressional and presidential stampede to honor her could not be separated from the tragedy of Hurricane Katrina two months earlier and the growing national outrage about the federal government's inaction and negligence. Searing, persistent racial and social inequality had pierced national and media consciousness in the aftermath of the storm, and Rosa Parks's coffin on display at the Capitol became a way to paper over those more unsettling images from New Orleans. Resurrected in the Capitol as a national saint, this honor for Parks became a way to lay the nation's history of racial injustice to rest—a gross distortion of what the lifelong freedom fighter had believed. This, however, necessitated a distorted, gendered image of a quiet, tired Parks confined to the bus on that long-ago December evening—an "accidental" heroine rather than a long-standing activist whose belief in the need for continuing struggle lasted until her death.

The outpouring of interest in *The Rebellious Life of Mrs. Rosa Parks* and in numerous other recently published civil rights histories suggest that many Americans hunger not only for a more substantive civil rights history but also for a critical analysis of the ways these popular fables are wielded in the present. As I have traveled around the country, it has become clear to me how much people crave analyses of the political uses of these fables and wish to know *why* we get the histories we get and what the stakes are in turning Rosa Parks into a quiet, meek, children's book character. There is a deep desire to understand the process by which she, and by extension the movement, are honored and simultaneously distorted in ways that diminish her legacy, the work of other activists, and the movement's disruptive, far-reaching challenge.

At the same time, I have seen a profound hunger for a fuller history of the modern Black freedom struggle—an abiding desire for a more accurate accounting of how it happened, to understand the long history of racial struggle in this country and *how* we might continue to build struggles for justice today. Over and over, I have heard people say that they suspected that there was more to the story; they describe feeling uneasy with popular accounts of the movement but didn't have the knowledge to upend them. Over and over, from fast-food workers in the Fight for $15 to activists of the Moral Mondays movement to BLM organizers across the country, I have heard how these fuller histories of Rosa Parks and the civil rights movement are more challenging and empowering for where we are today, sustaining community organizers in their work, identifying the forces of injustice more fully, and furthering their imagination in the struggle for a more just society. And so this book, *A More Beautiful and Terrible History*, seeks to accomplish a related goal—to deconstruct the stories and memorials of the civil rights movement we have received and construct new knowledge and the more robust and fuller history we need for today.

Rosa Parks plays a key role in this book, as does Martin Luther King Jr. Even after spending more than a dozen years researching and speaking about Parks, I continue to be astonished by the incessant, absurd, and chilling misuses of Parks and King. These two freedom fighters have been turned into Thanksgiving parade balloons—floating above us larger than life; unthreatening, happy patriots. Asking little of us, they bob along proud of our progress.[26] King and Parks are embraced yet simultaneously stripped of their political substance and courageous steadfastness (and what their legacies demand of us today). These elaborate spectacles of honor and tribute function to distract us from the responsibility of harnessing such resolve in ourselves and from reckoning with what Parks's and King's legacies reveal about the nation and its current policies and direction. An important trove of Rosa Parks's papers is finally open at the Library of Congress, providing new vantages for examining her work and the broader history of the movement. Similarly with King: the more we look, the more we see how misused and limited our views of him have become—particularly the ways King's work in the Jim Crow North and his critique of liberal racism have been largely ignored.

Included here too is a broader cast of characters—Barbara Johns, Ruth Batson, Ellen Jackson, Marnesba Tackett, Coretta Scott King, Gloria Richardson, Ella Baker, Mae Mallory, Milton Galamison, Claudette Colvin, Mary Louise Smith, Albert Cleage, Johnnie Tillmon, Julian Bond, Dan Aldridge, Pauli Murray, Anna Arnold Hedgeman, Lawrence Bible, E. D. Nixon, Johnnie Carr. Leadership and vision took many forms and grew in many places. Each chapter returns to a moment we are familiar with— the Montgomery bus boycott, Boston's busing crisis, the Watts riot, the March on Washington—and shows it anew, in wider context with richer detail and analysis to examine the distortions and silences that have been embedded in our popular understandings. At the same time, this book introduces lesser-known struggles—Black parent battles against unequal schooling in Los Angeles and New York, the welfare rights movement of the 1960s and the Poor People's Campaign, long-standing efforts challenging the injustices of law enforcement and the criminal justice system in the decade before the bus boycott and in the years before uprisings in Watts and Detroit. By showing how much larger, more beautiful, and more terrifying the Black freedom struggle was, it seeks to return the movement to those of us who need it now—so we might see a way forward in the perilous times in which we live.

THE "PROPAGANDA OF HISTORY"

Perhaps white America needs this form of hypocrisy to survive.

—E. Franklin Frazier, on viewing *The Birth of a Nation*[27]

National histories provide narratives about the past that ennoble the present. "Writing our national history," the late historian Nathan Huggins reminds, "we do so with a master narrative in our heads that sustains our collective sense of national purpose and identity, and resonates with our most compelling myths." What is needed, Huggins argued, is to "face the deforming mirror of truth."[28]

The popular histories of the civil rights movement do just the opposite, casting a flattering mirror on the nation. While produced under very different circumstances, they have served a function similar to the popular histories of Reconstruction that developed at the turn of the twentieth century to legitimize the rise of Jim Crow America.[29] Both have become the necessary glue that binds and justifies current public policy and national identity.

The distorted histories of Reconstruction that developed in the late nineteenth century were necessary for the establishment of a segregated American polity. Promoting reconciliation and national unity, early popular historical treatments explained Reconstruction as a corrupt and misguided experiment brought on by Northern carpetbaggers and misguided Black people.[30] By portraying American slavery as a relatively benign institution in which Black people were largely content, these versions demonstrated why no further federal government intervention was needed and allowed for Southern redemption and Northern indifference. These Reconstruction mis-histories reached their national pinnacle in D. W. Griffith's 1915 award-winning film, *The Birth of a Nation*, with its portrayal of two families on opposite sides of the Civil War and its positive account of the Klan. It was the first film ever to be screened at the White House.

By depicting newly freed Black people as angry, sexually promiscuous, and dangerous people who illegitimately sought special rights, popular histories of slavery and Reconstruction cast the changes of Reconstruction as unnecessary and presented Black people as in need of control. At the same time, popular treatments were nostalgic for the good Black people of the past, who had served well and happily. Showing white people in a largely flattering light, they framed Black people as undeserving of full rights and as being responsible for their own problems, thus necessitating an end to the changes of Reconstruction. W. E. B. Du Bois, in his 1935 classic *Black Reconstruction in America*, referred to these stories as "the propaganda of history" for "giving us a false but pleasurable sense of accomplishment."[31]

So too are these mis-histories of the civil rights movement necessary at the dawn of the twenty-first century in promoting the idea of an exceptional America moving past its own racism. Though vastly different on the surface (the latter seemingly positive, the former vicious and negative), popular histories of the civil rights movement operate similarly to show why no further government intervention is needed. A tribute to a quiet heroine and a dreamy hero proves that good values and individual acts are rewarded—that once revealed, real injustice is eradicated in a democracy like America. Excessive behavior (anger and recklessness, and refusal to behave respectably or to use proper methods for expressing grievances) by a new generation of Black people is again cast as the cause of many current problems, and such behavior must be checked and challenged to maintain this noble progress. Early histories of Reconstruction advanced national reconciliation and explained why no further action from the federal government was needed, while allowing for the criminalization of Black people and promoting a cheapened labor supply. And these recent civil rights commemorations and popular renderings of the civil rights movement often do the same.

Civil rights mis-histories give us a "pleasurable sense of accomplishment," thus becoming a key linchpin in the idea of an almost postracial America. US democracy, in this version, is a self-cleaning oven, powerful, strong, and constantly self-improving; injustice is aberrational and once revealed is eliminated in a country built to move past its own mistakes. Self-cleaning ovens work by burning up everything in them; so too is history incinerated to make room for the fable. This "self-cleaning America" fable conveniently makes it seem as if the United States was destined to have a great civil rights movement, and that most people did the right thing at the time. This is a pleasurable idea, to be sure, but one that obscures a much more sobering reality: how hard and infrequent such courage was; how tenacious and steadfast activists had to be; how much pressure people exerted against the movement; and how part of that counter-resistance has been to dim and diminish the movement's goals, trajectories, and visions.

A MORE BEAUTIFUL AND TERRIBLE HISTORY

The book opens with an analysis of the "Histories We Get," tracing the development of this national fable and its uses, from the establishment of a federal holiday honoring Martin Luther King Jr. to the avalanche of popular commemorations and memorials that occurred around the Obama presidency to the ways the civil rights movement has been invoked around Black Lives Matter and the turn of the Trump presidency. I use the word *fable* purposely, because fables are tales that provide morals on how to live or ways of understanding society. While containing real heroes and villains and nuggets of fact, they are stories embellished, fabricated, and distorted for a purpose. This history we get is a fable. Distorting and obscuring the truth, what has become the national story of the civil rights movement provides ways of understanding the past that have political uses in the present.

While in much of my previous work I have used the phrase the "Black freedom struggle" because it captures the movement's ideological, regional, and temporal expansiveness, I also use the phrase the "civil rights movement" here. The national fable consciously honors the "civil rights movement," and so the task here is to explicitly show that the civil rights movement was never what is now believed about it. Therefore, I consciously use the term "civil rights movement" to insist that the heart of the struggle, its most iconic people and moments, and the breadth of its vision, leaders, strategies, struggles, and accomplishments are far different from our popular renderings of them.

The nine chapters that follow, the "Histories We Need," will examine and fill in nine key silences and distortions in the popular fable of the movement to show how our past—and present—look different by reckoning with this much fuller history of the modern Black freedom struggle. These chapters draw on my own research, particularly on Los Angeles, Boston, Detroit, and New York, and the long history of racism outside the South, and on the role of women and high school students in the movement (including new research on Rosa Parks[32]). And they build on a vast body of historical studies published over the past two decades to address the gaps in these popular notions of the civil rights movement. In many ways, this history is hidden in plain sight—an avalanche of recent research has challenged the national fable of the movement and American racism from myriad angles.[33] The fable has grown more powerful at a time when academic scholarship, which decisively repudiates it, has gotten prodigiously richer.[34] And so the task of putting these popular tales in conversation with the scholarship is more necessary today than ever.

These chapters take on many of the accepted stories of the movement to show them in a far different light. We see a decade-long movement challenging school and housing segregation and police brutality in Los Angeles before the Watts riots, which in turn reveals the willfulness of the "surprise" of public officials and journalists over Black anger. We see twenty-five years of Black struggle attacking school segregation and educational inequality in the Cradle of Liberty before "Boston's busing crisis." We see Rosa Parks not simply as the bus lady but as a lifelong criminal justice activist; Martin Luther King Jr. challenging not only Southern sheriffs but also Northern liberals; and Coretta Scott King not just as Martin's "helpmate" but as a lifelong economic justice and peace activist pushing her husband's activism in those directions. And we see that far from being acceptable, passive, or unified, the civil rights movement was unpopular, disruptive, and deeply persevering. It had a broad vision for what justice looked like and what equality would entail. Those who drove it forward were old and young, women and men, and most were labeled troublemakers for their work, not just in Selma and Birmingham but also in Detroit and New York. A majority of Americans didn't like it, the federal government feared it, and many good people kept a distance. And we see the work and power of the organizing that made it possible, which shows that there was nothing natural or inevitable about the changes the movement wrought, highlighting the relentless courage, effort, and vision it took to imagine a different America.

These nine chapters revisit a set of events we think we know. The goal is to analyze gaps and omissions in how we have come to understand the civil rights movement, not to tell a comprehensive history of the movement. Many pivotal moments are not included, from the 1961 Freedom Rides to Milwaukee's open housing movement, and many crucial freedom fighters, such as Fannie Lou Hamer and Bayard Rustin, are mentioned only briefly or not at all. The book's focus on challenging certain key mythologies of the movement does not represent the sum total of important scholarship published over the past two decades on the modern Black freedom struggle but identifies some strands that are crucial to understanding what the movement encompassed and involved and how it has been distorted. It focuses on Black activism and does not cover the variety of struggles by Latinx, Asian Americans, and Native Americans occurring at the time. There is an emphasis on Rosa Parks and Martin Luther King Jr.—in part because these activists are so regularly invoked, distorted, and misappropriated that it seems necessary to set the record straight around the breadth of their political work and vision, and the ways their efforts were received at the time. And there is an emphasis on the struggle in the North because it is so excluded from our popular renderings of the movement.

Suggesting the urgent need to learn from the history of the modern Black freedom struggle and map continuities with present struggles is not meant to claim that the civil rights movement is the gold standard by which everything must be measured. Today's movements for racial justice do not have to be the civil rights movement. They face new conditions, innovate different strategies, build different webs of connections, use new technologies, and, particularly, embody intersectional justice in ways different from the movements detailed in this book.[35] But the civil rights movement occupies an increasingly central place in our national identity, so the need to analyze its misuses and grapple with its substance has grown more urgent. The scope of its vision has been narrowed in the service of those in power. The diversity of people who conceived, built, and led that struggle has been diminished, in part because their example offers such a potent challenge to where we are today. The extent of their courage has been obscured—because to see their imaginative relentlessness is to understand more fully the power of what they were up against and how they saw it could be changed.

While the civil rights movement is regularly celebrated for the way it demonstrates the power of ordinary Americans to change the course of the nation, what a host of activists did and how they did it is far more beautiful than we've been taught. The terrible diversity of people and forces that stood in the movement's way has been papered over as well. In an America of disproportionate Black poverty and persistent school inequality, with a criminal justice system riven with inequalities and an imperial foreign policy that justifies far-ranging constitutional abuses and record numbers of deportations, a fuller history of the movement is imperative for seeing a way forward. In an America that, across party lines, asserts its own exceptionalism, this history reveals long-standing investment in and deflection of racial injustice domestically and globally. In an America where Donald Trump's overt racial appeals now occupy the White House, the country requires a more serious and sober history to see clearly who we are and how we got here—and where we must go from here. We need this history more than ever.

The Histories We Get

The Political Uses and Misuses of Civil Rights History and Memorialization in the Present

Now that he is safely dead,
Let us Praise him,
Build monuments to his glory,
Sing Hosannas to his name.
Dead men make such convenient Heroes.
They cannot rise to challenge the images
We would fashion from their Lives.
And besides, it is easier to build monuments
Than to build a better world.

—Carl Wendell Hines Jr., "A Dead Man's Dream"

HOW THE HISTORY of the civil rights movement became a national fable begins with the struggle for a federal holiday honoring Martin Luther King Jr. Four days after King's assassination in 1968, Representative John Conyers introduced the first bill for a federal holiday in his honor. Three years later, the Southern Christian Leadership Conference (SCLC) delivered a petition with three million signatures calling for a holiday, but no action from Congress was forthcoming. Relentlessly carried forward by Coretta Scott King and a host of civil rights comrades over the next fifteen years, the proposed holiday garnered significant opposition. King had been deeply unpopular at his death. A 1966 Gallup poll found 72 percent of white Americans had an unfavorable opinion of the civil rights leader.[1] Major newspapers, including the *New York Times*, had editorialized against him, particularly when he publicly condemned US involvement in Vietnam. Many political leaders did not believe King's work rivaled that of Christopher Columbus and George Washington. Others admired King but did not feel like his legacy had been put to the test of time. Still others saw King as un-American and dangerous, and surely not someone to be honored.

Activists kept pressing through the 1970s, but the resistance continued. When Ronald Reagan was elected in 1980, he opposed the holiday, worried about the "cost" and fearing the United States would be "overrun with holidays." Jesse Helms and other conservatives raised concerns about whether King was a Communist—a belief Reagan was not willing to rule out. To secure the holiday, supporters highlighted King's transcendent value to America. In 1979, Stevie Wonder wrote a song, "Happy Birthday," in honor of King, focusing on "love and unity to all God's children." SCLC president Joseph Lowery argued that "the designation of Dr. King's birthday as a national holiday would transcend the issue of race and color.... If Washington established the Nation, Martin led the Nation to understand that there can be no nationhood without brotherhood."[2] The King holiday would be a way to celebrate America, Senator Ted Kennedy explained, "because Martin Luther King's dream is the American dream."[3]

Faced with growing public support for the holiday, opposition gave way to recognition of the holiday's political utility. Seeking reelection, President Reagan faced a "sensitivity gap" on racial issues. With the bill poised to pass Congress, signing it became a way to assuage moderate white voters, who now saw a holiday in their interest, as a way to show how open-minded they were. Reagan wrote New Hampshire's governor apologizing for not vetoing the bill: "On the national holiday you mentioned, I have the reservations you have, but here the perception of too many people is based on an image, not reality [of who King was]. Indeed to them, the perception is reality."[4] Symbolic acts, Reagan realized, could be used to defer more substantive action. Marking this history two decades after King's death could be a way to demonstrate racial sensitivity, pay tribute to the movement's successful and now completed battle against racism (in the process altering who King was), and thwart ongoing calls for racial justice.

And so, on November 2, 1983, Reagan signed the bill into law, explaining,

> Now our nation has decided to honor Dr. Martin Luther King Jr. by setting aside a day each year to remember him and the just cause he stood for. We've made historic strides since Rosa Parks refused to go to the

back of the bus. As a democratic people, we can take pride in the knowledge that we Americans recognized a grave injustice and took action to correct it. And we should remember that in far too many countries, people like Dr. King never have the opportunity to speak out at all.[5]

Reagan's remarks zeroed in on what would soon become key elements of the national fable of the civil rights movement: that there *had been* an injustice, but once these *courageous individuals freely* pointed it out, it was corrected, and so proved the *greatness of American democracy*. In the years following the signing, as historian Justin Gomer notes, Reagan "routinely position[ed] himself thereafter as the inheritor of King's color-blind 'dream'—a society in which 'all men are created equal' and should be judged 'not . . . by the color of their skin, but by the content of their character'—in order to attack civil rights."[6]

The holiday took on important national utility. As religion scholar Eddie Glaude observed, "For some the holiday effectively washed our national hands clean. The ritual act of disremembering became a ritual of expiation: the sins of our racial past gave way to an emphasis on individual merit and responsibility."[7] There would be outliers—Arizona for a while, and some states such as Arkansas, Alabama, and Mississippi combined the King holiday with Robert E. Lee Day—but these largely contrasted with the national celebration of progress.[8] As president after president celebrated King's "dream," the "domestication of Martin Luther King," as scholars Lewis Baldwin and Rufus Burrow have termed it, was cemented.[9] Americans, according to Baldwin and Burrow, had grown "comfortable with a domesticated King or one who is harmless, gentle, and a symbol of our own confused sense of what it means to be American."[10]

That narrative would be strengthened by the ways the country came to celebrate Black History Month. The idea of Black History Month began a half century earlier in 1926, when African American historian Carter G. Woodson, who founded the Association for the Study of Negro Life and History in 1915, designated a week in February for its observance. Its national consecration began when President Gerald Ford issued a "Message on the Observance of Black History Week" in 1975, calling on all Americans to "recognize the important contribution made to our nation's life and culture by black citizens." The next year, Ford officially recognized Black History Month, calling it a moment for the public to "seize the opportunity to honor the too-often neglected accomplishments of black Americans in every area of endeavor throughout our history." Since 1976, the month of February has been recognized by every president as Black History Month.[11]

Increasingly, Black History Month was observed in a celebratory, commercialized fashion. Schools rolled out the contributions of a largely preselected group of great Black individuals, while the greater arc of American history—of progress, time-honored democratic values, and American exceptionalism—remained intact. The focus on individual Black accomplishment, as needed as it was, narrowed the scope of what the month could mean for the country. By forgoing the uncomfortable reckoning an immersion in the nation's unvarnished past would entail, the ritual celebration of Black History Month—"the shortest month of the year and also the coldest," as comedian Chris Rock has put it—narrowed the history to one of inclusion and tolerance. Black History Month placed this history at a great distance from its young pupils, where long-ago heroes battled distant villains over faraway realities. Writer Christopher Emdin called it the "killing of Black history month," for "tell[ing] the same stories in the same way and the same time each year. . . . Connections that need to be made between the ancestors and the present generation cannot be made when history is told without context."[12]

Increasingly, movement memorializations became national events. In 1997, on the fortieth anniversary of the desegregation of Central High School, President Bill Clinton journeyed back to Arkansas to honor the Little Rock Nine, explaining, "They purchased more freedom for me, too, and for all white people." Marking his racial bona fides and personal journey as a Southerner who'd attended segregated schools, Clinton affirmed the work ahead. But then he claimed the "question of race is, in the end, still an affair of the heart." Increasingly racism would be defined as personal, matters of the heart rather than enduring matters of legislation and structure.

In the years before the trip back to Little Rock, Clinton had signed three landmark pieces of legislation—the 1994 Violent Crime Control and Law Enforcement Act, better known as the Crime Bill (which enshrined "three strikes" as federal policy and provided more money for building more prisons); the 1996 Personal Responsibility and Work Opportunity Reconciliation Act (which "ended welfare as we know it" and gutted the nation's social safety net); and the 1996 Anti-Terrorism and Effective

Death Penalty Act (which expanded federal power in law enforcement and cut off avenues by which people could challenge their convictions). All three traded on rampant stereotypes of people of color as dependent, debauched, and dangerous—"superpredators" and "deadbeats," in Clinton's words—to amplify criminalization, limit public assistance, foreclose avenues of due process and redress, and make good on Clinton's appeals to white voters.

Then, in 1999, Clinton presented Rosa Parks with a Congressional Gold Medal, asserting with a straight face that "Rosa Parks brought America home to our founders' dream." What the president also said, in so many words, was that the dream was complete—that it was so finite that the racial inequality in Clinton's own policies could be decisively separated from what civil rights activists like Parks had fought for. The "split screen" in action, Clinton celebrated the civil rights movement in the past, then claimed that the racial imagery at the heart of his legislative agenda (and its disproportionately damaging and targeted effects on Black people) were not racist but necessary for the Black community—and America—to progress.

Rosa Parks passed away on October 24, 2005, less than two months after the devastation of Hurricane Katrina. Amidst growing public outcry over federal negligence during the storm, and with racial fissures laid bare ("George Bush doesn't care about black people," Kanye West declared on national TV), Congress and President George W. Bush rushed to pay tribute to "the mother of the civil rights movement."[13] Parks became the first civilian, first woman, and second African American to lie in honor in the US Capitol.

A national funeral for the "mother of the civil rights movement" provided a way to sidestep questions on the enduring racial and social inequity that Katrina had exposed. Forty thousand Americans came to pay tribute, and President Bush laid a wreath at Parks's coffin. Six weeks later, Bush signed a bill ordering the placement of a permanent statue of Parks in the Capitol, the first ever of an African American there, explaining:

> Rosa Parks showed that one candle can light the darkness. . . . Like so many institutionalized evils, once the ugliness of these laws was held up to the light, they could not stand. Like so many institutionalized evils, these laws proved no match for the power of an awakened

conscience—and as a result, the cruelty and humiliation of the Jim Crow laws are now a thing of the past . . . By refusing to give in, Rosa Parks called America back to its founding promise of equality and justice for everyone.[14]

According to President Bush, Rosa Parks's dream was the founders' dream. And all it required was simply to shine a light on injustice and people were moved to change it. In 2006, Bush, in an address to the National Association for the Advancement of Colored People (NAACP), sealed this national redemption narrative with the idea of a second founding—America reborn from its former racism. "Nearly 200 years into our history as a nation, America experienced a second founding, the civil rights movement," he said. ". . . These second founders, led by the likes of Thurgood Marshall and Martin Luther King Jr., believed in the constitutional guarantees of liberty and equality."[15]

The election of Barack Obama took these national civil rights narratives to new heights. As *Time* magazine trumpeted in its cover story after Obama's victory, King's dream "is being fulfilled sooner than anyone imagined."[16] On numerous occasions during the campaign, candidate Obama located himself within this noble genealogy, referring to the civil rights movement activists as the "Moses generation" and to himself as the "Joshua generation." Throughout his campaign, Obama used the civil rights movement as a key signal of progress and the power of American democracy—as did many supporters, placing him within the long line of Black freedom fighters.[17] The journey of the movement was highlighted at Obama's first inauguration. "Our work is not yet finished," Senator Dianne Feinstein extolled, "but future generations will mark this morning . . . when the dream that once echoed across history from the steps of the Lincoln Memorial finally reached the halls of the White House."[18] The national praise at the heart of the fable had reached its zenith in the pride many Americans took in the historic election of the country's first African American president.

The civil rights movement also became one of the central ways, until Black Lives Matter changed this, that President Obama talked about racial injustice throughout his presidency—as a key part of America's history but also largely framed *in the past*. While he talked about the civil rights movement much more extensively than previous presidents, his framings had echoes of his predecessors'. From Reagan to Clinton to Bush to

Obama, the civil rights movement now embodied America's greatness, the noble sacrifice toward "a more perfect union."

MEMORIALS, ANNIVERSARIES, AND NATIONAL SELF-CONGRATULATION

The dedication of the memorial to Martin Luther King Jr. on the National Mall in Washington, DC, finally occurred on October 16, 2011. Affirming the progress of the past fifty years, President Obama capped off the dedication by extolling King's Americanism: "That is why Dr. King was so quintessentially American—because for all the hardships we've endured, for all our sometimes tragic history, ours is a story of optimism and achievement and constant striving that is unique upon this Earth."[19] The story of a movement created by thousands of people and of a man who had been surveilled relentlessly by the FBI was rendered as a Horatio Alger story of personal scrappiness and American exceptionalism.

The solitary stone statue of King towers above visitors. It bears little resemblance to the civil rights leader himself, or to the collective spirit of dissenting witness he embodied. The sculpture was modeled from a picture in which King was holding a pen, which was scrapped for a rolled-up "Dream" speech. The original plans for the monument had called for alcoves honoring other civil rights activists and martyrs, but they were not included because of insufficient funds. The sculpture is flanked by a granite wall. In no particular order, fourteen quotes are inscribed on it. Not one of them uses the words "racism" or "segregation" or "racial inequality." Not one.

King's searing description of the experience of racism from "Letter from Birmingham Jail," for instance, is missing. His moving, closing words from the first night of the Montgomery bus boycott, hailing a "race of people, a black people . . . who had the moral courage to stand up for their rights . . . inject[ing] a new meaning into the veins of history and of civilization" are missing. His indictment of America as "defaulting on this promissory note and . . . [having] given the Negro people a bad check"—which opened his speech at the 1963 March on Washington—is missing. Originally, this quote was selected to appear at the memorial, but it ultimately was deemed too "controversial."[20]

A man who risked his life and went to jail thirty times to challenge the scourge of American racism; who was quick to point out the racism of the North along with that of the South; who wrote from jail in 1963 that the biggest problem was not the KKK but the "white moderate" who "preferred order to justice"; who criticized the "giant triplets of racism, extreme materialism, and militarism"; whose sermon the Sunday after he was assassinated was going to be "Why America Is Going to Hell"—that man of God and courage is now honored with a memorial that refuses to speak the problem of racism. The quotes are arranged out of order (1955, 1964, 1963, 1967), and the context of the movements and mobilizations in which King was a part are invisible. The wall could have included a short sentence under each quote to explain where and in what context he spoke the words. But that sense of the history—of a movement unfolding in time and place, of a courageous person who was part of a collective movement of courageous people—was deemed unimportant.

President Obama himself consecrated the memorial as a celebration of the nation. While he noted that the work was "not complete" and spoke of the need for "world class" schools for all, a "fair" economic system for all, and "accessible" health care for all, he never once directly addressed the ongoing problem of racial inequality in schools, jobs, health care, or the criminal justice system. If there was a place and time where President Obama should have spoken forthrightly about the contemporary scourge of racial inequality and injustice, should it not have been at the dedication of the King memorial?

The year 2013 began with President Obama's second inauguration—where he took the oath of office on two Bibles, one of which was Martin Luther King Jr.'s traveling Bible. Calling it a "privilege" to use King's Bible, the president, as well as Supreme Court Chief Justice John Roberts, inscribed the Bible at the King family's request. Inscribing King's Bible marked the inauguration as a culmination of King's work. Traditionally, one of the few ways Bibles are written in is to record family events and milestones. Roberts's and Obama's inscriptions on the Bible figuratively made the inauguration a King family affair, and Roberts and Obama—and by extension Americans today—descendants of the civil rights leader.

Bitter congressional fighting had a brief respite at the end of February 2013, as leaders of both parties joined President Obama to dedicate the first full-size statue of a Black person in the Capitol's Statuary Hall.[21] The bronze statue of Rosa Parks—seated demurely, clutching her purse, and looking decades older than the forty-two she was on that December evening—is a meek and redemptive figure, and one of only a very few in Statuary Hall of a person sitting.[22] Nothing in how Parks is rendered suggests action or refusal; her posture is modest with slightly rounded shoulders and her purse is at the center of the pose. Because the bronze of the figure is lighter than that of other statues, the work stands apart from the other bronze and marble statues in the room—and tours gravitate to it, in part, according to guides, because it is one of the few that people immediately recognize. But the design of the statue turned Parks's fierce and dangerous refusal into a passive, ladylike affair.

Republican House Speaker John Boehner began the ceremony, noting how the statue's placement in the hall embodied "the vision of a more perfect union." "What a story, what a legacy, what a country," extolled Senator Mitch McConnell. "She did what was natural," Democratic Speaker of the House Nancy Pelosi said, quoting baseball star Willie Mays in her remarks. "She was tired, so she sat down." President Obama closed, proclaiming, "It is because of these men and women that I stand here today." He heralded Parks's "singular act of courage," obscuring her lifetime of courageous acts and the other stands that had preceded hers. Warning of the "fog [of] accepting injustice, rationalizing inequity, tolerating the intolerable," he nonetheless offered no program for change that day.

Across town the very same day of the statue dedication, the Supreme Court was hearing arguments in *Shelby County v. Holder*. The case brought by Shelby County, Alabama, amidst other voter suppression maneuvers throughout the country, challenged two portions of the 1965 Voting Rights Act (VRA)—Section 4(b) and Section 5—as no longer relevant, and sought a permanent injunction against their enforcement. These sections from the original act, which was ratified again in 2006, laid out a formula requiring certain states and municipalities with histories of voter discrimination to clear any changes in their voting procedures with the Department of Justice to ensure they did not repress the vote. The VRA largely, but not exclusively, targeted Southern states; the law had been expanded to address discrimination against various minority groups and remove language barriers, and to require action in areas of low-voter registration and turnout levels in other parts of the country.[23] In its June 2013 decision in *Shelby*, the Supreme Court struck down Section 4(b) of the act (the portion that determined which municipalities would face preclearance—federal preapproval to make changes to voting rules) as "based on 40-year-old facts having no logical relation to the present day," thus declaring that section unconstitutional.[24]

Rosa Parks was given a remarkable tribute, yet many public statements framed her action in ways at odds with the context of her bus stand and her lifelong political commitments, and offered no plan for addressing contemporary inequality. And the distinction was bestowed on a day when the Supreme Court was taking yet another step toward unraveling one of the accomplishments Parks and her comrades had struggled for decades to achieve. A memorial statue of the civil rights movement was deemed relevant to the present day, while the movement's goals of enforced voting rights protection were not. In many ways, the statue dedication embodied an increasingly familiar use of civil rights history as a national redemption story and Horatio Alger tale of American courage. In this way, the intersection of the Parks statue dedication and the Supreme Court hearing was not merely ironic but emblematic of a larger politics of historical memory at work for a nation that wanted to place this history firmly in the past and diminish the vision of its heroes now put on pedestals.

August 2013 saw a replay of such pageantry and shape-shifting history, as two fiftieth-anniversary commemorations of the March on Washington drew crowds—along with controversy about who got to speak, and how long. Attorney General Eric Holder spoke for thirty minutes; Julian Bond, cofounder of the Student Nonviolent Coordinating Committee (SNCC), two minutes. President Obama spoke, but young activists from the Dream Defenders and DREAMer movement were cut from the program due to time constraints. The original organizers of the March on Washington had made a series of compromises in 1963, eliminating civil disobedience from the day's plan and narrowing the scope of the demands. But as writer Gary Younge reminds, the one thing they did *not* compromise on was their plan that no politician was to speak; it would be the people speaking.[25] Fifty years later, the politicians dominated.

Huge celebrations commemorated the fiftieth anniversary of the Selma-to-Montgomery march in 2015. President Obama; First Lady Michelle Obama; their daughters, Sasha and Malia; and Michelle's mother, Marian Robinson, journeyed to Alabama to lead the march. With soaring speeches, moving commemorations, and a host of other festivities, from funnel cakes to a Black Entertainment Television (BET) concert, the civil rights movement was honored in epic fashion. The president gave a moving speech heralding the momentous change the civil rights struggle had wrought but fell into some familiar tropes of the civil rights fable. He reminded the crowd of how demonized these rebels had been: "Back then, they were called Communists, or half-breeds, or outside agitators, sexual and moral degenerates, and worse—they were called everything but the name their parents gave them. Their faith was questioned. Their lives were threatened. Their patriotism challenged." "Back then," President Obama explained—as if the experience bore no resemblance to the disparagement and dismissal of activists today. The history of the movement could provide a cautionary tale for how we treat today's rebels, but instead, the problem was framed in the past.[26]

Referencing Ferguson and the police killing of Mike Brown, the president made clear that the nation's work was not over. But in the speech's most troubling moment, he explicitly asserted that racial injustice was no longer systemic: "What happened in Ferguson may not be unique, but it's no longer endemic. It's no longer sanctioned by law or by custom." Just weeks before, the Department of Justice had issued its own report on the Ferguson police department, showing "African Americans experience disparate impact in nearly every aspect of Ferguson's law enforcement system"—but the president asserted that racial injustice was neither endemic nor legally or socially sanctioned.[27]

THE ENDLESS MISUSES OF ROSA PARKS

The popular history of the civil rights movement fixes it in time and place—a museum piece to be exalted from afar and a touchstone for all Americans. Rosa Parks's courageous bus stand had become America's stand. As 2012 drew to a close, President Obama tweeted a photo of himself in the classic Rosa Parks pose (seated in profile looking out the bus window) taken on the Rosa Parks bus. The picture had been taken months earlier by a White House photographer at a fund-raiser at the Henry Ford Museum in Dearborn, Michigan, which now displays the original bus. On the anniversary of her bus arrest, the president tweeted that photograph with the message "In a single moment 58 years ago today, Rosa Parks helped change this country."[28] Thus the day's honor included the president himself—her stance morphing into his.

Key to the Parks fable is the happy ending. On December 1, 2013, the fifty-eighth anniversary of Rosa Parks's bus arrest, the Republican National Committee made that message plain, tweeting: "Today we remember Rosa Parks' bold stand and her role in ending racism." The RNC's tweet—which was rapidly mocked and vilified—spoke more starkly what has been at the heart of many of the national tributes of Rosa Parks: honoring her is regularly accompanied by a celebration of American progress. This self-congratulation was on display at the second Republican presidential debate in 2015. When candidates were asked which woman they thought should be put on the ten-dollar bill, many seemed to flounder for a woman they wanted to honor: Jeb Bush picked foreign leader Margaret Thatcher, and John Kasich picked Mother Teresa. But three contenders—Marco Rubio, Ted Cruz, and Donald Trump—named Rosa Parks. Rubio, Cruz, and Trump picked a woman who spent her life doing things they disparaged in the present—galvanizing and helping sustain a disruptive yearlong consumer boycott against segregation, challenging the racial injustices of the criminal justice system and systemic police abuse, and fighting for voting rights, a robust social safety net, and reparations. These three men appeared to see political gain and little irony in honoring Rosa Parks, a woman who spent her life fighting for the racial and economic justice they oppose.

Three months later, Democratic presidential contender Hillary Clinton used Rosa Parks for her own campaign purposes, tweeting, "History often gets made on ordinary days by seemingly ordinary people—December 1, 1955 was one of them. Thank you, Rosa Parks. H." Her campaign logo had been transformed into a bizarre graphic rendering of Rosa Parks sitting in profile *on the back of* the Hillary Clinton for President logo. Compounding the problem, Clinton, campaigning in Alabama that day, observed: "It's always struck me how, depending on the way you look at it, Rosa Parks either did something tremendous or something rather humble"[29]— a deeply backhanded compliment, sidestepping the dangers Black women faced in being arrested, which Parks herself was well aware of, and the decade-long toll it had on the Parks family's economic well-being.

Adding to the absurdity, in 2015, Mike Huckabee, Ted Cruz, and the Values Voter Summit backing Kentucky clerk Kim Davis's claimed right not to issue marriage licenses to same-sex couples compared her stand to Rosa Parks's. Davis, writing from jail, did as well, proclaiming "Rosa

Parks had it easy" compared to what she was going through. Then, three weeks before the 2016 presidential election, the Trump campaign, amidst its rampant race-baiting, tried to cash in on its supposed connections to the civil rights movement. Trump's longtime attorney and campaign surrogate Michael Cohen tweeted a 1986 photo of Trump, Rosa Parks, and Muhammad Ali, claiming they were "receiving NAACP medals for helping America's inner cities. A man for ALL people!" The NAACP had given Trump no such honor; the photo was taken when all three won the Ellis Island Award, which Trump business associate William Fugazy had just created to honor "real Americans," after twelve recent immigrants had been awarded US Medals of Liberty.[30] The photo—with the corrected caption noting the Ellis Island Award—continued to circulate on social media, posted relentlessly by Trump supporters as proof that he wasn't racist. And when President-elect Trump's pick of Jeff Sessions for attorney general drew widespread controversy for Sessions's racial history of disturbing comments about Martin Luther King and the SCLC, his record as US attorney in Alabama, and his vociferous opposition to school funding equity, conservatives rolled out his "well-documented support of Rosa Parks," as Fox News put it.[31]

On International Women's History Day 2017, Snapchat featured a filter of Rosa Parks with hat and glasses.[32] Everyone could become Rosa Parks for a day, with a speech bubble appearing out of your mouth—"You must never be fearful about what you are doing when it is right." (Like all Snapchat, the filter was ephemeral and the picture would disappear in twenty-four hours.) Rosa Parks had, for all intents and purposes, become an empty vessel, to which any and all Americans could lay claim.[33]

THE POLITICAL USES OF THE CIVIL RIGHTS FABLE

The attraction of this national civil rights fable was palpable, and political gold in the hands of conservatives and liberals alike. From Reagan to Bush, it provided a shield against criticism of their race-based policies and approaches. A story of individual scrappiness and national progress, this tale of the civil rights movement served the nation well, underlining its ability to move past its problems with race. It held particular appeal for the Obama administration, which liked the historic resonances that framed his presidency—and for the public who elected him, to mark their own accomplishment.

The birth of the Tea Party movement, the relentless questioning of the president's birth certificate and citizenship, the scorched-earth attacks on Obama's economic stimulus plan, and the Affordable Care Act (often referred to as Obamacare) all kept a vicious race politics front and center from the minute President Obama entered the Oval Office, without his administration ever even tackling the ongoing scourge of racial injustice. As pollster Cornell Belcher observed upon Obama's historic 2008 election, "A black man can't be president in America, given the racial aversion and the history that's still out there. However, an extraordinary, gifted, and talented young man who happens to be black can be president."[34] Civil rights memorialization provided a way to approach this seemingly untenable task. Talking about racism through the history of the civil rights movement provided an easier way to speak about inequality, but then largely rendered the fight against it in the past.

This fit with the desire of many Americans to be proud of electing a Black man and to use his election to claim the country's sordid history of racial inequality was now largely over. Many Americans embraced these sorts of historical celebrations because they—and President Obama's presence in the White House—were feel-good moments of America becoming a "more perfect union."[35] But that combination produced a dangerous absolution; admiring the civil rights movement became a way to feel okay about opposing change in the present and to disregard those who insisted that the election of a Black president could go hand-in-hand with systemic racial inequality.

Part of the problem with these renderings of the movement are the ways they are steeped in American exceptionalism—and used to tell a story about the glorious evolution of US democracy and the scrappy Americans who prove its power. They cast civil rights activists in the cloak of sanctified, not-angry nobility, who struggled respectably and were destined to win because American democracy is an inspiration for the world. These tributes tell tales about the power of American values—of the disenfranchised's ability to use the levers of democracy and of the willingness of the powerful to change. The many ways Americans by their actions and inactions enabled, protected, and continue to maintain injustice at home and abroad fade into the background.

Part of what makes it difficult to see the gaps and distortions in these narratives is that these memorials operate on a very powerful set of registers. Because there is so little African American history in our schools and our public square, any bit that makes it in becomes precious. These historical tributes pay well-deserved honor to the courage and dedication of King, Parks, and their comrades, and to the significance of the civil rights movement to American history. They, importantly, encourage young people to identify with those who challenge the status quo to fight for justice, not simply to emulate and celebrate the rich and the powerful. The culmination of years of efforts to ensure the history of the movement and the legacy of these brave individuals are marked in significant public ways; they are inspiring tributes—wrongs exposed, terror defeated by courage, the power of ordinary citizens. By asserting in the most prominent spaces in the land that Black history is American history and Black leaders are American heroes, they help to desegregate the nation's public history. Their inclusion, given how dead and white publicly commemorated US history is, marks such a long-fought victory that sometimes it seems like the best that could be hoped for. All of this, then, makes the distortions embedded in them difficult to see and their dangers harder to recognize.

But these memorials and popular recountings contain perilous silences. They largely function as celebrations of individual courage, missing the collective struggle these victories took and forgoing national accountability by relegating the history of inequality to the past. They frame the issue in the South and only in the South, as these memorials and commemorations pay almost no attention to Northern segregation or the Northern struggles that Parks, King, and many, many others also pushed forward. They celebrate a small handful of individuals rather than a broad cast of characters. They suggest that the apex of the movement was the election of a Black president, rather than the "dismantling of all forms of oppression," as Rosa Parks put it. Memorializing the movement becomes a culminating task in the struggle for racial justice, obscuring the work needed in the present to dismantle various forms of injustice in schools, housing, jobs, policing, and US foreign policy.

By stripping King and Parks of the breadth of their politics—which interwove economic justice, desegregation, criminal justice, educational justice, and global justice—many of these national tributes render Parks and King meek and dreamy, not angry, intrepid, and relentless, and thus not relevant or, even worse, at odds with a new generation of young activists.

These memorials purposely forget the decades when these activists were surveilled, harassed, ostracized as troublemakers, and upbraided as "extremists"—how part of the way racial injustice flourished was through the demonization of those who called it out. The movement's heroism is also placed at a distance, rather than as a way to imagine how the young people visiting these monuments will grow up to be our next freedom-fighting heroes and heroines. By holding up a couple of heroic individuals separate from the movements in which they were a part, the ways the era is memorialized implicitly creates a distinction between the people we have today—too loud, too angry, too uncontrolled, too different—and the respectable likes of Parks and King.

These renderings make it seem as if the movement happened naturally or inevitably, missing the staggering resolve and perseverance of small groups of people who actually pressed it forward, and in so doing attracted larger groups of people to their cause. And in the process, these dilutions and distortions render the problems African Americans now face as largely their own doing, and contemporary activism as so very different from this hallowed past.

Invoking the movement has also become a way to maintain and distract from injustice in the present. In the midst of his first month in office, Trump recognized Black History Month, lauding the "museum on the National Mall where people can learn about Reverend King, so many other things." He stumbled on: "Frederick Douglass is an example of somebody who's done an amazing job and is being recognized more and more, I noticed. Harriet Tubman, Rosa Parks, and millions more black Americans who made America what it is today. Big impact."[36] As horrifying as it was that the president knew so little about Black history that he thought Frederick Douglass was still living (an error compounded by then press secretary Sean Spicer), the comments had eerie echoes of Reagan's idea that the movement was "based on an image."[37] Uttering the names of these heroes was deemed useful to the agenda President Trump was pursuing.

On the eve of Martin Luther King Jr. Day 2017, faced with criticism from Congressman John Lewis, who described him as not a "legitimate president," President-elect Trump hit back at Lewis. The congressman should fix his "crime-infested" district, Trump tweeted. "All talk, talk, talk—no action or results. Sad!" The controversy that ensued was important but predictable—Twitter exploded and Trump's slur of Lewis dominated the news all weekend (including the front page of the *New York Times*). But it was also useful bait amidst a week of exploding revelations on collusion with Russia and during the madcap rush to confirm Trump's nominees (many of whom had made direct racial appeals and supported practices steeped in racial inequality). While some claimed Trump "doesn't care that people think the civil rights movement was important," more likely, Trump, skilled in the politics of distraction—and waiting a day before responding—used its public importance to generate a massive, useful diversion.

Trump's tweet did inspire some congressional representatives to "stand with John Lewis" and sit out the inauguration.[38] But even then, the controversy centered on the heroism of the individual man. It was "standing with Lewis," rather than standing with the voting rights that Lewis had risked his life to try to ensure. Lewis himself had centered his comments not "around" the illegitimacy of Trump's presidency and the role of the Russia during the election—and had not included the significant voter disfranchisement and new voter ID laws that had certainly enabled Trump's victory. None of the members of Congress standing with him highlighted it either. This controversy could have been an opportunity to attack the dismantling of voting rights protections—fourteen states had new voting restrictions in place for the 2016 election—that had led to Trump's "illegitimate" win.[39] But the movement was placed in the past; what was to be defended was the honorable Congressman Lewis, not an enduring commitment to securing voting rights.

The misuse of history often provides distorted instruction on the process of change. In his commencement address at Howard University in 2016, President Obama explained to the graduates how change happens in the United States. He invoked the power of Mississippi freedom fighter Fannie Lou Hamer's challenge at the 1964 Democratic convention, which contested the racial exclusion embodied in the Mississippi Democratic Party, and her grassroots organizing in Mississippi. But he ended with this admonishment: "And democracy requires compromise, even when you are 100 percent right. This is hard to explain sometimes. . . . If you think that the only way forward is to be as uncompromising as possible, you will feel good about yourself, you will enjoy a certain moral purity, but you're not going to get what you want."[40] What the president did not mention to those Howard graduates was that a similar lecture had been given to Fannie Lou Hamer and other Mississippi Freedom Democratic Party activists by establishment civil rights leaders and Democratic Party operatives to encourage them to take a meager compromise in 1964, but they had rejected it.[41] It was this willingness not to bend to political expediency, but to insist on full rights, that characterized Fannie Lou Hamer's heroism that we now laud fifty years later.

At the same time, many civil rights memorials refigured civil rights history through a language of personal responsibility—what legal scholar James Forman has called the "politics of responsibility."[42] Increasingly, Black-on-Black crime and the need for the Black community to take responsibility for internal problems were cast as the new civil rights issue. On Martin Luther King Jr. Day 1995, then US attorney Eric Holder announced a massive crime-fighting initiative called Operation Ceasefire: "Did Martin Luther King successfully fight the likes of Bull Connor so that we could ultimately lose the struggle for civil rights to misguided or malicious members of our own race?"[43]

In 2004, Bill Cosby, speaking at an NAACP gala honoring the fiftieth anniversary of the *Brown v. Board of Education* decision, delivered a "blistering" diatribe on the behaviors and actions of Black parents and children to a mix of "astonishment, laughter and applause," according to the *Washington Post*.[44] Namechecking civil rights heroes from Dorothy Height to Julian Bond, Cosby lamented, "These people who marched and were hit in the face with rocks and punched in the face to get an education and now we got these knuckleheads walking around who don't want to learn English."[45] Much criticism of his remarks followed. But Cosby and Harvard psychiatrist Alvin Poussaint took the show on the road, underscoring how discipline, values, and personal responsibility were key to Black power today—to move Black people from "victims to victors."

Political scientist Fred Harris has described "the shift in the century-old ideology—the politics of respectability—to a public philosophy directed at policing the black poor" in the 1980s and 1990s, culminating in the campaign of Barack Obama.[46] Personal responsibility was also interwoven with his discussion of the movement in speeches candidate Obama made to Black audiences. At Brown Chapel in Selma, Alabama, in 2007, when he talked about the progress made by the movement and what it would take to complete the last 10 percent of the task, Obama pointed partly to individualized personal responsibility. Calling for responsible

Black fatherhood (decrying "daddies not acting like daddies"), he demanded a fictional, unreliable cousin Pookie "get off the couch," register, and go to the polls—locating much of the work in Black people themselves. Months later, at a speech to the NAACP, Obama again reiterated the "need to demand more from ourselves."[47] And as president, when he delivered the commencement address at Morehouse College in 2013, he made clear to Black men graduating that "there's no longer any room for excuses. . . . Nobody cares if you suffered some discrimination. And moreover, you have to remember that whatever you've gone through, it pales in comparison to the hardships previous generations endured. . . . And if they overcame them, you can overcome them, too." His allusion to "we shall overcome" as a message of "toughening up" and "not making excuses of racism" was aimed squarely at young Black men themselves (and was far different from the message he delivered at Barnard College's commencement the year before, in which he did not tell the young women graduates "there's no longer any room for excuses"). As historian Tom Sugrue observed, Obama's vision of the struggle turned on "individual initiative and self-transformation."[48] In many ways, this call was a perversion of the civil rights movement's outward organizing tradition (change "has to start with your action") into an inward self-help tradition ("we have to transform ourselves first").

Horrified by the ways popular histories of the movement have distorted its legacy for contemporary political interests, historians and social justice activists have sounded the alarm for years. SNCC organizer Julian Bond quipped that the narrative of the movement has been reduced to "Rosa sat down, Martin stood up, then the white folks saw the light and saved the day."[49] In 2004, the Organization of American Historians president at the time, Jacqueline Dowd Hall, delivered a powerful address, later turned into an article, warning that popular histories of the movement "prevent one of the most remarkable mass movements in American history from speaking effectively to the challenges of our time." Asserting that the dominant narrative "distorts and suppresses as much as it reveals," she argued for the need "to make civil rights harder. Harder to celebrate as a natural progression of American values. Harder to cast as a satisfying morality tale. Most of all, harder to simplify, appropriate, and contain."[50] And a growing body of movement voices and academic scholarship has emerged to interrogate the role of the movement in popular memory and culture.[51]

BE LIKE MLK: WEAPONIZING THE FABLES OF THE PAST

The loving, nonviolent approach is what wins allies and mollifies enemies. But what we have seen come out of Black Lives Matter is rage and anger—justifiable emotions, but questionable strategy. For months, it seemed that BLM hadn't thought beyond that raw emotion, hadn't questioned where it would all lead.[52]

—Barbara Reynolds

This ain't your grandparents' civil rights movement. . . . Get off your ass and join us![53]

—Tef Poe

Distorted renderings of movement history took on heightened danger as a new movement gained national attention. Galvanizing around the issues of police brutality, criminal injustice, and mass incarceration, Black Lives Matter came to national prominence after the killing of Trayvon Martin and subsequent acquittal of George Zimmerman in 2013, and the police killing of Michael Brown in Ferguson, Missouri, in 2014. The vision of Black Lives Matter was articulated by three Black queer women: Alicia Garza, Patrice Cullors, and Opal Tometi; its various local incarnations have encompassed a broad palette of issues affecting Black lives, from enduring school inequality to living-wage struggles, and from police accountability to gender justice. Taking to the streets, blocking traffic, disrupting political events and commerce, and launching die-ins on college campuses, this new leader-full movement, organized predominantly by young Black people but joined by a rainbow of others and Black people of all ages, has forced the nation to grapple with issues of racial injustice in law enforcement and the legal system.

The civil rights movement has lurked everywhere in public discussion of Black Lives Matter. While there have been notable connections and moments of camaraderie—for instance, Harry Belafonte's Justice League, as well as by many of the former members of the Student Nonviolent

Coordinating Committee—an undertone of concern and fear about the protesters and problems with the movement they are building have come from many corners, the criticism laced with problematic allusions to the civil rights movement. Former presidential candidate Mike Huckabee outrageously stated that Martin Luther King Jr. would be "appalled" by BLM's strategy and called on protesters to be more like King.[54] King's niece, Alveda King, referred to BLM's methods as "inappropriate." Oprah Winfrey called for "some kind of leadership to come out of this" and cautioned young activists "to take note of the strategic, peaceful intention if you want real change."[55] CNN's Wolf Blitzer criticized protests in Baltimore as not being "in the tradition of Martin Luther King." And Atlanta mayor Kasim Reed invoked the history of King to celebrate Atlanta's tradition of free speech, but then admonished protesters: "Dr. King would never take a freeway."

Even some former activists have gone this route. Congressman John Lewis, a former SNCC chair, initially spoke out against people critiquing BLM: "Those people should do something. Make their own movement."[56] But when BLM protesters disrupted a Hillary Clinton rally with Lewis in attendance, he cautioned: "Most of the things that we did back in the 1960s was good trouble; it was necessary trouble. . . . But we have to respect the right of everybody to be heard. And you do that in a nonviolent, orderly fashion."[57] Lewis cast these young activists' protests as being far different from the "necessary good" trouble he and his comrades had made. In July 2016, as protests flared again following police killings of Alton Sterling and Philando Castile, Lewis tweeted: "I was beaten bloody by police officers. But I never hated them. I said, 'Thank you for your service.'" And former SCLC organizer Andrew Young, at a pep talk at a police precinct, went a step further in his criticism of the protesters: "Those are some unlovable little brats out there. . . . They're showing off. And not even with a clear message."[58]

Casting the young protesters as reckless and not living up to the legacy of the civil rights movement, a number of prominent voices have measured Black Lives Matter against the movement and found it falling short. Many who claim sympathy with BLM's purpose have used the civil rights movement to decry their tactics—putting aside the fact that King took a highway many times over his life, that the movement was disruptive and unpopular, and that it made many Americans uncomfortable. The civil rights movement has become museum history, inaccessible for our grubby use today. While the actual civil rights movement was far more disruptive, demanding, contentious, and profound than it's depicted, the mythologies of it get in the way of seeing the continuities between these struggles, the shoulders current movements stand on, and the ways people can learn from past struggles to approach the problems we face as a nation today.

In response to the repeated invocation of the civil rights movement to criticize their work, some activists have challenged a set of older Black leaders, along with scores of white commentators, who disapprove of their approach. As Ferguson activist-musician Tef Poe retorted in his song "War Cry," "This ain't yo mama's civil rights movement," proudly distinguishing BLM from the civil rights movement (or at least from the myth being brandished against them). "Missouri is the new Mississippi," he explained.[59] They wanted to know what these critics were doing today and stressed the importance and distinctiveness of the movement they were building. Activist-writer Rahiel Tesfamariam donated a T-shirt with this slogan to the Smithsonian National Museum for African American History and Culture to document "the history being made" from this new movement: "This looks different; it sounds different. It's a comment of anger."[60]

Many saw the invocation of the civil rights movement against BLM as a way for critics to stand on the sidelines. "The burden of the brutalized is not to comfort the bystander," actor-activist Jesse Williams made clear at the 2016 BET awards, in a speech that went viral. "If you have a critique for the resistance, for our resistance, then you better have an established record of critique of our oppression."[61] "What I've learned from the [BLM] activists and what is going on today is, those of us who have lived almost a century, have no right to cynicism," Harry Belafonte joined in. "Mostly, the people who turn away from radical thought are people who don't like to be uncomfortable."[62] Recognizing the need to steep themselves in fuller histories of Black struggle, popular education and study groups have become an important but much less covered aspect of the many Black Lives Matter groups and mobilizations.[63] And many BLM activists have partnered with a set of elders willing to build on those lineages. But that has not caused commentators to stop using the civil rights movement to chastise the work of BLM activists.

Fed up with the prominent misuse of history against Black Lives Matter, sixty-six former SNCC activists published a statement in July 2016 marking the continuities of struggle:

> "Fortunately, today, as in the past, the protesters who have taken to the streets against police violence will not be intimidated by slander or mischaracterization as 'racist' or 'terrorist sympathizers' born of the fear, ignorance and malice of their would-be critics. . . . We, the still-active radicals who were SNCC, salute today's Movement for Black Lives for taking hold of the torch to continue to light this flame of truth for a knowingly forgetful world."[64]

As these SNCC activists made clear, memorializing a civil rights movement without young people in the vanguard, without anger, without its long-standing critique of the criminal justice system, missed what the movement was actually about. Julian Bond, visiting a class at Morehouse College in 2009, critiqued the respectability politics being pushed on this new generation, which many young activists were also rejecting: "A nice suit is a nice suit. Get one. But it won't stop a bullet, son."[65]

Key similarities exist between the civil rights movement and BLM—from the forces they are up against to the criticisms they encounter to the expansive vision of justice they seek. Like the young activists propelling BLM, civil rights activists were regarded as dangerous and reckless by many and as downright seditious by others. The movement was pushed forward by young people, who made many people nervous sixty years ago, just as they do today. Thus, substantively considering new movements for racial justice in the context of the civil rights movement means seeing the ways they are tied to, rather than set apart from, this longer movement history.

More significantly, these mis-histories of the civil rights movement impoverish people fighting for social justice today by separating them from the perspectives and experiences of a long line of courageous freedom fighters. Sixty years ago, Rosa Parks drew solace and sustenance from the long history of Black resistance before her time, placing her action and the Montgomery bus boycott in the continuum of Black protest. Her speech notes during the boycott read: "Reading histories of others—Crispus Attucks through all wars—Richard Allen—Dr. Adam Clayton Powell

Sr. and Jr. Women Phillis Wheatley—Sojourner Truth—Harriet Tubman, Mary McLeod Bethune."⁶⁶ For Parks, the ability to keep going, to know that the struggle for justice was possible amidst all the setbacks they encountered, was partly possible through reading and referencing the long Black struggle before her. By denying a new generation their place in that lineage, a key form of sustenance is taken away.

And perhaps most consequentially, the mythologizing of the civil rights movement deprives Americans of honest history that shows us where we are today in this country. The task, as James Baldwin put it, is "to describe us to ourselves as we are now"—to honestly reckon with the way the country feared the civil rights movement and its disruptiveness; to fully grasp the movement's scope and tenacity; to understand the diversity of freedom fighters and what they did and imagined; to grapple with the robust resistance to change, not just in the redneck South but in the liberal North; and to examine what learning from that struggle shows us about the country today.

THE HISTORIES WE NEED

In 2009, President Obama journeyed to Norway to accept the Nobel Peace Prize. In a speech replete with references to Martin Luther King Jr., Obama began by calling his own accomplishments "slight," foregrounding that he was there as a culmination of the efforts of many movement activists: "As someone who stands here as a direct consequence of Dr. King's life work, I am living testimony to the moral force of nonviolence. I know there's nothing weak—nothing passive—nothing naïve—in the creed and lives of Gandhi and King." He reminded those gathered of the Americanness of the civil rights movement. But then he made an interesting pivot: "As a head of state sworn to protect and defend my nation, I cannot be guided by their examples alone. . . . The nonviolence practiced by men like Gandhi and King may not have been practical or possible in every circumstance, but the love that they preached—their fundamental faith in human progress—that must always be the North Star that guides us on our journey."

President Obama's Nobel speech made explicit that which tends to be more implicit in national tributes to the civil rights movement. As a nation, we honor these courageous men and women, then dismiss them as "impractical" when their example asks things of us that we do not want to provide—rendering the times and issues we confront as very different from those old injustices. In short, we prefer our heroes and heroines in the past and will cast aside the parts of the story that raise questions about our current directions.

The rest of this book focuses directly on these absences—the histories unmarked in popular understandings of the movement—and on what the national fable of the civil rights movement justifies and hides. Identifying nine key distortions in popular renderings of the movement, each chapter examines what a fuller history then shows us. These fuller histories of the modern Black freedom struggle are more uncomfortable histories—unsettling because they show the nation in a much more painful light and point out our current responsibilities more vividly.

The first two chapters show the extensive and diverse movements for desegregation and racial equality outside of the South and the long history of political organizing in Northern cities that preceded the uprisings of the mid-1960s. The next two chapters confront the power of polite racism—the variety of tactics that helped legitimate and obscure racial inequality—and the role the media played in disparaging Black struggle and dismissing racial injustice, segregation, and police brutality, particularly outside of the South. Chapter 5 gets off the bus to show the movement's broader demands regarding desegregation, criminal justice, economic justice, and global justice. Chapters 6 and 7 get beyond the "great man" view of history, examining the central role young people—in particular high school students—played in pushing the movement forward, and the adult discomfort with it, as well as the breadth of women's leadership and the various barriers and gendered assumptions those women encountered. Chapter 8 focuses on the unpopularity of the movement, the toll this chilling climate took on activists, and the immense political repression they faced. Finally, chapter 9 revisits the iconic Montgomery bus boycott to return the story of organizing and the role of disruption, perseverance, and anger to our understanding of the movement.

By illustrating the ways the story of the movement has been stripped and narrowed, these nine chapters offer a much broader vision of what the fight for justice and equality entails and the ways activists imagined and implemented it. By providing a more sobering account of what racism is and how injustice and inequality are maintained, this fuller history gives us the tools to approach the task of racial justice today.

The Histories We Need

CHAPTER ONE

The Long Movement Outside the South

Fighting for School Desegregation in the "Liberal" North

— FOR ADINA BACK[1] —

There is a pressing need for a liberalism in the North that is truly liberal, that firmly believes in integration in its own community as well as in the deep South.

—Martin Luther King Jr., 1960[2]

The man'll shoot you in the face in Mississippi, and you turn around he'll shoot you in the back here [in New York].

—Fannie Lou Hamer[3]

SELMA, MONTGOMERY, BIRMINGHAM—our popular history of the era tells an epic story of a Southern movement born on a Montgomery bus, nurtured in Mississippi jails, and filled with resounding faith and mind-bending courage as ordinary Black citizens braved prison and violence to change the Deep South. Their determined efforts culminated in the passage of the Civil Rights Act in 1964 and then, a year later, the Voting Rights Act. Martin Luther King Jr. and Rosa Parks looked on as President Lyndon Johnson signed the Voting Rights Act on August 6, 1965. Moving and heroic, the nationally celebrated narrative of the movement is exclusively Southern.

President Obama and his family traveled to Alabama in March 2015 to mark the fiftieth anniversary of the Selma-to-Montgomery march. But the president did not journey to New York City in February 2014 to mark the fiftieth anniversary of the largest civil rights protest of the decade. On February 3, 1964, nearly half a million students and teachers stayed out of school to challenge the New York City Board of Education's refusal to make a plan for comprehensive desegregation. Obama did not even make a presidential announcement, as he did for the sixtieth anniversary of Rosa Parks's bus arrest, to mark the anniversary. The movement commemorated was depicted only in the South.

Southern cities such as Montgomery, Birmingham, Memphis, and Atlanta, in fact, now market themselves partly through civil rights tourism—at times right alongside Confederate tourism, as in the case of Montgomery. But come to New York, Boston, or Detroit and historical markers to local civil rights movements are hard to find. The country, then and now, fixated on the problem in the South, framing racial injustice as a regional sickness rather than a national malady. Many Northern whites at the time encouraged this focus on the South, preferring to advocate change below the Mason–Dixon Line rather than in their own backyards—a tendency many Southerners found hypocritical. Accordingly, the "real" movement was taking place in the South—and that is what we remember and celebrate today.

Yet tens of thousands of people were active in civil rights struggles outside the South, from the 1940s to the 1980s. Movements in Northern cities, like those in their Southern counterparts, used many tactics—nonviolent civil disobedience and marches, meetings with city officials and disruptive direct action, boycotts and door-to-door canvassing. They took on redlining and housing segregation, school segregation, job exclusion, discriminatory public services, welfare exclusion, police brutality, and criminalization. And these movements were repeatedly met with similar claims, from public officials and citizens alike: this is not the South; we don't have that kind of racism here; disparities exist because Black people haven't adopted the right behaviors for success. Northern activists struggled to have their efforts recognized and taken seriously—and that same problem is reflected in our popular histories, which again background these movements.

In the popular imagination, *Brown v. Board* is posited as a challenge only to Southern school systems; resistance to the decision is pictured in the form of Southerners from Little Rock to Birmingham, not as Northern mothers, politicians, and parent groups, who also labored mightily to ensure that school desegregation would not come to their schools as well. "Boston's busing crisis" is treated very differently from white resistance to the desegregation of Central High School in Little Rock, Arkansas; there is almost no recognition of the three-decades-long civil rights movement in Boston, which led to the 1974 judicial order for system-wide desegregation. When the actions of Northern Black people appear in popular tributes to the era, they tend to show up in the later 1960s, in the form of the riots and a naïve King discovering Northern Black issues, or as a contrast drawn between groups like the Black Panther Party and the Southern movement. Such framings reinforce the idea that Northern Black people were of a different character and didn't engage in sustained organizing, and that Black Power emerged out of nowhere. A distorted view of the era, these public accounts miss nonviolent, disruptive struggles from New York to Boston to Los Angeles that took place concurrently with those in the South, and the massive efforts of political leaders and white citizens to dismiss the movements and blame Black people for the conditions of their schooling, neighborhoods, and law enforcement.

And so, fifty years later, a parade of memorials pays tribute to the movement only in the South. This is particularly curious, given an avalanche of scholarship over the past two decades that has dramatically documented the vibrancy of movements outside the South.[4] Given the ways the public fable has grown more prominent at a time when scholarship documenting Northern racism and Black organizing outside the South has dramatically departed from this narrative, the political uses of ignoring the North come into view. There was no national honor or memorial event for the 1964 school boycott, perhaps because the movement did not prevail, and New York City never comprehensively desegregated its schools. To recognize the long movement in New York and Boston to desegregate schools would have opened a much more uncomfortable set of questions on the limits of Northern liberalism and the pervasive nature of school segregation. It would disrupt the happy ending and challenge the easy morality tale the fable gives us—of Northern good guys who went South to support the movement—and show how white Northerners disparaged and quelled movements in their own backyards.

Grappling with this larger landscape of segregation and struggle in the "liberal" North—and with the variety of "good guys" who helped justify and hide injustice in their own cities—brings into sharp relief the national character of American apartheid. Focusing on the North also makes clear that there was nothing accidental or "de facto" (or simply, in fact) about Northern segregation. As historian Matthew Lassiter documents, the framework of "de facto" segregation (as compared to "de jure," or by law) was created to appeal to Northern sensibilities, to make a distinction between the segregation so evident in many Northern cities from the segregation many Northerners decried in the South. Thus Northern "de facto" segregation was cast outside the law, despite the many government policies that supported and legalized these practices (and judges from Boston to California would find intentional segregation in these school districts as well). Many scholars and journalists since the 1960s have clung to this false distinction between a Southern "de jure" segregation and a Northern "de facto" segregation, making Northern segregation more innocent and missing the various ways such segregation was supported and maintained through the law and political process.[5]

At the same time, looking carefully at these Northern movements reveals how hard community activists fought—not just in the South but across the country—to unveil and challenge segregation and racial inequality. Alongside their Southern counterparts, Black people and their allies built movements from the Northeast to the Midwest to the West to challenge inequality. Courage and relentlessness ran from Birmingham to Boston, Little Rock to Los Angeles. Confronting the extent of the Northern struggle, as Newark activist and historian Komozi Woodard explains, is to see "how much we loved our children." Black parents and community members built movements to challenge school segregation and inequality, protest housing segregation, confront police brutality, highlight job and union exclusion, and equalize public and social services. They took on cultural arguments blaming Black families and children for the conditions of their neighborhoods and schools, and relentlessly worked to pressure city officials for equity. Trying tactic after tactic to get change, they innovated strategies, shamed city officials, disrupted municipal life, and labored to bridge class and ideological divisions. They were red-baited and smeared, and they persisted—like their Southern counterparts. But their stories are much less publicly known.

"WHAT DO YOU DO ABOUT THE POOR CHILDREN RIGHT HERE?": THE CIVIL RIGHTS MOVEMENT IN NEW YORK CITY

On February 3, 1964, more than 460,000 students and teachers stayed out of school to protest the New York City Board of Education's refusal to create a comprehensive school desegregation plan. Bigger even than the 1963 March on Washington, New York's school boycott was the culmination of a decade of work by Northern organizers such as the Reverend Milton Galamison and Ella Baker, along with Black parents including Mae Mallory and Viola Waddy, who demanded an equal education for their children. And it was the result of a decade of delay, obfuscation, and obstructionism by New York City leaders and white New Yorkers who might have praised the *Brown* decision but didn't think it applied to them.[6]

A decade earlier, the Supreme Court had handed down its ruling in *Brown v. Board* outlawing segregation in schools, determining that separate could never be equal and laying out a promise of equal education: "In these days it is doubtful that any child may reasonably be expected to succeed in life if he is denied the opportunity of an education. Such an opportunity, where the state has undertaken to provide it, is a right which must be made available to all on equal terms." Northern Black people, like their Southern counterparts, rejoiced in the ruling, hoping it would bring change to their segregated and unequal schools. Schools educating Black children in New York were heavily overcrowded and decrepit, with underqualified teachers (in many Black schools, most of the teachers were substitutes) and often lacking in sufficient materials or up-to-date facilities.

Since the 1930s, government-made Home Owners' Loan Corporation (HOLC) maps had sought to expand home ownership by creating a neighborhood ratings system to encourage bank lending and real estate development. Every neighborhood was rated from A to D, with D neighborhoods marked in red and deemed unsafe for loans and development to encourage bank lending and real estate development. These ratings were based not just on the quality of housing stock but also on racial homogeneity and room for further business development. So, neighborhoods in New York with more than 5 percent Black people, according to historian Craig Wilder's research, were given C and D ratings.[7] As a result, this government-sponsored process of facilitating development and home loans rewarded suburban development and white New Yorkers while trapping Black and

Puerto Rican people into certain neighborhoods in the city, limiting investment in those neighborhoods and maintaining school segregation.[8]

Between 1940 and 1960, about 2.5 million Black people and nearly a million Puerto Rican people migrated to New York City. They were shut out of many neighborhoods across the city, and Harlem and Bedford Stuyvesant schools grew impossibly crowded. Rather than relieve the crowding by zoning schools differently, sending Black students to less crowded white schools, school leaders instituted part-time school days, so two different groups of Black students would attend the same school in staggered succession. Parents found this appalling, viewing it as further evidence of the city's segregationist impulses. Meanwhile, students of color were regularly channeled into vocational or trade schools and classes, and college options were limited. Part of the issue was also hiring discrimination. Black and Puerto Rican teachers were hired at much lower rates than were white teachers. The hiring process included an oral, in-person test designed to weed out people with "foreign" or "Southern" accents, which led to the screening out of most Black and Puerto Rican candidates.[9]

A variety of New Yorkers, some more typically associated with Southern struggles, took on New York's segregated schools. Before *Brown*, New York-based organizer Ella Baker and Black psychologist and researcher Kenneth Clark had pointed out the deep inequities and visible segregation in New York's schools, and they pressured the city to make good on *Brown*'s mandate. Clark's research, in which he studied the doll preferences of Black children in South Carolina, illustrated the harms of segregation. His experiments became famous when they were cited in the *Brown* decision, but, according to historian Adina Back, "some of his most poignant, though lesser known research with black children and the ways they saw white dolls as smarter and more beautiful came from his work with Northern black children."[10] After the Supreme Court's decision, Clark and Baker pressed harder—determined that New York would have to comply and desegregate its schools as well.

Ella Baker had grown up in Norfolk, Virginia, and attended Shaw University. After graduation, in 1927, she moved to Harlem, where she worked in a variety of community organizations. In 1940, she began working with the NAACP, serving as the NAACP's director of branches from 1943 to 1946, but she left the position because she saw the organization as too hierarchical and not committed to the work of its branches. Baker remained active in the NAACP, heading its Harlem branch in 1952 and moving the office to the heart of Harlem to embed it in the community. Baker believed in the importance of local leadership and in empowering people to "participate in the decisions over their lives."[11] In the face of New York City's stonewalling on desegregation in the mid-1950s, she traveled throughout the city urging parents to see that they could be involved and could insist that their children's rights were recognized.

Like its Southern counterparts, New York City did not want to desegregate its schools after *Brown*. But it pursued a different strategy than outright resistance. The city's board of education (BOE) adopted an integration resolution that did *not* call on schools to move toward desegregation or craft a plan for how that would proceed; rather, the board formed a committee to investigate what action might or might not be necessary:[12]

> The Board of Education of the City of New York is determined to accept the challenge implicit in the language and spirit of the decision of the United States Supreme Court. . . . We believe that an effective method for obtaining these ends is to set up a Commission of the Board of Education charged with the responsibility of determining the facts and recommending whatever further action is necessary to come closer to the ideal, viz., the racially integrated school.[13]

In other words, New York celebrated the importance of the *Brown* decision but then cast the Supreme Court's mandate as not necessarily applying to the city's schools. "New York City didn't act right after the '54 decision. It didn't have any reason to act, so you had to help it to realize it," noted Baker.[14] School officials purposely sidestepped the fact that the ways they zoned schools produced overwhelmingly white and overwhelmingly Black schools—and cast the issue of segregation as something beyond its control. The commission would investigate whether there was anything to be done. In part to deflect criticism by Baker and Clark, the two were invited to be part of this newly established commission to study the problem.

New York City was invested in depicting its own segregation in terms that were different from those applied to schools in the South. New York Superintendent of Schools William Jansen directly instructed his staff to refer to the city's segregated schools as "separate" or "racially imbalanced." He explained: "The use of the word 'segregation' in releases is always unfortunate." Jansen directly attacked Kenneth Clark's charges of systemic segregation in New York schools. "In Kenneth Clark's allegation, he alleges that we deliberately segregated children which is false . . . [and] implies that racial segregation exists in our schools. There is no justification for charging this to our schools."[15] The board repeatedly claimed that whatever segregation existed was merely the result of housing segregation, and that it was powerless to do anything. As Jansen explained it, New York's segregation was "natural" and not caused by anyone in the city: "We did not provide Harlem with segregation. We have natural segregation here. It's accidental."[16] According to school officials, people just chose to live with their own. Clark's public critique of the segregated nature of New York schools was dismissed by school officials, including Jansen, who questioned Clark's Americanism as a way to discredit his criticisms.

As criticisms mounted from community leaders about his lack of leadership on desegregation, Jansen defended himself: "I know that my friendliness and respect for the Negro people is as great as that of anyone in the school system."[17] Public officials invested in maintaining the status quo saw how language mattered, and thus deliberately tried to use different words to describe what was happening in New York's schools; along with labeling segregation "racial imbalance" and "separation," they referred to New Yorkers opposed to desegregation as parents committed to "neighborhood schools" and opposed to "forced busing."[18] At the same time, they labeled Black students and their parents as "culturally deprived" and not possessing the proper cultural values and practices for success.

The concept of Northern segregation as "de facto"—in contrast to the "de jure" segregation found in the South—was perhaps the slipperiest and most long-lasting way of masking the intentional nature of school segregation in Northern cities. Partly an effort to appease Northern sensibilities and mark certain forms of segregation as innocent, Northern segregation had come to be termed "de facto." As Black lawyer Paul Zuber, who litigated cases in New York and New Jersey, wrote in 1963:

> The word *de facto segregation* was never heard until the historic Supreme Court decision of 1954. . . . Now the law is clear, segregation by legislative act was illegal and in violation of the Constitution of the

United States. Now the North needed a rationalization to continue its brand of racial segregation.[19]

This renaming by New York officials was strategic, because it acknowledged what was obvious to the eye—that New York City's schools were resolutely segregated—but claimed it was the case merely in "fact" not "law'" (and thus not due to state action). As historian Matthew Lassiter explains, "A broad spectrum of white actors seized upon the 'de facto' rationale through a 'color blind' discourse that defended neighborhood schools and segregated housing as the products of private action and free-market forces alone, a sphere in which government had not caused and therefore had no right or obligation to remedy." It became a way of describing Northern segregation that placated Northern sensibilities and required no action—despite ample evidence, Lassiter explains, "of comprehensive State action in producing deeply entrenched patterns of residential and educational segregation."[20] Trying to appeal to city leaders, some activists began to use the term as well to press their cause—unwittingly giving force to a specious distinction between Northern and Southern segregation that city officials were eager to exploit.

The city commissioned the independent Public Education Association to do the study. The PEA concluded that, on average, facilities in predominantly Black and Puerto Rican schools were older, had fewer adequate classrooms and materials, and were not maintained as well as facilities of predominantly white schools.[21] Nonetheless, it stuck to the board's framing of "separation" and not "segregation." In its assessment of the BOE's responsibility, it adopted a tone sympathetic to the challenges that school administrators faced, as if zoning were created by some faraway potentate and not New York City officials: "To suggest that these lines be drawn to consider the possibility for integration is to make more difficult that which is already too difficult."[22] By placing the responsibility for deciding whether the schools were morally bound to zone for integration in the realm of social philosophers, rather than at the feet of the school officials who had done the zoning, it provided the city an effective escape hatch.

The board's commission on integration was charged with creating a plan to implement the PEA report; Ella Baker served on its subcommittees on zoning and teacher placement, the two most controversial groups. The subcommittees found that BOE policy—specifically the way zoning lines had been drawn and teachers placed—directly contributed to the city's school segregation. When it recommended dramatic changes to the city's zoning and teacher placement policy, the BOE and other city leadership rejected the proposal.

Black parents and local activists had rejoiced at the *Brown* decision, believing it would finally result in change in the city's schools. With the city's stonewalling, however, they began to turn to more direct protest. Meanwhile, the national NAACP in the decade after the *Brown* decision was focused largely on the South. "They were always talking about the poor people down South," lamented Ella Baker, who ran Harlem's NAACP in the 1950s. "And so the question was, what do you do about the poor children right here?"[23]

In September 1957, seeking to draw attention to the fact that another school year was starting without any comprehensive desegregation plan, Baker helped organize a picket of over five hundred Black and Latino parents in front of city hall. Calling themselves Parents in Action, the group spearheading the picket drew parent activists from across the city. They demanded the end of the "neighborhood school" concept if it got in the way of desegregating and getting more experienced teachers, smaller class sizes, and an end to part-time school days.[24]

At a 1957 public hearing on school integration, Black parent-activist Mae Mallory asserted that the Harlem public school her daughter attended was "just as 'Jim Crow' as the Hazel Street School that I attended in Macon, Georgia."[25] Mallory was part of a growing parents' movement. "We were trying to shame New York because they would always talk about the South and segregation, when their hands were dirty too."[26] She objected to the ways New York officials tried to portray themselves as so very different from their Southern counterparts.

Conditions were miserable. Historian Adina Back interviewed Mallory in 2000 about her experiences in trying to get change at her child's school, PS 10 in Harlem. Mallory recounted how shocked she was by the dirt and stench she encountered there. "There were only two bathrooms for sixteen hundred kids. They were very old fashioned, with one single wood sheet that went from one end of the place to the other with holes cut in it. You couldn't flush it. So whatever the children did, it had to stay there until the next time the water came to flush. And that made the school smell terrible."[27] Mallory found conditions intolerable and took her case to Albany, where she spoke about "the miserable condition of P.S. 10. They were not prepared for this angry Black woman. Brand new toilets were put in immediately."[28]

For her efforts to address the situation, Mallory told Back, school officials cast her as "dangerous." A school representative "stood in the doorway with her arms akimbo, and she told me that Mr. Principal told her to keep me out of the school." Hardly one to be dissuaded, Mallory confronted the principal directly: "I explained that he had to have contempt for the children because I'm sure that he didn't want to be there under those conditions. And it seems that the Board of Education had contempt for him to put him there."[29] After her son Keefer, a fifth grader, came home with an assignment to count the pipes under the sink, Mallory confronted her children's teachers about their low expectations of their students. The teacher bristled: "'Are you questioning my integrity as a teacher?'" recounted Mallory. "So I told her you god damn right. Are you challenging my integrity as a parent? This child isn't a moron. What does he need to count pipes under the sink for? The teacher answered, 'How do you know he is not going to be a plumber.'" This incident propelled Mallory to get involved in the school's curriculum and ultimately to file a suit against the BOE, "the first suit in the North against *de facto* segregation."[30]

Mallory became part of a group of mothers who came to be known as the Harlem Nine. They kept their kids out of school in the fall of 1958 to protest the segregated, unequal schools their children had been assigned to.[31] The mothers had been told their kids were culturally deprived, and that was why they didn't learn—not that their schools were unequal. The women were determined to fight back against the ways they and their kids were being blamed for the substandard education. In 1956, twelve mothers in Harlem formed the Parents Committee for Better Education, which would grow to hundreds and challenge the New York City Board of Education to improve the resources and conditions at Harlem's schools.

These nine mothers took decisive action, according to Mallory, to "demand a fair share of the pie, that our children be educated the same way as everybody else's."[32] They had tried to get the city to take their grievances seriously, but getting nowhere, they decided to pull their kids out of these schools to homeschool them. The city still didn't care—and the mothers decided to stop schooling them entirely. "We will go to jail and rot there, if necessary, but our children will not go to Jr. High Schools 136, 139, or 120," Viola Waddy explained.[33] Some of the mothers, including Bernice Skipworth and Shirley Rector, lived in Harlem's Lincoln Houses. The *Amsterdam News* called them the "Little Rock Nine of Harlem." Challenging school officials who tried to cast them as the problem, these mothers asserted a "responsible" motherhood by seeking equality for their children. Adina Back explains: "Their sense of entitlement extended beyond the boundaries of class, race and gender as they described their activism as the struggle for human rights."[34]

The city brought the nine mothers up on charges for failure to comply with compulsory education requirements. At the time, the FBI was heavily monitoring Mallory's actions and those of the other Harlem Nine mothers. According to historian Ashley Farmer, despite Mallory's organizing activities with the Communist Party, "it doesn't appear that the Bureau really took notice of her until she began organizing with school desegregation groups and with the Harlem 9. This suggests that she was more of a threat to them as a grassroots leader than as a participant in other kinds of CP activities."[35]

A young Black lawyer, Paul Zuber, defended the Harlem Nine and represented Mallory in her suit against the New York City Board of Education. Zuber, who'd grown up in Harlem and attended Brown University and Brooklyn Law School, was fearless. "He moves like a Sherman Tank where others fear to tread," the *Chicago Defender* observed.[36] Zuber called out the racism of New York alongside that of the South: "Down home [in the South], our bigots come in white sheets. Up here, they come in Brooks Brothers suits and ties."[37] The cases against the mothers ended up in two courtrooms. Judge Lewis Kaplan found four of them guilty of violating state compulsory education law. But Judge Justine Polier refused to find Skipworth and Rector guilty, dismissing their charges and citing their "constitutionally guaranteed right to elect no education for their children rather than subject them to discriminatorily inferior education."[38]

When the city decided to appeal Polier's decision, the Reverend Gardner Taylor—the only African American member of the BOE—was disgusted by the city's desire to punish those who highlighted New York's segregation: "Never again can the City of New York rebuke or admonish any other section of the country on this question, the board has . . . now made it one nation indivisible, with little difference between New York and Little Rock."[39] Ultimately, the board dropped the appeal, but segregation in the city's schools remained.

In fact, as in other Northern cities, segregation *worsened* in New York City schools in the decade after *Brown*, particularly in response to large-scale Black and Puerto Rican migration to the city. As the civil rights leader Milton Galamison told the board in 1958, "It is alarming to observe that over so long a period of time, and in the face of so many resolutions, not a single Negro school in Brooklyn has been desegregated; that the number of segregated junior high schools has increased from 17 to 25; and that the pattern of segregation is rising rather than diminishing."[40] Galamison had grown up in Philadelphia, attended Lincoln University and Princeton University, and become pastor of Siloam Presbyterian Church in the Bedford-Stuyvesant section of Brooklyn in 1949.[41] He was clear the goal was much more than a seat for a Black child next to a white one: "The Negro wants integration into American life in terms of jobs, in terms of education, in terms of the ability to really partake of the fruits and advantages of American society. He doesn't want to sacrifice, however, being a Negro. . . . Short of his participation in the mainstream of American life in terms of the same education that everyone is getting, in terms of the same kind of housing that everyone else is getting, and in terms of the same kind of employment that everyone else is getting, he can't have any kind of equality."[42] Galamison's relentlessness made political leaders and journalists nervous. As biographer Clarence Taylor notes, one of Galamison's greatest contributions was "making many New Yorkers aware of the duplicity of New York City's established liberal elite."[43]

Black parents pushed on. They formed separate parent organizations when they were excluded from official school Parent Teacher Associations and tried to break through the doublespeak and bureaucracy that New York City officials employed to protect their segregated and unequal schools. They also sought to demonstrate their commitment to their children's education and to challenge the ways many teachers and school administrators treated them and their children as the problem. School officials often deflected protests highlighting the city's inequalities by casting Black and Latino students as lacking the right cultural values and behaviors for educational success and thus requiring a different sort of education to learn. The term of the time was "cultural deprivation," and so what was needed was cultural remediation. One white parent spoke it plainly: "Clean up the Jungle Homes and you won't have Blackboard Jungle Children; sending them to other schools won't change their stripes."[44] Vehemently denying any racism, many residents of the city's white communities laid claim to "their" neighborhood schools and decried the "crime" and "cultural deprivation" of other communities, which they said caused the lack of success of children living there. They weren't racist, residents claimed, but they simply didn't want their children "bused." Teachers in schools in white communities often echoed these ideas, referring to students from Black communities as "problem children" who suffered from "cultural handicaps" and came from "culturally deprived homes."[45]

Indeed, the rhetoric of "neighborhood schools" and "busing" originated in struggles to oppose desegregation. White parents didn't talk about their schools as "neighborhood schools" or profess the value of the "neighborhood school" until they were faced with the possibility of desegregation, as historian Matthew Delmont demonstrates.[46] Similarly, few white parents were opposed to putting their kids on school buses—and indeed did so without complaint—until those buses were used for desegregation. In 1972, the US Commission on Civil Rights reached that conclusion, pointing out that the school bus had been a "friendly figure in the North" for fifty years.[47]

Alongside a growing Black parents' movement, there had long been white teachers who saw the scourge of segregation in New York and tried to demand change from the BOE. Most were called Communists for their trouble and marginalized, and many were fired. Some of these teachers had gotten their start in multiracial movements or labor organizations affiliated with the Communist Party, and some had no connection to the Communist Party whatsoever—regardless, it was considered a "red" idea to advocate desegregation. As the New York Age, one of the city's African American newspapers, noted in 1952, many of the teachers being labeled subversives were Jewish people who actively worked on behalf of Black students: "Two disturbing facts about the continued firing and suspension of teachers in the Board of Education's drive against subversives are that the ax appears directed primarily at Jews and that most of these teachers have been active in fighting against discrimination and for school improvements among minority groups."[48]

Unlike other organizations of teachers in the city, the radical Teachers Union (TU) had joined Black community calls for teacher rotation (calling for the board of education to establish a policy of rotating better, permanent teachers into Black schools) and increased hiring of Black and Puerto Rican teachers. Such ideas were considered dangerous and possibly seditious, and the TU was resoundingly attacked and red-baited for this work.[49]

Faced with the intransigence of the New York City Board of Education and city leaders, Black parent groups across the city, along with civil rights organizations and white and Puerto Rican activists, moved to a bigger action. Bayard Rustin, one of the key organizers of the 1963 March on Washington, brought his organizing skills to the task. On February 3, 1964, more than 460,000 students and thousands of teachers (about 43 percent of students and 8 percent of teachers) stayed out of school in response to the BOE's unwillingness to formulate a comprehensive school desegregation plan. Many students attended Freedom Schools, created by parents and activists to demonstrate how much students desired an equal and excellent education. Their numbers far outstripped—and nearly doubled—the number of people who had marched in DC in August 1963.

But the protest met with much criticism from the media, little change from the BOE, and no pressure from the federal government.[50] Many white New Yorkers were aghast at the protests—and stepped up their counter-organizing to ensure that change did not come to New York schools. While newspapers such as the *New York Times* were covering the Southern civil rights movement extensively and sympathetically by 1964, they took a very different, much more critical approach to a growing desegregation movement at home. The BOE initially compiled a list of teachers who had participated in the boycott, and board president James B. Donovan threatened to take into account these teacher absences in considering promotion decisions. The board later retracted the threat—and destroyed its record of participants.[51]

Understanding the history of the 1964 New York school boycott requires grappling with the fact that civil rights activists did not succeed in moving public officials to remedy the city's segregated and unequal schools. Quite the contrary, in fact; it was white parents who opposed desegregation who saw their demands recognized. An umbrella group calling itself

Parents and Taxpayers formed to protect New York's segregated "neighborhood schools." While smaller in number than Black protesters, these white parents commanded a great deal of political power both locally and nationally, and garnered a tremendous amount of media attention. A month after the exponentially larger school boycott, more than ten thousand white New Yorkers, 70 percent of them women, marched over the Brooklyn Bridge in the rain to protest a very limited desegregation plan that was to pair forty elementary schools and twenty junior high schools. This white counterprotest was widely and sympathetically covered on the newly emerging television news. "This is the greatest day of my life," said one woman marcher.[52] TV footage of the protest formed the visual backdrop as Congress debated the Civil Rights Act, and the march succeeded in affecting the structure of the bill.[53]

Emanuel Celler, a Democratic congressman from Brooklyn, helped ensure a loophole in the 1964 Civil Rights Act that would keep federal enforcement away from—and federal money flowing into—New York's segregated schools. (The law would tie federal funding to school desegregation.) In drafting the act, the bill's Northern and Western sponsors, mindful of their white constituents back home, drew a sharp distinction between segregation by law in the South and so-called "racial imbalance" in the North, amending Title IV, section 401(b), to read: "'Desegregation' means the assignment of students to public schools and within such schools without regard to their race, color, religion, or national origin, but *'desegregation' shall not mean the assignment of students to public schools in order to overcome racial imbalance*" (emphasis added). In the years after passage of the law, white politicians and parents in Boston, Chicago, New York, and elsewhere regularly pointed to this portion of the Civil Rights Act to justify the maintenance of their segregated schools.[54] New York City never implemented a comprehensive desegregation plan.

Northern and Western members of Congress purposely kept enforcement away from their own schools, a fact that was clear at the time, even though it has largely been lost to history. Southern politicians noted the hypocrisy of the bill's supporters in carving out the loophole for their own schools. Praising New York's senators as "pretty good segregationists at heart," Mississippi senator James O. Eastland "[did] not blame the two distinguished Senators from New York for their desire to protect New

York City, as well as Chicago, Detroit, and similar areas. But why should they attempt to penalize our part of the country?"[55] Eastland did not point out this hypocrisy because he cared about Northern Black students' educations, yet his observation about how enforcement would come to the South but not the North was sadly on target. Contextualizing why many African American communities rioted the summer after the bill passed, civil rights organizer Bayard Rustin observed, "People have to understand that although the civil rights bill was good and something for which I worked arduously, there was nothing in it that had any effect whatsoever on the three major problems Negroes face in the North: housing, jobs, and integrated schools . . . the civil-rights bill, because of this failure, has caused an even deeper frustration in the North."[56]

In the years following the passage of the Civil Rights Act, the Department of Health, Education, and Welfare (HEW, now the Department of Health and Human Services), the federal office charged with enforcing school desegregation policies, lacked the political support and resources needed to successfully hold Northern cities accountable for school segregation. HEW's limitations placed the burden of proving that Northern schools were intentionally segregated largely on Black parents and civil rights lawyers.[57] The task of school desegregation would not fall equally across the nation—many Northern cities would never be forced to desegregate their persistently separate and unequal schools. But that history finds no place in fiftieth-anniversary commemorations.

So if the nation was going to mark New York's 1964 school boycott, a number of uncomfortable truths would have to be confronted: First, that there was a long-standing, diverse movement challenging New York City's unequal and segregated school system, but many New Yorkers—including city leaders, journalists, and ordinary citizens—engaged in myriad actions to thwart and demonize it. Second, one of the most important pieces of civil rights legislation ever passed in the United States—the 1964 Civil Rights Act—was purposely designed to keep school desegregation away from the North. And finally, despite decades of efforts by Black parents and civil rights activists, the struggle against school segregation did not succeed, and many school districts, including New York's, never comprehensively desegregated.[58] But that more sordid version of the era finds little place in our public imagination or national self-interest because it would require reckoning with a much more sobering history and entail more sustained action in the present.

"IT'S NOT THE BUS, IT'S US": THE CIVIL RIGHTS MOVEMENT IN BOSTON

In 2014, Boston was poised to mark an important anniversary. That September marked the fortieth anniversary of the implementation of Boston's court-ordered school desegregation, the result of decades of civil rights agitation in the city. The vast majority of articles and events on the anniversary of the so-called "Boston busing crisis," however, commemorated the city's "troubles" with busing, and not the twenty-five-year Black struggle that compelled the city to face its own entrenched racial inequality. As they had done forty years earlier, most city officials, citizens, and journalists ignored the three decades of Black organizing against segregation and educational inequality that had led to the federal case, *Morgan v. Hennigan*, and Judge W. Arthur Garrity Jr.'s far-reaching 1974 decision. By sidestepping this history and the racial inequality that had long defined Boston, they framed "busing" as difficult for everyone in the city and thus a collective—and perhaps unnecessary—trauma.

Bostonians have long refused to face the city's record of ingrained racism. Before the 2017 Super Bowl between the New England Patriots and Atlanta Falcons, controversy erupted when *Saturday Night Live* "Weekend Update" co-anchor Michael Che quipped, "I just want to relax . . . and watch the blackest city in America beat the most racist city I've ever been to." Despite escalating criticism, Che refused to back down. *Boston Globe* columnist Renee Graham defended him: "Perhaps a solid first step will be for people to be as outraged by the racism that clings to Boston like a second skin as they are by a comedian who had the audacity to call it out."[59]

Framing the issue around "busing" has long been a way to maintain that silence and to cover up the pervasive, state-sponsored segregation in the city and the decades-long movement that sought to challenge it. Throughout the 1960s and 1970s, liberal journalists, political leaders, and white parents employed the idea of "forced busing" to evade public responsibility for Boston's deeply inequitable and segregated school system and to foreground the perspectives of white constituents who wanted a more acceptable way to explain their opposition to desegregation. It has become one of the few ways Northern race relations enter school textbooks—with "Boston's busing crisis" treated as different from the struggles to desegregate Little Rock's public schools. Through this framing, the inequality of Boston's schools was obscured and court-ordered desegregation in Boston was treated as perhaps unnecessary; racism in Boston was reduced to class alienation and ethnic parochialism of working-class white people who simply sought to protect "their neighborhood schools," instead of systemic racial inequality broadly supported in the city's schools, policing, housing, and jobs.

A fuller history of Boston's court-ordered desegregation has to begin decades before the NAACP's case came before Judge Garrity. From its formation in 1950, the Boston NAACP's public school subcommittee sought to demonstrate the segregated nature of the city's schools but faced opposition from whites and some Black people over whether segregation even existed in the northern city. As NAACP subcommittee leader and longtime activist Ruth Batson explained, "We were 'raising a false issue.'"[60] A mother of three kids, Batson had become active when she discovered a white friend's kids had science in school but her daughters didn't. She called the NAACP to report the problem but was told that the organization didn't have a subcommittee on education. The next day, the NAACP called her back and asked her to chair one. She said yes, and her life "changed profoundly."

The NAACP subcommittee saw firsthand that keeping Black students in separate facilities was a way for the Boston School Committee, the elected body that runs the Boston Public Schools (BPS), to provide Black students with an inferior education. Six of the city's nine predominantly Black elementary schools were overcrowded. Four of the district's thirteen Black schools had been recommended for closure for health and safety reasons, while eight needed repairs to meet city standards.[61] Per pupil spending averaged $340 for white students but only $240 for Black students. Teachers at predominantly Black schools were more likely to be substitutes and often less experienced than those assigned to white schools. The curriculum at many Black schools was outdated and frequently blatantly racist, and the school district overwhelmingly tracked Black students into manual arts and trade classes, rather than college-preparatory ones. The school district also segregated through pupil assignment policies that fed Black students into high school in ninth grade and whites in tenth—and often into different junior high schools before that. "You could live on the same street and have a white neighbor, as I did," parent-activist Ellen Jackson explained, "and you went to one junior high school and she went to another junior high school. . . . It was not de facto at all."[62] In addition to the racial gerrymandering of attendance zones (many schools were located at the edges of irregularly shaped districts and were not the "neighborhood schools" they were professed to be), the Boston School Committee reserved the overwhelming majority of jobs for white applicants through racially discriminatory hiring and promotion practices. Many schools had no Black faculty (Black educators made up only one half of 1 percent of the city's teachers), and there were no Black principals in the system.[63] As in New York, the struggle for desegregation in Boston was about educational equality and jobs.

According to Batson, in the years following the Supreme Court's landmark decision in *Brown v. Board of Education*, "Northern states were very smug" and did not think the decision applied to them.[64] In the early 1960s, the Boston NAACP tried to persuade the Massachusetts Commission Against Discrimination (MCAD) to recognize the existence of racial segregation in Boston's schools. But MCAD refused, claiming that racial segregation was not a problem in the city. While the existence of public commissions such as MCAD seems to attest to a more open racial climate in Massachusetts and did provide openings at other junctures for advancement, its unwillingness to investigate institutions such as the Boston Public Schools—and its proclamation that they were, to the contrary, *not segregated*—protected the city's discriminatory practices.

The NAACP responded by taking its case en masse to the Boston School Committee in June 1963. Supporters packed the hearing, while more than eight hundred congregated outside the building singing freedom songs.[65] Saying it was "too late for pleading," Ruth Batson laid out the NAACP's fourteen-point program, decrying the existence of "de facto segregation," curriculum bias, and tracking and hiring discrimination in BPS.[66] In response, according to Batson, "we were insulted. We were told our kids were stupid and this was why they didn't learn."[67]

To continue the pressure on the Boston School Committee, Black community leaders turned to direct action. A week after the hearing, they organized a school boycott and nearly half of the city's Black high school students stayed out of school, participating in Freedom Schools instead.[68] The school committee then agreed to a second hearing with the NAACP, but shut the meeting down when civil rights leaders used the phrase "de facto segregation." Calling it "a horrible time to live in Boston," Batson explained: "The press came out: NAACP is wrong. . . . We got very little public support and we got absolutely no political support. . . . All kinds of hate mail . . . There were people who could not accept the fact that this horrible thing was happening in Boston."[69]

According to Batson, the subcommittee also found a "general consensus" among principals that Black students did not do as well as white students because "the parents did not seem to care."[70] Similar to public officials in New York, Boston school officials did not defend segregation on its face, but blamed the problems in Black schools on Black children's motivation and their parents' values. While many of their white Southern counterparts in the 1950s and early 1960s explicitly defended segregation and states' rights, a different lexicon of race emerged in Northern cities like Boston—one that framed white resistance to racial integration in a language of "neighborhood control," "taxpayer's rights," and "forced busing," and cast African American and Latino youth as "problem students" whose "cultural deprivations" hampered their educational success. In 1964, William O'Connor became the new head of the Boston School Committee, declaring, "We have no inferior education in our schools. What we've been getting is an inferior type of student."[71] Fellow school committee member Joseph Lee concurred: "The Negro can make their schools the best in the city if they attend schools more often, on time and apply themselves."[72] Such cultural arguments blamed Black students and their parents for their educational underattainment and provided a palatable way for Boston's liberal sensibilities to justify disparities in terms different from those applied to the South.

By the mid-1960s, the term "busing" had emerged as a useful political phrase and organizing tool for white Bostonians. School committee member Louise Day Hicks (who later won a city council seat and became the public leader of the antidesegregation movement) played on fears of "forced busing." She characterized those pushing for desegregation as "outsiders," while asserting "there has never been any discrimination in the city of Boston and those who say there is are doing a great disservice to this great city."[73] Politicians such as Hicks, by employing the disingenuous phrases "forced busing" and "problem students," helped advance their own political careers and galvanize white support against desegregation.

Children were already being bused to Boston public schools without objection from white parents or politicians—often to *maintain* segregation. But from the early 1960s, white leaders in Boston had found decrying "forced busing" an effective and palatable way to oppose desegregation and were taking more deliberate and costly steps to avoid any desegregation. The Boston School Committee decided to use an old synagogue, Beth El (which cost $125,000 to buy, $10,000 to repair, and $90,000 a year to operate), rather than bus nearly two hundred Black students from the crowded Endicott District to white schools (which would have cost only $40,000). Claiming that busing was an infringement on the rights of "taxpaying families" (read, white families), the school committee moved to institute double-session days in Black schools, rather than bus Black children from overcrowded schools to white schools—though white children were bused to other white schools to eliminate overcrowding. When Black parents protested the double-session days, the committee gave up the idea but did nothing to alleviate the overcrowding.[74] In this way, busing in the 1960s was regularly used by the school committee to enable and protect segregated schools. And white parents did *not* object to this sort of busing. By 1972, 85 percent of Boston's high school students were already being bused—a fact that the media conveniently ignored as it repeatedly validated white opposition to "busing" as the problem.

To appear compliant with federal mandates, Boston passed an open-enrollment policy in 1961, much like the freedom-of-choice plans that popped up across the South in the mid-1960s. Black students were entitled to open seats in white schools. In reality, there were numerous barriers for Black families seeking to actually use open enrollment to access seats in less-crowded, better-resourced schools, while white families sometimes took advantage of it to transfer out of schools in transitional neighborhoods. The school committee forbade the use of school funds to bus children to these seven thousand open seats throughout the city, even though students were being bused to maintain segregated schools.

Black parents sought to challenge the idea that they did not care about their children's education—to counter, as one mother put it, the school committee's "ideas as to what they'd do with our 'poor, culturally deprived

children.'"[75] In 1965, Black parents led by Ellen Jackson took the unprec-
edented step of creating Operation Exodus, in which they paid for buses
to take their children to schools with open seats in other parts of the city.
Parents believed that if they began busing Black students to these open
seats, they would shame the school district into complying with the state
law and taking over the operation and funding of the buses. According to
Batson, Operation Exodus parents "gave lie to the stereotypes applied to
them: 'deprived . . . lack of education interest . . . laziness . . . lack of ambi-
tion and worse, 'a disregard for their children's education.'"[76] But school
officials continued to exhibit a disregard for their children's educational
futures. Despite publicly celebrating Operation Exodus in an effort to look
compliant and racially balanced (the district in fact cited the program in
its court filings in its defense), BPS never took over the operation or funding of the program.

As historian Gerald Gill observes, Boston's escalating protests took
place alongside Southern movements: "Boston's activists were equally determined to confront a powerful and racially insensitive institution and
were firmly empowered to press forward, not retreat."[77] Other parents
and activists took up a variety of strategies to secure educational equity.
In 1966, Batson and others formed the Metropolitan Council for Educational Opportunity (METCO) to enable Black students to attend suburban schools. In addition, by the late 1960s, some parents and community
leaders had formed independent Black schools, such as the Highland Park
Free School, Roxbury Community School, and the New School. Meanwhile, by the late 1960s and early 1970s, Black students in more than a
dozen high schools had staged school boycotts and walkouts to protest
school disciplinary and dress-code policies, a lack of Black teachers and
administrators, the need for Black studies, and the need for an independent assessment of patterns of segregation in the city. By pressing for an
independent study of racial patterns within city schools, students clearly
were aware of the difficulty community activists and adult leaders had
been having in establishing the problem of system-wide segregation with
the Boston School Committee and took up the fight.[78]

Latino children experienced similar problems. Excluded and underserved in BPS, five thousand Latino students, according to a 1970 report,
were systematically excluded from school completely. Language barriers (including the lack of bilingual education), inadequate teachers and

counselors, dilapidated buildings, shortages of books and other materials, and racist curricula meant that Latino students were receiving a separate and distinctly unequal education. Latino students were treated as deficient and were regularly cast as the problem in discourses that were similar to those used against Black students. Latino parents and community groups began to sound the alarm, exposing the problem and pushing for bilingual instruction and access.[79]

After two decades of meetings, rallies, student walkouts, parent organizing efforts, community initiatives, and independent schools, there was still little change in BPS. And so Black parents with the NAACP decided as a last resort in 1972 to file a federal suit against the school committee, *Tallulah Morgan v. James W. Hennigan*. At the time, 59 of the 201 schools in BPS taught the majority of the city's Black students, and only 356 of 4,500 teachers in BPS were Black.[80] By 1972, there were few neighborhood schools in Boston; 85 percent of high school students in Boston were already being bused, and thousands of white students not ensconced in all-white neighborhoods were bused past Black schools to white schools.[81] In 81 of Boston's 201 schools, no Black teacher had ever been assigned, and another 35 schools had only one Black teacher.[82] In 1973, the Boston School Committee willingly gave up $65 million in state and federal funds rather than desegregate schools.[83]

In June 1974, Judge Garrity found the Boston School Committee had "knowingly carried out a systematic program of segregation affecting all of the city's students, teachers, and school facilities." He explicitly rejected the school committee's rhetoric of protecting "neighborhood schools," citing open enrollment, magnet schools, city-wide schools, and widespread high school feeder programs as "antithetical" to a neighborhood school system. He ordered comprehensive desegregation to begin in September. This included mandates for hiring more Black and Latino teachers, the elimination of the feeder system that sent Black students to high school in ninth grade and white students in tenth, and the desegregation of twenty-three of the sixty-five racially imbalanced schools through school pairings and busing (with schools close to each other, such as Roxbury and South Boston High Schools, paired to minimize busing).[84] Yet, in extensive coverage of school opening and "busing," many news outlets, including the *Boston Globe*, refused to grapple with Boston's long history of school segregation and the fact that vast numbers of Boston students had already been bused before "busing." They ignored three decades of Black activism (protests the *Globe* itself had covered over the years) that challenged the structures of segregation in school resources, zoning, hiring practices, and curriculum, as well as the sustained white resistance to desegregation and refusal to follow either state or federal law that had brought the city to this juncture.

In the face of Garrity's order, public officials and journalists repeatedly ignored well-established Black grievances and persistently claimed that systematic segregation did not exist in the Cradle of Liberty. They treated Garrity's decision as surprising and unexpected, with many casting it as extreme and drastically out-of-line. (Garrity received so many death threats that a federal marshall was assigned to protect him.)

Over the summer, white parents had begun organizing a boycott, and many kept their kids home—with the support of a number of Boston City Council members, including Louise Day Hicks, Albert "Dapper" O'Neil, Christopher Iannella, and Patrick McDonough. Each of these council members displayed a letter—R-O-A-R—in the windows of their office, spelling the acronym of the antidesegregation organization Restore Our Alienated Rights, and the council let the group use its chambers to meet. The police union had publicly opposed the court's order, and many police officers were not committed to peaceful and effective school desegregation. According to Batson, many white Bostonians "believed that it all belonged to them, their school, their sidewalk."[85]

The start of school on September 12, 1974, provoked some of the ugliest antidesegregation demonstrations in the history of the civil rights movement, though desegregation happened in many Boston schools without incident. Crowds of whites harassed Black students trying to desegregate white schools, and often their harassment turned violent. Thousands of white families kept their children home rather than send them to a desegregated school. Buses carrying elementary school students were stoned. Nine Black children were injured and eighteen buses were damaged. Black students desegregating South Boston High were met by a mob of whites throwing rocks, bottles, eggs, and rotten tomatoes, yelling "Niggers go home!"[86] The situation grew worse over the weeks: fights broke out in the schools, and white crowds continued their attacks on Black students and bystanders. The courage of Black students who braved these schools continued as well. "If they run us out of that school, they can run us out of

the city," one Black student said, explaining her decision to keep attending school despite the violence. "They will be able to stop access wherever
they want."[87]

Most of the city council proudly stood with the resistance, and Boston's mayor, Kevin White, had committed $200,000 of city money in a
fruitless appeal of Garrity's order. A month after the school year started
in Boston, President Gerald Ford joined in, pronouncing "I respectfully
disagree with the judge's orders"[88]—and Mayor White quickly followed
suit. Even though resistance was happening all over the city with support
from political leaders all the way to the White House, and though white
middle-class neighborhoods known as the High Wards experienced significant racial violence, working-class South Boston was pictured as the
problem. It was easier to lay the blame then and even forty years later on
working-class South Boston than focus on the middle-class whites who
also resisted desegregation and the levers of power that supported and encouraged white opposition to court-ordered desegregation.[89] Spotlighting
the racism of South Boston helped make it seem as though what was happening in Boston wasn't systemic, despite its similarities to white opposition to desegregation in Little Rock and Birmingham.

Massive organizing and marches by Black residents and their allies
in 1974 and 1975 received much less attention in the news. Most of the
national media attention focused on white parents and children, not on
Black organizers who had spent decades trying to demonstrate how racist
Boston was. Black people became bit players in Boston's most famous civil
rights event—even though their organizing continued unabated.

Following the discursive strategies of the time, many historians have
continued to treat white Northern opposition to homegrown civil rights
movements differently from Southern resistance. While "Southern segregationists" sought to prevent school desegregation, similar movements
in Northern cities are often described as "white backlash" or "antibusing movements"; rarely are they termed "segregationist." Southern white
assumptions about the culture and behavior of Blacks are interrogated
more vigorously than Northern officials' explanations of "problem students" and "cultural deprivation." Historians have treated as calculated
and contrived the Southern "surprise" when sit-ins erupted in 1960, but
not Northern "surprise" over Garrity's ruling. The violence and upheaval
that accompanied school desegregation in Little Rock (and the federal

intervention it required) is treated as horrible but necessary; in Boston, it is seen as horrible but not quite as necessary. The attempts to "understand" Northern white residents' overt opposition to desegregation—as historian Ronald Formisano writes, "Thousands of decent, moderate whites across the city [of Boston] cannot be said to have been racists"[90]—reflect the problematic assumption that racism did not pervade Northern consciousness as it did the Southern one.

Such framings reached their height in J. Anthony Lukas's Pulitzer Prize–winning *Common Ground*, which helped engrave the public mythologies of "Boston's busing crisis" into historical common sense.[91] Still cited as an indispensable source (in 2016, the *New York Times* named it *the* book to read to understand Boston), Lukas's book examines "Boston's busing crisis" by tracing the experiences of three Boston families—the working-class Black Twymons, the working-class Irish McGoffs, and the middle-class Yankee Divers—from 1968 to 1978.[92] Seven years in the writing, *Common Ground* discounted the role of Black leaders and parent activists as key players of the decade and focused on a Black family that was not active in the community and whose children embodied a variety of social ills. The pathological lens through which Lukas viewed the Twymons made enduring educational problems in the city largely the fault of Black culture and behaviors. By framing it as the "busing crisis" and not as massive white resistance—supported by all levels of power—to school desegregation, Lukas's book rendered understandable Northern white defense of "their neighborhood schools." It invisibilized what segregation meant in the city, and fit with contemporary political interests to render Northern "busing" (read, desegregation) as perhaps unnecessary and hard on everyone. *Common Ground* continues to be celebrated as "great history"—in ways that a text that normalized the segregationist school practices Southern white families clung to would not be.

The attachment to the busing story follows from an attachment to a story of the civil rights movement as a rousing *Southern* story—one born on the dusty roads of the South, nurtured by noble Southern students, church ladies, and ministers, and concluded with the signing of the Civil and Voting Rights Acts. Struggles for school desegregation that rippled through the North were less rousing: they were met over and over with denials and surprise: this is not the South; we don't have systemic segregation; we like "our neighborhood schools." Repeatedly, Black parents and civil rights activists pressed for desegregation and were told their children were the problem. Repeatedly, school zones were redrawn in ways that maintained segregation, Black and Puerto Rican teaching applicants were screened out, and Black and Latino students tracked into vocational classes, in schools with more policing and punishment. And yet, time and again, activists were asked to prove that there was segregation in these liberal Northern cities.

Increasingly, school segregation came to be interpreted as an interpersonal problem between Blacks and whites, a matter of racial attitudes and who sits next to whom. Questions about fundamental inequalities in education and who benefited from these disparities receded further from the conversation, in a discussion that reduced integration to a seat next to a white child. Alongside local resistance to more substantive desegregation, the US Supreme Court by the 1970s also limited the implementation of *Brown*'s promise of equality. In 1973, in *San Antonio Independent School District v. Rodriguez*, the Supreme Court reversed a Texas district court's decision that education was a fundamental right that rendered inequalities of school financing constitutionally pressing. While the Supreme Court acknowledged that *Brown* had affirmed that "education is perhaps the most important function of state and local governments," it found that "education, of course, is not among the rights afforded explicit protection under our Federal Constitution. Nor do we find any basis for saying it is implicitly so protected." Having ruled that education was not a "fundamental" right or interest, the court maintained that reliance on local property taxes to fund public schools, even while causing significant disparities, was constitutional because local control over schools represented a legitimate state interest.

This decision, in effect, ensured that poorer districts would never receive equal funding to build equal schools—and that having a right to equal protection did not extend to attending an equally funded school. Thurgood Marshall, in his dissent, noted:

> that a child forced to attend an underfunded school with poorer physical facilities, less experienced teachers, larger classes and a narrower range of courses than a school with substantially more funds—and thus with greater choice in educational planning—may nevertheless excel is to the credit of the child, not the State. Indeed, who can ever measure

for such a child the opportunities lost and the talents wasted for want of a broader, more enriched education? Discrimination in the opportunity to learn that is afforded a child must be our standard.[93]

In *Milliken v. Bradley* the next year, the court reversed a district remedy that had created metropolitan superdistricts linking the city of Detroit with its suburbs to remedy the widespread, institutionalized segregation found in Detroit's schools. Despite extensive evidence of the intentional nature of metro Detroit's school segregation, the decision exempted suburban districts from any role in or responsibility for remedying school segregation and subsequently reinforced the existing trend of white flight from city public schools to suburban school districts. Calling the decision "a giant step backwards" from *Brown* and an "emasculation of our constitutional guarantee of equal protection of the laws," Thurgood Marshall in his dissent observed, "Notwithstanding a record showing a widespread and pervasive racial segregation . . . this Court holds that the District Court was powerless to require the State to remedy its constitutional violation in any meaningful fashion . . . thereby guaranteeing that Negro children in Detroit will receive the same separate and inherently unequal education in the future as they have been unconstitutionally afforded in the past."[94]

Rodriguez and *Milliken* had far-reaching consequences for school children in suburban, urban, and rural areas, as they sheltered inequality through a legal claim of local preference and control. Alongside the ways President Ford and mainstream news outlets naturalized the resistance to Boston's court-ordered desegregation, this spelled an end to any substantial national commitment to school desegregation and provided comfort to those who wanted to preserve the "quality" of "their schools" by denying access to other children.

Racial inequities in schooling have continued to widen in the four decades since *Milliken*. In 2007, the Supreme Court, in *Community Schools v. Seattle*, went a step further. Asserting that *Brown*'s goal had long since been realized and even voluntary school desegregation programs in Seattle and Louisville were an "extreme approach," it struck down these programs as "more faithful to the heritage of *Brown*." The fable made flesh, Justice John Roberts explained the court's decision: "When it comes to using race to assign children to schools, history will be heard. . . . It was not the inequality of the facilities but the fact of legally separating children

based on race on which the Court relied to find a constitutional violation in that case [*Brown*]." Ignoring the explicit language of the *Brown*
decision that "the right of the opportunity of an education . . . must be
made available to all on equal terms," the court stated that *Brown* had
only sought to address the use of race in school assignment rather than
the ways the use of race was a mechanism to promote inequality. In other
words, fundamental school inequality didn't pose a constitutional problem, only the explicit denial of a seat next to a white kid did. Thus, the
ways the story of the movement had been shrunken and distorted helped
shape a much narrower idea of what the problem was, and emboldened
this court backsliding.

Given this history, then, it should not be surprising that a 2014 University of California, Los Angeles, study found that New York had the most
segregated schools in the country (with charter schools in New York City
some of the most segregated)—and that many Northern metropolises
were more segregated than Southern ones.[95] After a decades-long struggle involving school inequities and state funding, the Campaign for Fiscal
Equity brought suit in 1993, challenging the inequitable funding of New
York's schools using the state's constitutional guarantee of a sound and
basic education for all students. In 2001, Judge Leland de Grasse found
deep racial inequities in terms of funding, but New York State appealed
the case. When a court of appeals sided with de Grasse in 2003, the state
refused to comply. De Grasse determined that $5.6 billion in operating aid
and $9.2 billion in capital funding were needed, but the state committed
only $2.3 billion in 2007–2009, then froze the funding with the recession.
New York City students are still owed billions of dollars.

Grappling with a fuller history of the Northern movement that steadfastly challenged educational inequality and school segregation raises
important and unsettling questions. The problem did not rest with the
poor values of Black parents or poor behaviors of Black students (as many
Northern officials tried to claim) but with a deeply inequitable school system that provided educational resources, small class size, up-to-date facilities, and jobs disproportionately to white people. Like their Southern
counterparts, many Black parents in the North built movements, trying
tactic after tactic, to call attention to the problem and demand desegregation and equality for their children. Seeing these efforts, and the racial
inequality left to fester in many places, raises questions about the narrow

ways the civil rights movement is understood. Many commentators now talk about how schools are "resegregating," highlighting the ways that civil rights era progress in desegregating schools in the South has been significantly eroded.[96] But this ignores—and erases—the fact that many school systems, including New York's, never desegregated. According to a 2013 report, nine of the top ten most segregated US cities are in the North, with Detroit being the most segregated city and New York, Boston, and Los Angeles (despite their reputations for cosmopolitanism) at numbers three, nine, and ten, respectively.[97]

Systemic school inequality extended above the Mason–Dixon Line, and activists fought for decades to challenge it, but city elites, white citizens, and much of the mainstream media—with tacit and sometimes explicit support from the federal government—protected systemic inequality in Northern cities. By ignoring this history, the fable makes it seem as though injustice is vanquished in the end, and that society, in time, appreciates those who fight injustice through proper channels. Despite a massive show of organized, persistent, and peaceful direct action in New York and Boston (two cities that pride themselves on their openness and liberalism), white officials and citizens resisted change. They continued to cast Black and Latino youth as the problem, amplifying criminalization and programs for "juvenile delinquency," while persistently ignoring or demonizing Black and Latino demands for equitable resources, open hiring, and desegregation. The kinds of movements built by parents such as Mae Mallory, Ruth Batson, and Ellen Jackson, and by community leaders including Ella Baker and Milton Galamison, and by 460,000 student boycotters, help us see their relentless dreams for excellent schools for all in the city.

The fuller history of Northern struggle reveals the ways the fable has helped maintain the idea that the problem rests in the behaviors and values present in urban communities of color today, as opposed to the lack of will to change in society more broadly. Seeing these long-standing Black movements in these cities, and the institutions and citizens that resisted them, forces us to reexamine the ways we talk about the uprisings of the 1960s and where our cities are today.

CHAPTER TWO

Revisiting the Uprisings of the 1960s and the Long History of Injustice and Struggle That Preceded Them

People can cry much easier than they can change.

—James Baldwin[1]

In my travels in the North I was increasingly becoming disillusioned with the power structures there . . . [who] welcome[d] me to their cities and showered praise on the heroism of Southern Negroes. Yet when the issues were joined concerning local conditions only the language was polite; the rejection was firm and unequivocal.

—Martin Luther King Jr., November 1965[2]

THE SUMMER OF 2017 marked fifty years since the Newark and Detroit uprisings. Scores of anniversary articles, podcasts, radio interviews, op-eds, public events, and even a Hollywood movie reflected on Black life in these cities, on the uprisings and their causes, on what happened and how it changed life in these cities and the nation, and on enduring issues such as police brutality today. And while many thoughtfully excavated a larger history of systemic racial injustice and Black life in both cities, nearly all replicated a glaring erasure: leaving out the long history of activism in these cities *before* these uprisings. Perhaps the worst was Kathryn Bigelow's film *Detroit*, written by Mark Boal, which focused on the police killings of three Black teenagers at the Algiers Motel early on the fourth morning of the Detroit uprising. The movie literally started with the police raid of the bar that touched off the riot, completely erasing the history of Black life and activism in the city before that night. In Bigelow and Boal's *Detroit*, there was no Black community life in the city before the riot or well-established Black grievances, let alone a long-standing Black movement that repeatedly raised issues of police brutality, housing and school segregation, urban renewal, and job exclusion but had been disparaged and dismissed for years before the uprising.

Fifty years earlier, both Martin Luther King Jr. and Parks had pointedly criticized the willful disregard of movements and "resistance to change" in Los Angeles and Detroit in the years leading up to the uprisings in both cities. While both King and Parks are regularly invoked in discussions of racial politics today, their work in the North and particularly the way they framed the uprisings of the 1960s are hardly acknowledged. Both had pressed for change and joined with movements in these cities demanding housing and school desegregation, jobs and public assistance, and an end to police brutality for years before the uprisings—and were attacked for it. And both insisted that the story did not begin with the riots of the mid-1960s, as the media and political officials suggested, but with the long history of injustice and frustrated Black struggle in the North that preceded them.

In November 1965, King took to the pages of the *Saturday Review* to criticize the surprise evinced by California officials in the wake of the Watts riot three months earlier. Given widespread segregation and inequality in Los Angeles and a freedom movement long opposed and dismissed there, King found the shock dishonest; Northern city leaders like those in LA in the years before the uprising embraced his efforts in the South but were "firm" and "unequivocal" in rejecting local demands for change.[3] By refusing to recognize the long history of Black struggle in the city challenging school and housing segregation, job exclusion, and police brutality and own up to the massive white resistance to it, Angelenos conveniently avoided their responsibility. While offering concern about civil rights in the South, they had maintained and defended systems of inequality at home that had created the conditions for the uprising. King found this double standard deeply troubling.

This willful blindness that King critiqued in the *Saturday Review* has been replicated in popular narratives and in many textbooks: as the story goes, a movement of courageous Southern Black people, with the help of liberal Northern whites, pushed the nation to confront the Jim Crow South and succeeded in passing two landmark laws, the 1964 Civil Rights Act and 1965 Voting Rights Act. But just days after the signing of the VRA,

Watts erupted. In this version, systemic racial injustice and a noble movement are located in the South. The Watts riot becomes the first introduction to the Northern racial landscape outside the South—and Black communities there are cast as angry, alienated, and unwilling to work through "proper channels." The problems of Northern Blacks are treated as much more complicated—cultural as much as structural; Northern youth pictured as inherently rejecting nonviolence and organized struggle; and no civil rights movement depicted in these cities before the riots.

In this version, King's work in and perspectives on the North are mistakenly understood to start only after these riots—a gross distortion of his actual political life, in which he had crisscrossed the North in the early 1960s to highlight not only Southern inequality but also Northern injustice. By 1960, King was publicly making clear "the racial issue that we confront in America is not a sectional but a national problem."[4] Throughout the early 1960s, he took part in rallies, meetings, and marches from Boston to Los Angeles highlighting the problems of school and housing segregation, job discrimination, and police brutality in those cities. In April 1965, in a speech to the Massachusetts legislature, King pointedly explained that "segregation, whether it is de jure segregation of certain sections of the South or de facto segregation of the North, is a new form of slavery covered up with certain niceties."[5] And in the *Saturday Review* piece, King pointed out that most Northern white people who praised his efforts challenging segregation and racial injustice in the South resisted those efforts and his own work in their own backyards. But the media covered his criticisms of Northern racism very little—until after the riots, when it began soliciting King for his comments. In other words, King was highlighting Northern racial injustice long before the riots, but reporters often reported it as new after these uprisings.

Indeed, in the decade *before* 1965, Black Angelenos, like their counterparts in New York City, Boston, Detroit, Birmingham, and Montgomery, took to meeting rooms, mass gatherings, and the streets to protest the systemic racial inequality at the city's core. They held regular demonstrations demanding desegregation and equity in Los Angeles's public schools, protested widespread police brutality in the city, and fought racially exclusive housing developments and a segregationist 1964 state ballot initiative, Proposition 14, which sought to repeal the hard-won 1963 Rumford Fair Housing Act. King journeyed to the city a number of times to join with them. They were met with white intransigence around school inequality and segregation, an unwillingness to reform police practices, and the decisive victory of Proposition 14 in November 1964, which returned to Californians their right to discriminate in the sale and rental of their property.

Focusing on that decade of struggle before the uprising reveals that in the face of mounting Black protests, white leaders and citizens developed a variety of mechanisms to ignore them: diminishing the problem, refusing to listen, reshaping the problem, asking for proof, demonizing activists as "troublemakers," blaming Black culture as the problem, and refusing to even acknowledge incidences of police abuse. Surprise following the uprisings in both Watts and Detroit became the ultimate way to ignore the long-standing nature of these grievances. Reckoning with the history of Black organizing before the uprisings in those cities upends our popular narrative of the era and forces us to confront the years of white disregard and opposition to Black demands for justice that laid the groundwork for these rebellions of the mid-1960s. It requires us to see movements in each of these cities that were long ignored, often because many city leaders and white citizens saw themselves as open and progressive.

LA: MORE SEGREGATED THAN LITTLE ROCK

Los Angeles's commitment to segregation was deep-seated. "Los Angeles hurt me racially as much as any city I have ever known," novelist Chester Himes observed. "Black people were treated much the same as they were in any industrial city of the South.... The difference was the white people of Los Angeles seemed to be saying, 'Nigger, ain't we good to you?'"[6] Indeed, Marnesba Tackett, who migrated to Los Angeles in 1952 and soon became a leading civil rights activist, "found . . . very little better than what I found in the South."[7] In the early 1950s, Tackett led the Los Angeles NAACP's Education Committee, which began attacking school segregation, the lack of Black teachers, and the presence of racial stereotypes in the city's school curriculum.[8] The Los Angeles Unified School District (LAUSD) Board of Education vehemently denied the charges, claiming that it maintained a color-blind policy that kept no records of the racial distribution of students or teachers. As in Boston, in Los Angeles the need to *prove* the existence of segregation would be a persistent challenge for civil rights groups such as the NAACP, the Congress of Racial

Equality (CORE), and the American Civil Liberties Union (ACLU), who demanded on countless occasions that LAUSD administer a racial census to document the obviously segregated nature of its schools. The board resisted calls for a school census until it was forced by the state to conduct one in 1966, claiming Black parents would object to inscribing race on individual student records. Subsequent access to school records in a later desegregation lawsuit, according to white ACLU activist and UCLA professor John Caughey, showed that the board of education (BOE) had been "reliably informed about where Blacks were" and thus had purposely "misrepresented its own knowledge of school segregation in LAUSD."[9] Similar to what occurred in New York and Boston, in Los Angeles, there were white community activists who joined the struggle for racial equality in the city, who also consistently pointed out the state-sponsored nature of the city's segregation and were consistently ignored and in some cases red-baited for their criticisms.

The 1960 US Census revealed Los Angeles was more segregated than any city in the South, and the *California Eagle* reported, "more Negro children attend all-Negro schools in Los Angeles than attend such schools in Little Rock."[10] School segregation worsened in Los Angeles, as it did in many Northern and Western cities, after the *Brown* decision. As Black migration to the city increased, the board kept readjusting zoning lines to keep Black students ensconced in increasingly overcrowded Black schools. Many were forced to have double-session days, a policy LAUSD pursued in Black schools to accommodate increasing numbers of students, while a great number of seats went empty in other parts of the city. Teachers and administrators often called Black students "monkeys," "thugs," and "tramps."[11] Textbooks were old and often contained "happy slave tales" and other demeaning portrayals of Black people in history and literature.[12]

Patterns of school segregation did not derive simply from racialized housing patterns, as school officials liked to claim. Rather they resulted from these officials' own actions gerrymandering school zoning lines, restricting the hiring of Black and Chicano teachers, apportioning school resources unequally, tracking Black and Chicano students into vocational rather than college programs, and providing few college-preparation classes in Black and Chicano schools.

By 1961, the Southern California ACLU, NAACP, and CORE all were highlighting the dramatic overcrowding plaguing many Black and Latino schools and pressing school officials to address pervasive school segregation in the city. That year, King made the first of many trips to the city to speak to a Los Angeles freedom rally. More than twenty-eight thousand people heard King highlight the issues facing African Americans in the city and draw connections between Southern struggles and the Los Angeles movement. Shortly after getting out of a Birmingham jail in May 1963, King returned to Los Angeles and spoke to crowd of more than thirty-five thousand people at Wrigley Field. "You asked me what Los Angeles can do to help us in Birmingham," he told the audience. "The most important thing that you can do is to set Los Angeles free because you have segregation and discrimination here, and police brutality."[13]

The turnout at these events and the tenor of the coverage in local Black newspapers indicate that African Americans in Los Angeles viewed themselves as part of a national freedom movement. While the fable paints King as out of touch with racial issues in the North and West before Watts erupted, his repeated appearances in the early 1960s decrying education inequity, housing segregation, and police injustice in Los Angeles reveal this as a dangerous, if convenient, distortion.

As for local civil rights leaders, the NAACP's Marnesba Tackett critiqued the idea that Black people in Los Angeles largely viewed the civil rights movement from afar.

> Of course, Los Angeles was very sympathetic toward what was going on in the South . . . [but] my priority was in trying to get equal education right here in Los Angeles, where we had a lot of discrimination, a lot of work done in terms of the way boundaries were drawn. . . . It all needed to be worked on at one and the same time.[14]

Inspired by King's visit to create a united front movement in Los Angeles, seventy-six community and political groups formed the United Civil Rights Council in June 1963. Tackett was unanimously selected as the UCRC's education chair.[15] Attacking the BOE's claim of color blindness, she compared Los Angeles schools to "those of Alabama and Mississippi."[16] The UCRC drew up a list of demands, calling on the board to redraw district lines, transfer Black students out of overcrowded schools, diversify the curriculum, and change the teacher-hiring process to increase the number of nonwhite teachers and distribute them throughout the entire district. But the board did nothing, preferring to study the issue.

Most board members publicly asserted that the city's schools were not segregated. They blamed nonwhite families for "negative attitudes toward education," regularly referred to majority-Black schools as "culturally-disadvantaged schools," and "resent[ed] pressure put on the board. . . . We represent majorities." Instead of desegregation, Los Angeles school officials proposed increased funding to "culturally disadvantaged" schools, including money for new programs aimed at addressing "juvenile delinquency" and reducing dropout rates, and blamed "the lack of hope and motivation among some of these families which leads them into negative attitudes toward education and the demands the school makes on their children."[17]

In response, the UCRC began holding marches downtown throughout the summer of 1963, and held sit-ins, sleep-ins, and study-ins in the fall. Purposely echoing King's "Letter from Birmingham Jail," a group of the city's Black leaders issued a critical statement in June 1963: "All deliberate speed has meant no speed at all. The spirit of Birmingham means integration now in every way."[18] Hundreds of student protesters marched; they lined the halls of the BOE building with a study-in, and disrupted a meeting with a sing-in in the fall. But the board remained intransigent. Writer James Baldwin, at a 1963 press conference, took Los Angeles's leadership to task: "I doubt that a single Negro in Los Angeles would agree that conditions are improving. . . . The real Negro leaders have been trying to speak to you for years. . . . You won't listen."[19]

Such confrontational tactics were not popular in a city proud of its liberalism. In November, national director of CORE James Farmer was barred from speaking at the University of Southern California because the dean deemed him "too controversial."[20] That same month, CORE launched "Operation Jericho," a door-to-door campaign in the Watts neighborhood to counter petition campaigns by adjacent white South Gate residents to prevent school desegregation. Many Black students lived closer to South Gate High School than Jordan High School, and "the education at South Gate was so much better," Tackett explained at the time. "We noticed the school board kept expanding Jordan's boundary as more black children moved in instead of sending them to South Gate."[21] At the end of the month, the board acquiesced to South Gate parents and refused to redraw the school boundary between South Gate and Watts, making available a meager thirty-four high school transfer spots for Black students to attend South Gate and Huntington High Schools—a move the *California Eagle* termed a "fraud of the worst kind."[22]

The city remained intractable as well on the issue of police brutality. In 1961, the NAACP brought a tabulation of incidences of police brutality in the city to the Los Angeles Police Commission.[23] Nothing was done. On April 27, 1962, Los Angeles police killed the twenty-nine-year-old unarmed secretary of the local Nation of Islam (NOI), Ronald Stokes, and wounded six others outside Muslim Temple 27. None of the seven men were armed. The fracas began when officers stopped two men, claiming they were suspicious because they were loading clothes into their car and there had been burglaries nearby. Stokes was shot at close range with his hands up. Police arrested seventeen members of the NOI, including those wounded, and blamed them for the trouble.[24] Yet despite an autopsy that established that Stokes was shot at close range and had been stomped, kicked, and bludgeoned while dead or dying, the public inquest into his death found that the police shooting was "justified" in "self-defense."[25]

Making an emergency trip to Los Angeles to hold city authorities accountable for Stokes's death, Malcolm X joined NOI members, Christian ministers, Black politicians, the NAACP, and thousands of Angelenos to work toward creating a united front movement against police brutality in the city.[26] Three thousand people packed a joint mass meeting at Second Avenue Baptist Church with Malcolm X, NAACP leaders, the Reverend Maurice Dawkins, Cyril Briggs, and Mervyn Dymally. National NAACP head Roy Wilkins called attention to the city's "long reputation" under Chief William Parker for police brutality.[27] Loren Miller, who owned the *California Eagle*, and Earl Broady provided legal assistance for the fourteen NOI members, and Celes King of the NAACP provided $160,000 for their bail. Working with local activists, Malcolm X accused the LAPD of "Gestapo like tactics and false propaganda." He also began reaching out to African leaders on the matter of US police brutality and many, including Ghana's president Kwame Nkrumah and Egypt's president Gamal Abdel Nasser, condemned Stokes's murder. The lack of justice in the Stokes case spurred Malcolm X, in conversation with New York lawyer Paul Zuber, to pursue the idea of filing a petition to the United Nations protesting police brutality.[28]

When Nation of Islam head Elijah Muhammad called Malcolm X out of Los Angeles, local activists continued pressing forward, documenting a widespread pattern of police abuse in the city and calling for Chief Parker's resignation. Parker had become chief in 1950 and gained a national reputation for professionalizing the Los Angeles Police Department. Locally, however, he was known for amplifying an us-versus-them police culture and for a pattern of police brutality and harassment of Black Angelenos. His attitude toward the city's Black community was stark: "They came in and flooded a community that wasn't prepared to meet them. . . . We didn't ask these people to come here."[29]

In response to rising Black complaints of police misconduct, Mayor Sam Yorty criticized the NAACP for "bringing about the very condition they are complaining about." He asked for federal help around the "unrest" and created a blue ribbon committee to look into the issue.[30] Little change in police practices resulted. Local NAACP head Christopher Taylor blasted the committee's report: "We're right back where we started from. . . . They've ignored all complaints of the community and now they can keep on doing the same thing."[31] When Malcolm X returned to Los Angeles in 1964, he again condemned the ongoing pattern of police brutality in the city. Thus, Black grievances against the police were amply highlighted for years before the uprising.

In 1964, the burgeoning Black freedom movement in Los Angeles had to shift its organizational energies in an effort to defeat a menacing ballot initiative. Proposition 14 sought to repeal the new Rumford Housing Act, which banned racial discrimination in the sale and rental of property—a law activists had fought for years to achieve. Supporters of Proposition 14 explicitly denied any racial animus but asserted their property rights and claimed the 1963 act, by mandating antidiscrimination, denied them equal protection under the law. The proposition's confusing language would provide a template for citizen movements seeking to maintain segregation by asserting the right to private property and freedom from government intrusion: "Neither the state nor any subdivision or agency thereof shall . . . limit or abridge . . . the right of any person . . . to decline to sell, lease, or rent property to such . . . persons as he, in his absolute discretion, chooses."

The NAACP, UCRC, and CORE, along with student groups from a number of LA colleges, conducted voter registration workshops, called for a boycott of the Southwest Realty Board for backing the initiative, and worked to pressure Governor Edmund Brown to oppose the ballot initiative. The Japanese American Citizens League and the Mexican American Political Association joined the fight, as did Martin Luther King Jr., who came to Los Angeles multiple times to campaign against Proposition 14, saying its passage would be "one of the most shameful developments in our nation's history."[32] Many white Angelenos labeled him a Communist for this work, picketing the SCLC's western office with signs reading "King Has Hate, Does Travel" and "Thank God for Chief Parker."[33]

Supporters of Proposition 14 drew on "culture of poverty" images to justify patterns of racial inequality in the city. LA County Young Republicans president Robert Gaston claimed, "Negroes are not accepted [in white neighborhoods] because they haven't made themselves acceptable."[34] Calling the 1963 Fair Housing Act "the Forced Housing Act," supporters raised contrasting images of happy, suburban Anglo families and dysfunctional, deviant families of color. In November, California became the first to "take away gains Negroes had won," as King put it, when 75 percent of white Californians "voted for ghettos."[35] The proposition passed by a two-to-one margin, even as Californians voted by similar margin to return Lyndon Johnson to the White House.[36] The message from the majority of white voters was stark: civil rights were good, as long as they didn't come home to California.

Los Angeles branch NAACP vice president Celes King observed the irony of Proposition 14's passage and the lack of change in Los Angeles, despite its sunny reputation: "[With] the models in the other part of the country where they appeared to be making progress, here in Los Angeles we were supposed to be the satisfied blacks. Well, [we] really weren't satisfied."[37] Nine months later, on August 11, 1965, a California Highway Patrol officer pulled over twenty-one-year-old Marquette Frye for drunk driving. Frye had moved to Los Angeles at the age of thirteen and struggled with the city's segregated schools: "When we came to Los Angeles, we got into an all-Negro school. . . . I made 'A's and 'B's back in Wyoming but here I began getting suspended for fighting."[38] Frye subsequently dropped out of high school.

When another police officer began hitting Frye and his mother, who had arrived on the scene, onlookers started throwing stones and bottles at

the officers, and the unrest escalated to the looting and burning of buildings. In response, the police cracked down on the Black community at
large. The city curfew only covered Black LA—an area the media began
calling "Watts," although it covered the neighborhoods of Watts, Central,
Avalon, Florence, Green Meadow, Exposition, and Willowbrook. That
this swatch of 250,000 residents could be effectively cordoned off from
the rest of the city is a testament to the degree of segregation in LA. At
the end of seven days, thirty-four people had died and hundreds more
were injured, many at the hands of the local police or the California National Guard.

Many public officials and local residents were "shocked" by the Watts
riot, as it came to be called. Proclaiming California as a "state without racial discrimination," Governor Brown flew home immediately, informing
reporters that "nobody told me there was an explosive situation in Los
Angeles."[39] It was a willful, comforting shock. Even though the *Los Angeles Times* had covered many of the protests of the past decade, reporters
and editors refused to call city leaders to account for their long deafness
to Black grievances and instead helped legitimate this frame of surprise.
As King made clear a few months later in the *Saturday Review*, this frame
of surprise conveniently erased the multitude of organizations that had
long highlighted and challenged racial injustice in the city, and his own
efforts to draw attention to inequality and police injustice in Los Angeles
and across the North. (The year before, following the 1964 Harlem uprising, King had similarly called for a civilian-complaint review board to
monitor the New York Police Department—and been roundly criticized
by city leaders.)[40]

The "surprise" also obscured the role many in the city had played in
dismissing Black protest and maintaining inequality. By erasing this long
history of struggle, many Angelenos could conveniently evade responsibility for maintaining these systems of inequality and creating the conditions for the uprising.

The anger and frustration that burst forth during the uprising demonstrated the expectation and resulting frustration that had grown within
Los Angeles's African American community. NAACP chapter vice president Celes King, a bail bondsman, risked his business to post bond for
hundreds of people, eliminating the standards usually used to agree to
post for someone. That the vice president of the city's NAACP was willing

to affiliate his economic future to protect the rights of those arrested is telling: "The community was, I would say, generally supportive of the blacks that were the so-called rioters."[41]

The uprising was more targeted than public officials suggested. Aimed at commercial interests (such as banks that charged Black people high rates, and grocery stores that marked up prices and sold rotten food), most housing was untouched, as were many Black businesses, Simon Rodia's artistic Watts Tower, and the Urban League's Watts project.[42] The Los Angeles Riot Study, conducted by UCLA, on Black attitudes about the riot found that 58 percent of the Black people surveyed felt that favorable results would follow the riot, 62 percent considered the riot a Negro protest, and 64 percent thought the attack was deserved.[43] This is not to say that every Black Angeleno saw the riots as a form of protest (a significant minority of the Black community clearly did not), nor that those who did linked it directly to the long-ignored activism of the previous decade. But understanding how nearly two-thirds of Black Angelenos surveyed saw the riots as "deserved" necessitates seeing both the inequities in the city and the long history of struggle to address these problems by other means.

Nearly incessantly at first, and for years following the uprising, journalists repeatedly asked King about Watts, giving him much more room to expound on these issues than they ever had before 1965. King critiqued the frame of shock but at other times went along with it, because it provided him space to talk about interlocking issues of race and class oppression that he'd been trying to emphasize for years. As Black bookstore owner Alfred Ligon explained, "It was only because of the [Watts] uprising that they became interested in the blacks."[44]

While many city and state officials, along with the media, blamed Black culture and underclass alienation to explain what had produced the uprising, a mountain of evidence from the research, testimony, and investigation that followed the uprising, including that of the McCone Commission convened to investigate it, made the case that the "riots" were political rebellions against racism in the city and nation. The social profile of the "rioters" culled from the arrest data indicates that they had better than average educations, and that they were employed, socially conscious, and aware of international news. But researchers for both the McCone Commission and the Kerner Commission (convened after the uprisings in Detroit and Newark in 1967) were disciplined when they tried to put forth this more political thesis.[45]

DETROIT AND THE "RESISTANCE TO CHANGE LONG BEFORE"

Both Martin Luther King Jr. and Rosa Parks had a similar criticism of the reactions of many Detroiters and public officials to the 1967 Detroit uprising. For years, Black people in Detroit had highlighted and challenged Motown's injustices: deep housing and school segregation, job discrimination, and patterns of police harassment and brutality.

On June 20, 1963, four years before the uprising, nearly two hundred thousand Black people marched through Detroit highlighting pervasive inequality in the city and the unwillingness of city leaders to recognize Black grievances and address segregated schools, housing, or job exclusion. March co-organizer Reverend C. L. Franklin explained to the *Detroit News* that the march would serve as a "warning to the city that what has transpired in the past is no longer acceptable to the Negro community."[46] Active in union and open housing movements in the city, Rosa Parks appeared at the front of Detroit's Great March alongside Franklin, the Reverend Al Cleage Jr., and Martin Luther King Jr.

The Parks family had been forced to leave Montgomery in 1957, still unable to find work and facing death threats after the boycott's successful end eight months earlier. They moved to Detroit, where her brother and cousins lived. Parks described Detroit as the "Northern promised land that wasn't."[47] While a number of the public displays of segregation on buses, at drinking fountains, and on elevators were thankfully gone, she didn't find "too much difference" in race relations between Montgomery and Detroit and the systems of school segregation, housing segregation, job discrimination, and police brutality in both cities.[48] For years after they arrived, both Rosa and husband Raymond Parks had tremendous difficulty finding either steady work or decent housing, their experience paralleling those of many other Black people in the city. And like she had in Montgomery, she would spend the next four decades fighting the racism of Jim Crow Detroit.

Finally in 1961, the Parkses secured a ground-floor flat in the Virginia Park neighborhood along Detroit's Twelfth Street corridor—"the heart of the ghetto," as she described it. By the 1960s, twice as many people would be crowded into the Twelfth Street corridor, as these neighborhoods shifted from about 95 percent white in 1940 to 95 percent Black in 1960.[49] Like the Parkses, many Black people couldn't afford their own places. Decent housing for Black people to rent or buy was in desperately short supply. During the 1960s, the city began using urban renewal to clear Black neighborhoods to make room for development, gobbling up many Black homes and neighborhoods in the process. Forty-three thousand Detroiters were displaced by urban renewal—70 percent of them Black. Activists began calling it "Negro Removal."[50] Detroit's liberal mayor, Jerome Cavanagh, had brought in $38 million in federal funds for urban renewal.[51]

After years of trying to draw attention to issues relating to jobs, schools, housing, and city planning, the 1963 march was organized as a way to disrupt the indifference of most white Detroiters to the inequalities and injustices that shaped Black life in the city. The numbers of marchers rivaled those at the March on Washington in DC two months later. Labor activist General Baker remembered the Great March's massiveness: "We didn't have to walk but were pushed up Jefferson."[52] The size signaled a growing impatience with the lack of change in the Motor City. After King spoke, Reverend Cleage took to the stage at Cobo Hall, highlighting the landscape of local inequality and urging Detroiters to boycott A&P supermarkets until the company agreed to hire Black managers.[53]

Thirteen days after Detroit's Great March, a police officer killed a young Black woman, Cynthia Scott. Cutting an impressive figure at six foot four and 198 pounds, "Saint Cynthia," as she was known, a sex worker, was shot twice in the back and once in the stomach by police officer Theodore Spicher. Three days later, the prosecutor ruled that Spicher shot the "fleeing suspect" in self-defense and no charges would be filed. While the police claimed that Scott had pulled out a knife, an acquaintance who was with her said that she didn't have a weapon; rather, the police had been harassing her, and when she walked away from them after telling them they had no grounds to arrest her, they shot her.

Five thousand people demonstrated outside police headquarters, yelling "Stop killer cops!" and threatening to storm the building.[54] Petitions were circulated to recall the prosecutor, and the Detroit NAACP demanded a full investigation.[55] Hundreds of people continued picketing and sitting-in at police headquarters. Richard Henry, whose brother Milton served as the lawyer on Scott's case, and Al Cleage helped organize a picket line outside police headquarters a week later. Cleage's Christian militancy would be a key driving force in Detroit's growing freedom movement. Growing up in Detroit, Cleage attended Wayne State University and Oberlin Graduate School of Theology, in Ohio. Returning to Detroit in 1954, he formed his own congregation, Central Congregational, later renamed Central United Church of Christ. In 1957, the church purchased a building on Twelfth Street. In the early 1960s, Cleage joined with Richard and Milton Henry to build the Group on Advanced Leadership, an all-Black organization, "because something more needed to be done about police brutality, Negro removal disguised as urban renewal, Negro-hating textbooks, and the lack of black business."[56]

Scott's case became a touchstone for young activists in Detroit and led to the emergence of the Black political party, the Freedom Now Party. Henry Cleage, Al Cleage's brother, ran for Wayne County prosecutor in 1964 on the Freedom Now ticket, promising if elected to reopen the case.[57] As Al Cleage wrote in the *Illustrated News* (the bimonthly newspaper he founded in 1961 that developed a circulation of more than 35,000), "All Negroes are not automatically suspicious because of the fact that they are Negroes. . . . No grounds were given for the arrest for Cynthia Scott. Her arrest was therefore illegal and she had the right to walk away. An officer who kills a citizen who refuses to submit to an illegal arrest is guilty of murder and must be brought to trial!"[58] Young activists sat-in at the mayor's office, calling for a Black chief of police to be appointed.[59]

Public schools, urban renewal, housing, policing, jobs—these were the issues that animated Detroit's freedom struggle. Critical of the racial blinders of Detroit's liberalism, Cleage split from some other Black leaders to oppose a tax increase for schools, on the grounds that school segregation meant that Black people would pay more but Black children would get less. In November 1963, Black leaders held a meeting to create a Northern Christian Leadership Conference, but when they refused to let Cleage invite Malcolm X, he broke away and spearheaded his own parallel conference, the Grassroots Leadership Conference with Malcolm X as the keynote.

Since the late 1940s, Black people and the Detroit NAACP had brought a pattern of police harassment and brutality to the city's attention. But these injustices were repeatedly denied and swept under the rug by city officals. In 1960, the Detroit NAACP lambasted the "chronic" nature of the problem and presented its own records of 244 cases of police brutality between 1955 and 1960, with 47 resulting in hospitalization.[60] In 1964,

NAACP executive director Roy Wilkins sounded the alarm that police relations in Detroit had worsened drastically.[61] In 1965, people marched to protest five police killings in two years—Cynthia Scott, Kenneth Evans, Clifton Allen, Nathaniel Williams, and Arthur Barrington—and the brutal beatings of six others.[62]

On top of outright brutality, police officers regularly took money and other items of value from Black people they stopped. Any note of protest could lead to a beating, according to Detroit NAACP leader Arthur Johnson, and a trumped-up charge of drunkenness, disorderly conduct, or resisting arrest.[63] Police expanded the practice of arresting Black people simply on "investigation"; about a third of their arrests were made for this reason.[64] And they gave scores of tickets to increase revenue. "There's a certain time of month . . . that you can't hardly drive around the block. They follow you around just waiting for you to do something wrong," one young man explained.[65] Following the Watts uprising, Detroit police grew more aggressive, using new federal money to create a Tactical Mobile Unit for "crowd control" that Black Detroiters found to be "Gestapo-like."[66]

Again and again, Black Detroiters raised these injustices, but Detroit's leadership repeatedly ignored them. Detroit's Black newspapers, the *Michigan Chronicle* and Cleage's *Illustrated News*, recorded a steady stream of police abuse and harassment of Black Detroiters, but according to Johnson, the city's major newspapers, the *Detroit News* and *Detroit Free Press*, "had a standing agreement" not to cover issues of police brutality."[67]

Despite local calls, protests, rallies, and walkouts for concrete action to remedy Detroit's segregated schools and housing, reform police practice, and open up job possibilities, little changed.[68] Yet many whites in the city, including the city's white political leadership, believed Detroit the apex of racial progress, with two Black congressmen, a strong NAACP, a liberal mayor, and a prosperous auto industry that appeared to offer Black and white workers economic opportunity. In 1966, *Look* magazine and the National Civic League named Detroit an "All-America City."[69]

But such sunny pronouncements masked an unjust reality. Beginning August 9, 1966, a three-day mini-uprising erupted on Detroit's eastside on Kercheval Avenue following harassment by a specialized police unit known as the "Big Four" (four white plainclothes police officers who moved through the city and were known for intimidating Black people) and the quick arrival of the Tactical Mobile Unit.[70] Saying it had been building up for ten years, one young man explained their frustration with how police treated Black Detroiters. "If you're just standing on the street, no matter how long, they run you off. If you're in your car, they tell you to move on. If you drag your eyes, you're wrong."[71] But city leadership downplayed the episode and continued to celebrate the city's racial openness.

The 1967 uprising began following a massive police reaction when patrons refused to disperse after police tried to shut down an after-hours bar. People had gathered that night to celebrate the safe return of two men from Vietnam. Because many Detroit establishments refused to serve Black people, and many Black business owners had difficulty securing the paperwork and capital for an official establishment, after-hours bars, or "blind pigs" as they were called, represented a crucial space for Black community leisure. Police raids on these bars had been, according to a Department of Justice report, a "chief source of complaint" before the uprising—and that night would be the third time this particular establishment would be raided in less than two years. In the early morning hours, police began arresting people at the blind pig at 9125 Twelfth Street (Detroit's Twelfth Street corridor served as a hub of working-class Black leisure). The crowd grew larger and more angry as morning dawned and the day went on. The police grew more violent and forceful, as well. At the peak of the unrest, the uprising encompassed fourteen square miles. The governor requested federal help, and 2,700 army paratroopers descended on the city. Law enforcement was given wide latitude to "subdue" the uprising by any means necessary.

"What really went on was a police riot," Congressman John Conyers would later observe.[72] In certain neighborhoods, police shot out the streetlights, causing further chaos. The only Black bookstore in Detroit, Vaughn's Bookstore—a frequent gathering place for young activists—was intentionally destroyed by police, witnesses reported. Police firebombed the building, mutilated the artwork, damaged many photographs, and left the water running, ruining the vast majority of books.[73] Police arrested over seven thousand people during the uprising, but most of these arrests were ultimately shown to be baseless. In perhaps the most egregious event, police killed three young men at the Algiers Motel; while the officers claimed self-defense, no weapons were ever found and witnesses said the young men were deliberately murdered. At the end of five days, forty-three people were dead—thirty at the hands of the police—and property damage was estimated at $45 million, with 412 buildings completely burned.

The abusive policing that took place during the uprising was supported by prosecutors and the courts. Wayne County prosecutor William Cahalan not only supported police tactics but insisted on high bail to keep people "off the streets."[74] As historian Say Burgin documents, judges "ran roughshod over defendants' Eighth Amendment rights—at the explicit request of Wayne County prosecutor William Cahalan—by routinely denying counsel, setting impossibly high bails (often for whole groups of people at once), and bringing spurious charges for which there was little to no evidence."[75] Ultimately, according to the Kerner Commission, 24 percent of those arrested for felonies were never prosecuted, and half of those prosecuted were dismissed at preliminary examination for lack of evidence.[76] By spring of 1968, with half the 3,200 looting cases cleared, 60 percent had resulted in dismissal and *only two* had resulted in convictions on the original charge.[77]

Understanding that these maneuvers were aimed at keeping Black and poor people "off of the streets," newly elected Recorder's Court judge George Crockett was sickened by the ways in which the judiciary acted as an extension of the police and the mayor's office during the uprising. Crockett, who had served as a criminal defense lawyer and vice president of the National Lawyers Guild, represented Communists accused under the Smith Act before deciding to run for Detroit's Recorder's Court in 1966. He observed: "There is no equal justice for black people in our criminal courts today, and what's more, there never has been. And this is the shame of our whole judicial system. . . . And this is so, not because the written law says it shall be so, rather it is so because our judges, by their rulings, make it so."[78] Crockett would use his powers as judge very differently than his colleagues and try to right the scales of justice, often freeing or giving lenient sentences to first-time offenders and for nonviolent offenses, and refusing to collude with prosecutors on how justice should proceed.

Rosa Parks, who lived a mile from where the uprising began and worked serving constituent needs in Congressman John Conyers's Detroit office, sought to contextualize the Detroit uprising as "the result of resistance to change that was needed long beforehand."[79] Patterns of police harassment and brutality had been documented for years with no change in police practice. Parks thus located the uprising in the context of white resistance and deafness to Black grievances in Detroit: "The establishment of white people . . . will antagonize and provoke violence. When the young people want to present themselves as human beings and come into their own as men, there is always something to cut them down."[80] Bookstore owner Ed Vaughn echoed this in an interview with Black reporter Louis Lomax: "You told them; Martin Luther King told them; everybody who cares, white and black told them. They did not listen."[81] A few months later, in a talk before the American Psychological Association, King reframed the question of riots by highlighting the injustice and white illegality that produced the conditions in Northern cities: "When we ask Negroes to abide by the law, let us also demand that the white man abide by law in the ghettos. Day-in and day-out he violates welfare laws to deprive the poor of their meager allotments; he flagrantly violates building codes and regulations; his police make a mockery of law; and he violates laws on equal employment and education and the provisions for civic services."[82]

As King made clear, the police themselves were doing illegal and immoral things, as were landlords and city officials, often protected by the cloak of whiteness. Despite rampant police harassment and brutality during the uprising, a pattern of impunity followed—and it became clear that there would be no accountability for police misconduct. Following a speech by H. Rap Brown in Detroit, young militants took up the call for a "People's Tribunal" to bring the evidence of what happened in front of the community and hold the police accountable for their actions during the riot, particularly the killings of the three young men—Carl Cooper (age seventeen), Aubrey Pollard (age nineteen), and Fred Temple (age eighteen)—at the Algiers Motel. Dan Aldridge, one of the organizers, said, "We wanted to bring out all the facts and the truth about what actually happened." They asked the fifty-four-year-old Rosa Parks if she would be willing to serve on the jury. Believing that it was "better to protest than to accept injustice," she agreed and joined their attempts to get justice—understanding the importance of the older generation in nurturing the spirit of resistance emerging with young people.[83] Ed Vaughn, African American writer John Killens, and white activist Frank Joyce also served on the jury. Attorney Milton R. Henry served as prosecutor; Solomon A. Plapkin, a white attorney, and Central Church member Russell L. Brown Jr. acted as defense counsel. (The Detroit Bar Association considered disbarring the lawyers who participated.)

Organizers were forced to hold the tribunal in Reverend Cleage's church (later known as the Shrine of the Black Madonna, for the eighteen-foot brown-skinned Madonna and Child that artist Glanton Dowdell painted and Cleage installed in the front of the sanctuary on Easter Sunday 1967) when the original site, the Dexter Theater—fearing police would attack the place—backed out. They kept the witnesses out of sight, fearing police retaliation.

On the evening of August 30, 1967, people began arriving early and the church was packed to the rafters—with the sidewalks overflowing as well. "The brothers and sisters don't know what fear is any more," Cleage wrote after in the *Michigan Chronicle*. "There is no way to put down on paper the sheer horror of the recital of events by witness after witness. . . . The packed auditorium became more quiet than a courtroom."[84] Hearing the evidence, the tribunal's jury found the police guilty of all charges. According to Aldridge, the reaction was "joy. . . . Because they heard the truth."

The last time Rosa Parks saw Martin Luther King was seven months later, in the elite Detroit suburb of Grosse Pointe. Repeatedly interrupted, heckled, and called a traitor that night, King made a point of contextualizing the riot the year before:

> I'm absolutely convinced that a riot merely intensifies the fears of the white community while relieving the guilt. . . . But it is not enough for me to stand before you tonight and condemn riots . . . without, at the same time, condemning the contingent, intolerable conditions that exist in our society. . . . [A] riot is the language of the unheard. And what is it America has failed to hear? It has failed to hear that the plight of the negro poor has worsened over the last twelve or fifteen years. It has failed to hear that the promises of freedom and justice have not been met. And it has failed to hear that large segments of white society are more concerned about tranquility and the status quo than about justice and humanity.[85]

In the years following these uprisings, California and Michigan became key sites in the development of Black Power. Groups such as the Black Panther Party, the Dodge Revolutionary Union Movement, and the Republic of New Afrika took the Black freedom struggle to new places in the later 1960s—foregrounding access to health care, affordable housing and liberatory education, the right to self-defense, the need both for reparations and fundamental economic transformation, and a changed relationship between law enforcement and the Black community. But the urge was to present this militancy as coming out of nowhere, rather than as having emerged from years of work, struggle, and reflection by local organizers, from reflection, and from the "resistance to change long before." Seeing a protracted movement in these cities before the uprisings reveals how long and hard people fought to reveal and challenge these injustices—and the investments Northern political elites and many ordinary white citizens had in ignoring or dismissing those movements. Surprise and sadness, as Baldwin points out, were easier than changing.

A similar surprise has accompanied uprisings from Ferguson to Baltimore today—as has a similar refusal to grapple with long-standing Black demands and movements that preceded them. While recent uprisings in Ferguson, Cleveland, Milwaukee, and Baltimore have prompted much important reporting on the nature of injustice in law enforcement, municipal policy, and the court system in these places, few stories have focused on the groups and organizers in these cities that have highlighted problems *for years*. Much like after the Watts and Detroit uprisings, journalists today have not forced city leaders and citizens to grapple with the reasons why these movements and the issues they amply highlighted for years have been neglected for so long.

Such silences are comfortable. As King and Parks pointed out fifty years ago, it is easier to cast people as unwilling to work through the proper channels than wrestle with the ways society didn't listen and wouldn't change, even when people did work through the proper channels. It is easier to cast protesters as reckless and dangerous than face the comfort and cruel convenience of those on the sidelines of injustice. And it is easier to frame the situation as unfortunate but outside of our control, rather than come to grips with the ways the country has maintained an unjust criminal justice system and the long-standing protest that preceded these moments.

CHAPTER THREE

Beyond the Redneck

Polite Racism and the "White Moderate"

I have been gravely disappointed with the white moderate. I have almost reached the regrettable conclusion that the Negro's great stumbling block in his stride toward freedom is not the White Citizen's Counciler or the Ku Klux Klanner, but the white moderate, who is more devoted to "order" than to justice . . . who constantly says: "I agree with you in the goal you seek, but I cannot agree with your methods of direct action."

—Martin Luther King Jr.,
"Letter from Birmingham Jail," 1963

PART OF WHAT MAKES these memorials and tributes so powerful is that they highlight the courageous successes of ordinary citizens against systems of power and injustice. It is a David-and-Goliath story and David wins. "When the history of this country is written," Senator Barack Obama eulogized at Rosa Parks's funeral, "when a final accounting is done, it is this small, quiet woman whose name will be remembered long after the names of senators and presidents have been forgotten." Such invocations invite all Americans to identify with and be inspired by the power of ordinary people to change the course of the nation.

The danger in such identification is that the forces of injustice, complicity, and complacency—the Goliath—are placed at a distance. With the exception of a few ubervillains like Eugene "Bull" Connor and J. Edgar Hoover, the perpetrators go unmarked. "That's because so much of Black History Month takes place in the passive voice," writer Gary Younge observed. "Leaders 'get assassinated,' patrons 'are refused' service, women 'are ejected' from public transport. So the objects of racism are many but the subjects few. In removing the instigators, the historians remove the agency and, in the final reckoning, the historical responsibility."[1] Our popular history of the movement largely sidesteps how and by whom racial inequality was perpetrated and maintained. Without understanding how and why a system of racial injustice was propelled not only by people who were yelling but by people who were silent, not just by violence but by state bureaucracy, and by refusing to grapple with the various interests and benefits this system accrued for many and the fears people harbored of standing up against it, we miss a key lesson from this history.

Key to popular understandings of the civil rights movement is a view of racism as personal hatefulness—"Southern backwardness," as civil rights historian Charles Payne has termed it. Racism is pictured as the governor snarling at the University of Alabama entrance, the Mississippi voter registrar continually slamming the door on would-be Black voters, the white mother spitting at Black children—key embodiments of those who perpetrated racial injustice but not the only manifestations of it. Our image of racism is violent, aggressively personalized, and continually located in the "barbaric South," historian Heather Ann Thompson argues.[2] There has been a tendency to personify racism in the figure of a working-class white redneck who dislikes Black people and spouts hateful things, as opposed to the middle- or upper-class white person who might decry such hatefulness but still embraces racially unjust policies.[3]

The focus on the redneck racism of the Jim Crow South and its epithets and violence blinds us to the venality of "polite" racism and the "firm" resistance to Black demands, as King aptly characterized it. Other "polite" embodiments of racism were endemic across the country in maintaining white supremacy—public officials and citizens who preferred framings like "separation" and "neighborhood schools"; who utilized sociological theories of crime and "cultural dysfunction" to justify inequalities in city schools, services, housing, and policing; and who denied jobs, limited access to government programs, and maintained segregation through bureaucratic means. Yet these perpetrators find little place in these fables. By making racism only about bombing, blocking, and spitting, the nation gets off easy.

With its roots in the nineteenth century, this "barbaric South" framing of racism was a strategic and purposeful Cold War construct that has carried into our present-day understandings. With the United States seeking to appeal to the hearts and minds of the Third World during the Cold War (and with the Soviet Union highlighting America's racism), the nation was invested in casting the race problem as a regional Southern anachronism at odds with the liberal American way. In a paradigm born before the Civil War, the Deep South was portrayed as distinct and separate. Then, in the 1950s and 1960s, when a movement courageously built by ordinary Black people with support from the courts and the federal government took on these premodern racists, it was increasingly broadcast around the world, as legal historian Mary Dudziak demonstrates.[4] In other words, the Southern civil rights movement came to signify the power of American democracy, where ordinary citizens (with the help of Northern liberals) could challenge the antidemocratic elements within it and succeed. To show the Northern struggle, to show racism embedded across the nation in far more liberal places often through more "polite" means, would have disrupted this framework.

The redneckification of racism today provides a form of national catharsis. If racism is pictured as mean Southern ladies who decide they want a separate bathroom for the Black women who work for them (as in Hollywood's *The Help*) or as fat Southern sheriffs who block tiny children from entering school buildings, then most Americans can rest easy. In *The Help*, the main white villain is mean to her own kids and insists on having a separate toilet built for her Black maid. While certainly such people existed, racism also lurked in white people who loved their children and would never expect their Black maid to use a separate bathroom, who liked individual Black people and even were inspired by the Southern civil rights movement but didn't want change in their own backyard (whether in New York or Alabama).[5] Maneuvering and fighting to maintain the status quo, many people treated Black protest as unfair and excessive. Or they stayed silent when bad things happened to others, assuming people must have done something to bring these problems on themselves.

While many White Americans supported segregation with their actions, others supported it through their inaction—their unwillingness to see how their home, neighborhood, school, or desire for police protection derived from disparity. Many refused to prioritize antiracism, looking the other way when friends, coworkers, or politicians labored to preserve racially inequitable systems. Still, other Americans knew that this system was deeply wrong but felt there was little they could do about it or feared risking their family's safety and security, so they hung back. This history is humbling—showing how hard it is to do the right thing and exposing the many barriers to unseating the status quo. It reveals that the perpetration of injustice is not always about hatred but often about indifference, fear, and personal comfort.

Partly, it is easier to think about racism as the provenance of hate-filled individuals—J. Edgar Hoover, or a parade of racist Southern governors, or South Boston mothers who attacked Black children, or Klan members who set fire to churches and homes—because it lets a lot of people off the hook. When racism is portrayed only in spitting and screaming, torches and vigilante justice, many people can rest easy, believing they share little responsibility in its maintenance. When racism is cast as the actions of a small cast of mean individuals, the rest of the people who supported, allowed, or stood aside for it are harder to see, and the solutions often become about changing hearts, about diversity training and tolerance. And when the focus is on individual prejudice, the systems people support that maintain and excuse injustice recede into the background.

But if racism is pictured as parents asserting their rights as taxpayers and questioning whether the *Brown* decision applies to "their schools"; if it is shown in calls for more "law and order" and "fiscal responsibility"; if it is demonstrated in the lack of public will to address differentials in resources and services in schools, streets, policing, and housing; if it is revealed in the kinds of issues the news media chooses not to cover; if it is illustrated in who stays silent when inequality is brought to light—then it raises questions about where we are today. If racism is understood not just as an affair of the heart but about material advantage and personal comfort, then the remedy is much different because it means it will cost something to alter.

The redneckification of racism also puts the focus on vigilante violence and misses the other ways white supremacy survived. Violence was one tactic in the South *and* in the North. White citizens made their opposition to movement activism known and sent a message to Black people who "got out of their place." Black people moving into "their neighborhoods" or "their schools" from Michigan to Mississippi often faced arson, property destruction, and physical attacks.[6] But increasingly in the North and in the South, white people turned to state violence and the police to maintain the status quo. Law enforcement—and its use of force and control—held power, legitimacy, and palatability, allowing local citizens to see their own hands as clean.

Economic violence was even more widespread. Many movement activists, North and South, lost their jobs. Historian Charles Payne, in his study of Mississippi, found that *every* woman he interviewed who was active in the movement lost her job.[7] Demonizing dissent was another tactic. The red-baiting most longtime civil rights activists encountered, and the firings that sometimes accompanied it, were convenient weapons of the "civilized," because they demonized the protester and sent a message to an entire community about the costs of dissent. When Kenneth Clark raised issues about New York's segregation in the early 1950s, he was called a Communist. When King spoke out against Proposition 14 in California or addressed suburban Detroiters, he was called a Communist. When Rosa Parks helped launch the Montgomery bus boycott, she was called a Communist, and a decade later, when John Conyers hired her to work in his Detroit office, he was slammed for hiring a Communist and the office received voodoo dolls, rotten watermelons, and all sorts of hate mail. Time and again, from north to south to west, those who challenged the racial status quo were called extremists and investigated by local police and the FBI, in part intended to curb and control their activities.

Alongside red-baiting, one of the most potent weapons of racial inequality was disregard. European historian Tony Judt highlights "the dilemmas of incompatible memories" to consider how popular renderings of historical injustice often gloss over how evil is actually perpetrated: "It is hard for us to accept that the Holocaust occupies a more important role in our own lives than it did in the wartime experience of occupied lands. But if we wish to grasp the true significance of evil—what Hannah Arendt intended by calling it 'banal'—then we must remember that what is truly awful about the destruction of the Jews is not that it mattered so much but that it mattered so little."[8] As Judt illuminates in his examination of World War II and the rise of Nazism, what was required was both many people's obsession with the Jews and many other people's indifference about the unjust conditions and suffering Jewish people were encountering. Similarly, the way racial injustice flourished in the United States required people obsessed with racial difference and the maintenance of white rights who were willing to construct whole systems to delineate, hierarchize, and police it. But it also required—and continues to require—many people to care so little, who would not get involved, and who saw little urgency in the fact of Black suffering.[9] It required many to believe that they had gained what they had through hard work and that other people hadn't fared as well because they lacked the right values and work ethic. And it stemmed from the inaction of people who saw inequality and injustice as unfortunate—or even horrible—but out of their control (unconnected to *their* neighborhood, *their* school, *their* municipal services, or *their* law enforcement). And it rested upon law enforcement and an us-versus-them police culture that produced police abuse; many would find the incidences of law enforcement "overreacting" wrong but consider them the unfortunate aberration of fighting crime.

To understand fully how systems of white supremacy functioned means taking into account all the people who allowed inequality to happen and the practices, policies, and cultures they created and supported that countenanced it. Segregation flourished in part because "polite" people stood back to make room for it. When movement activists pushed desegregation of schools and housing and jobs, some people attacked, but others stood by and let them attack. Many asserted their rights as "parents and taxpayers" and thought a lot about their children and little about other people's children. They said, "Prove there's a harm being done; we all just like to live with our own." Then, faced with a growing movement, they wondered, "Why are those people being so disorderly and angry?" "Polite racism" worked through multiple means: through language that disguised it, through government bureaucracy and the leveraging of channels of power that enabled it, and through sociological framings of cultural dysfunction that explained and justified inequity and the need for punitive approaches.

The first tool of "polite" racism involved language. While many white Southerners in the 1950s and early 1960s defended "segregation now and forever" and "states' rights" and called Black people horrible names, a different vocabulary of race emerged in the North in the postwar period, and increasingly over the 1960s in Southern metropolises. The lexicon they employed celebrated "color blindness" and expressed "surprise" at Black anger; it cast African American and Latino youth as "problem students" whose behavior (and that of their parents) hampered their educational success and whose communities were filled with "crime;" and it highlighted "property rights" and framed resistance to desegregation in the language of "neighborhood schools," "taxpayer's rights," and "forced busing." Many of these people decried "racism" and took offense at the notion that their actions and perspectives were at all racist, in part because they too saw racism as being steeped in personal hatred.

Many city leaders knew what they were doing; as seen with New York superintendent of schools William Jansen, political leaders explicitly instructed city officials to use "separation" not "segregation" because of the connotations of the latter and the responsibilities it might entail. Movements to oppose racial equality in large cities like New York and Los Angeles were often described as "backlashes," or "antibusing" activism, rather than as "segregationist," conveniently distinguishing them from their Southern counterparts and, ideally, from federal mandates. Such language simultaneously spoke and obscured race, constantly forcing community activists outside the South to prove that racial segregation and inequity in these liberal cities was real and harmful, and that it was the product of official policies.

Historian Karen Miller has documented the ways "color-blind" discourses originated in the early twentieth century among Northern white political leaders eager to distinguish their modern municipal leadership even as they maintained segregationist urban structures.[10] "Northern racial liberalism," Miller contends, "is the notion that all Americans, regardless of race, should be politically equal, but that the state cannot and indeed should not enforce racial equality by interfering with existing social or economic relations."[11] In the early twentieth century, Miller found, white liberal Detroiters saw themselves as "color-blind," believed their practices would ultimately lead to racial equality, but were willing to accept racial inequality and segregation, even when protests emerged from African Americans highlighting the inequality embedded in city institutions. This frame of color blindness became the Northern way to not see school and housing segregation, differential employment rates, or brutal policing. With public support of racial segregation viewed as the distasteful purview of Southern racists, "color-blind" discourses provided a socially acceptable rhetoric to harness many Northern whites' contentment with the status quo (and opposition to housing, school, and job desegregation).

Increasingly in the 1950s and 1960s, these discourses provided a supple way for liberals to distinguish themselves from "segregationist" politicians while promoting and maintaining segregationist policies. US racism was a double act; Southern open-call racism provided an alibi for Northern "polite" racism; liberal Northern hypocrisy created a rationale for Southern white defensiveness. Part of the appeal of these "color-blind" discourses, then, is the cloak of deniability they provided for Northerners (a hypocrisy that Southern leaders often called out).

In this way, New York City school officials praised the *Brown* decision but claimed they weren't sure how it applied to them. They gave the matter to a committee to study, miring civil rights activists like Ella Baker and Kenneth Clark in work to demonstrate the problem existed but ultimately refusing to take action on the recommendations in terms of zoning and teacher placement. They said: "This isn't the South; we don't have that kind of racism here." Similarly, in Boston and Los Angeles, civil rights activists spent years on studies to "prove" that the problem existed, even as the segregated nature of schools was evident to the naked eye. And even when they provided reams of documentation, school officials refused to rezone, claiming the problem was not their doing, while offering money for programs to address juvenile delinquency (preferring to cast Black and Latino students and their families as the problem that needed fixing).

These "polite" discourses were also then mobilized to claim plausible deniability. When Black people grew increasingly insistent and angry through the 1960s about the lack of change, and about the dishonesty of being asked to constantly prove injustice, Northern liberals acted surprised. "California is a state where there is no racial discrimination," California governor Edmund Brown had the gall to claim as he flew home in August 1965, when the Watts uprising was beginning. Such claims of surprise and bewilderment framed these "crises" as reckless and Black grievances as excessive—the veiled language over and over serving to hide and dissemble what was actually occurring. As Martin Luther King observed in 1968,

> Negroes have proceeded from a premise that equality means what it says, and they have taken white America at their word when they talked of it as an objective. But most whites in America, including many of goodwill, proceed from a premise that equality is a loose expression for improvement. White America is not even psychologically organized to close the gap—essentially, it seeks only to make it less painful and less obvious but in most respects retain it. Most abrasions between Negroes and white liberals arise from this fact.[12]

The second tool of "polite racism" involved the workings of government bureaucracy and policy, and the use of political sway to maintain it.

Historian Carol Anderson has termed this "white rage." According to Anderson, "White rage is not about visible violence, but rather it works its way through the courts, the legislatures, and a range of government bureaucracies. . . . It's not the Klan. White rage doesn't have to wear sheets, burn crosses or take to the streets. Working the halls of power, it can achieve its ends far more effectively, far more destructively."[13] Many white Northerners wielded their power and voting pressure at home, even as they might have pressed for desegregation in the South, understanding that you didn't need a governor at a schoolhouse door if you had BOE officials constantly adjusting school zoning lines to maintain segregated schools. You didn't need a burning cross if the bank used maps made by the Federal Housing Authority to mark Black neighborhoods as "dangerous" for investment and deny Black people access to home loans. You didn't need white vigilantes if the police were willing to protect and serve certain communities while containing and controlling others.

School officials used attendance boundaries, feeder patterns, transportation policies, teacher-hiring practices, and other methods to ensure that the vast majority of students of color attended segregated, under-resourced schools. And when school officials made moves to adjust those lines even a bit for Black children (from South Gate, California, to Brooklyn, New York), white parents fought back. HOLC ratings, restrictive covenants, veterans' loan policies, block associations, and banks all worked together to solidify and maintain housing segregation. Many employers refused to hire Black workers or restricted the number or types of jobs they could hold; many unions excluded Blacks altogether, and government officials granting contracts turned a blind eye to the hiring practices of those they awarded. Much of this was done bureaucratically, with the force of the state and of lawmakers who didn't shout segregation from the rafters but instead used the levers of bureaucracy and intricacies of policy to protect "their constituents'" (read, just their white constituents') needs.

This was an ongoing, dynamic process. Throughout the 1960s, as court documents later revealed, school officials in Boston and Los Angeles constantly adjusted school-district and zoning lines to preserve segregated schools and used busing to maintain these segregated schools. In Boston, activists encountered an additional barrier: the Massachusetts Commission Against Discrimination. Civil rights activists brought a complaint to MCAD hoping for the force of the state commission in pushing forward their cause—and in 1960, MCAD literally declared Boston's schools *not segregated*. In 1961, in order to seem compliant with *Brown*, Boston Public Schools passed an open enrollment policy—which was used initially mostly by white parents to avoid changing schools, while Black parents found it difficult to use. The appearance of adherence, rather than substantive change, was paramount. Four years later, Black Bostonians began Operation Exodus, a busing program that made it possible for Black families to take advantage of open seats in the district. They assumed they would shame the school system into taking over the program, once they demonstrated the need and desire to use this policy. BPS never took over or provided funding for the program but repeatedly cited the existence of Operation Exodus, both publicly and in legal briefs, to appear compliant with federal desegregation mandates. The willfulness was evident.

Many Southerners at the time reacted angrily to this hypocrisy, seeing Northern liberals as eager to criticize the South without being willing to examine, much less change, their systems. During the bus boycott, for instance, Montgomery's main newspaper, the *Montgomery Advertiser* (which was opposed to the boycott), took to running stories on segregated Northern locales to demonstrate that the racial systems in Montgomery that were highlighted by outside media were actually rife throughout the country.[14] Southern congressmen decried the hypocrisy of Civil Rights Act section 401(b) provisions on school desegregation, correctly realizing that the enforcement was purposely designed to target them and leave Northern schools untouched. But it was easy to dismiss these Southerners as hypocrites themselves—since they cared little about Black people in Detroit or Boston or New York—and sidestep the nugget of truth in their complaints.

Shortly after the passage of the Civil Rights Act, which gave the federal government the power to withhold federal funds if a district was found noncompliant, civil rights advocates in Chicago filed a complaint with the US Office of Education. They laid out how the Chicago Board of Education had violated Title VI of the Civil Rights Act: 90 percent of Black students attended segregated schools in Chicago, and these schools were more overcrowded, had more uncredentialed teachers, and had fewer educational resources or honors classes than other schools in the city. The US Department of Health, Education, and Welfare briefly withheld $30 million from the city, but as historian Matthew Delmont powerfully documents, the full weight of the Chicago and Illinois political classes came down upon them.[15] Ultimately, HEW retreated, and Chicago's schools remained as segregated as they had been. Following HEW's capitulation, New York congressman Adam Clayton Powell aptly observed, "When the United States Office of Education was pressured into restoring Federal funds to Chicago's segregated public school system, it represented the first abject surrender to the principle that separate but equal is wrong in the South, but acceptable in the North—particularly if a city can muster enough Northern politicians and educators with a segregationist mentality to practice this shameful hypocrisy."[16] Boston rested easy seeing how Chicago had prevailed. Indeed, Northerners repeatedly used political power and pressure to evade desegregation and federal mandates, with white parents using discourses of "neighborhood schools" and "forced busing" to assert their political will to defend their segregated schools.

In their manipulation of the Civil Rights Act, Northern liberals used the veiled language of "racial imbalance" and "neighborhood schools" and applied their political power to keep desegregation away from their schools. In time, Southerners came to follow suit. Suburban Southern whites, as historian Kevin Kruse argues, "abandon[ed] their traditional, populist, and often starkly racist demagoguery [by the late 1960s], and instead craft[ed] a new conservatism predicated on a language of rights, freedoms, and individualism."[17] Thus, in many ways, Northerners developed the tactics that are now associated with some of the reddest Southern states in the union.

These strategies paved the way for Richard Nixon's "Southern strategy" to win the White House in 1968. This is an oft-cited misnomer historians and political scientists have repeated over the last fifty years to describe how Nixon and Republican Party operatives learned from Barry Goldwater's resounding defeat in 1964 and adjusted their racial approach to win the White House four years later. Given how Goldwater's stark racial appeals had proven unsuccessful, Nixon savvily repackaged racially driven policy goals in more polite, obscured language palatable to American Cold War sensibilities to win areas that hadn't been traditional Republican strongholds.[18]

As Lee Atwater explained, "You start out in 1954 by saying, 'Nigger, nigger, nigger.' By 1968 you can't say 'nigger'—that hurts you, backfires. So you say stuff like, uh, forced busing, states' rights, and all that stuff, and you're getting so abstract. Now, you're talking about cutting taxes, and all these things you're talking about are totally economic things and a byproduct of them is, blacks get hurt worse than whites."[19] These cloaked racial politics proved effective for Nixon, but it wasn't a particularly Southern strategy that won him the White House. In 1968, George Wallace won the Deep South. Nixon secured the presidency by winning swaths of the Midwest, Northeast, West, and border states—including Wisconsin, Illinois, Iowa, New Jersey, Vermont, New Hampshire, Oregon, and California. What proved successful in this Northern-Midwestern-Western-Southern-border-state strategy was an appeal to voters who still wanted racial policy but wanted it cloaked in euphemistic frames of "law and order," "forced busing," and "cultural deprivation."[20] As Nixon explained to his domestic advisor H. R. Haldeman, "You have to face the fact that the whole problem is really the Blacks. The key is to devise a system that recognizes this while not appearing to."[21] What Nixon introduced to the national stage, and what Ronald Reagan later crystallized with the "Reagan Democrats," were strategies that Northern politicians already had employed successfully for two decades. Professions of the value and importance of equality, married with sustained resistance to the methods by which it might be implemented, were a political gold mine to be tapped by both Republicans and Democrats—and criminalization and cultural arguments were instrumental to explaining away existing inequalities.[22]

Perhaps the most important tool of "polite racism" was the mobilization of a discourse seemingly steeped in the objectivity of social science that posited the dysfunctional cultural adaptations Black people had developed in the urban North as key to existing social and economic inequities. The need to address "cultural deprivation," as it was often termed in the 1950s and 1960s, provided a way to explain and deflect movements for racial equality by saying that the most important task was to change the behaviors and values of Black people themselves. With public support for racial segregation and discrimination viewed as the distasteful purview of Southern racists, "culture of poverty" explanations provided a socially acceptable rationale to harness many Northern whites' virulent opposition to housing, school, and job desegregation. A way to blame Black people for their own situation in the "neutral" language of social science, "culture of poverty" framings necessitated strategies to "uplift" the Black community, rather than desegregation, which, political officials claimed, wouldn't address the real problem. Rather, what was needed were programs to address "juvenile delinquency," teach positive cultural adaptations and good work habits, and support family values. And if these didn't work, more punitive approaches would be required.

Repeatedly, in cities including Boston and Los Angeles, cultural arguments were used directly to thwart demands for desegregation. When the NAACP subcommittee took its case against Boston's school segregation to the school committee, "they told us our kids were stupid," Batson recalled, "and this was why they didn't learn."[23] When William O'Connor became the new Boston School Committee chair, in 1964, he declared, "We have no inferior education in our schools. What we have been getting is an inferior type of student."[24] Three thousand miles away, Los Angeles Board of Education members expressed similar sentiments around the "negative attitudes towards education" that Black and Latino families supposedly held. School officials didn't publicly endorse segregation; they found a more palatable way to criticize certain families for their "negative attitudes" and "lack of motivation" and to use that to explain away disparities in schooling. Over and over, from Boston to Los Angeles to New York to Detroit, Black parents' demands for equity and desegregation were met with resistance from school officials who said their kids lacked the proper cultural habits to learn and who would only provide money for programs for cultural remediation and to fight juvenile delinquency.

The use of cultural arguments to deflect demands for policy change was not limited to struggles relating to schools. When the Brooklyn chapter of the Congress of Racial Equality began a campaign highlighting disparate practices of sanitation removal in Bedford-Stuyvesant from other parts of the borough, the habits of Black working-class communities were blamed. CORE activists discovered that other, predominantly white neighborhoods in Brooklyn (with less population density) got five-day pickup, while the pickup in Bedford-Stuyvesant was two days a week and substandard, with garbage often left strewn on the streets, even after the trucks went through. As historian Brian Purnell demonstrates, after protracted attempts to demonstrate the inequity of sanitation services and numerous unsuccessful meetings with city officials, Brooklyn CORE launched Operation Cleansweep on September 25, 1962. Activists followed sanitation trucks through Bedford-Stuyvesant, picking up the piles of trash the trucks left behind, then dumping the garbage on the steps of Brooklyn

Borough Hall to demonstrate the poor quality of sanitation removal in the neighborhoods. The city responded that people in Bedford-Stuyvesant didn't understand how to keep their neighborhood clean and suggested classes to instruct them on how to use garbage cans.[25]

These cultural explanations were taken up by certain Black voices who also sought to further Black progress and foreground Black agency. The politics of respectability had a long history across the twentieth century as many Black elites focused on remediating the behaviors of the Black poor as a way to uplift the community. But this took on heightened power and danger as those discourses and strategies moved into public policy.[26] With biological arguments discredited after World War II, culture became the way to talk about race, in part aided by the rise of academic social science.[27] Deriving partly from the rise of midcentury sociological theories of some Black and white social scientists (which gained further prominence in 1965 with the publication of the US Department of Labor's *The Negro Family: The Case for National Action*, known as the Moynihan Report), this formulation cast Northern Blacks as undone by the structural barriers of the Northern urban landscape.[28] These scholars argued that, untethered from the values of religion, family, and community that anchored Southern Black communities and faced with the racist structures of urban political economies, Northern Black people developed cultural responses that led to educational and job underattainment.[29]

By the 1960s, urban social science was booming, and scholar after scholar went to the "ghetto" to investigate this "other America."[30] While many portrayed these cultural adaptations in the context of systemic discrimination, poverty, and disfranchisement, they still depicted a dysfunctional culture holding Black people back.[31] They lamented the "tangle of pathologies," "family structures," and "cultural deprivation/dysfunction" that were said to explain persistent inequalities and promote particular policy solutions. Political expediencies led many public officials to focus on the cultural part and jettison the focus on structural factors such as unemployment and unequal public services.[32] As the Moynihan Report put it so starkly, "At the heart of the deterioration of the fabric of Negro society is the deterioration of the Negro family."[33] This set of Black and white academic voices dovetailed with white political elites' notions of the problem, and so their approaches were elevated. What followed was the idea that the Black community needed uplift, mentoring initiatives, programs to encourage cultural success, marriage, and jobs for men (the report's main author, Daniel Patrick Moynihan, recommended the military).

Using this framing, many white liberals, with support from some Black middle-class leaders, sponsored programs addressing juvenile delinquency, job readiness skills, and cultural remediation to facilitate Black educational and economic attainment and remediate these "cultural adaptations." In 1967, Martin Luther King Jr., in his speech to the American Psychological Association, took American social science to task for its role in maintaining injustice: "All too many white Americans are horrified not with conditions of Negro life but with the product of these conditions—the Negro himself." King faulted the "white majority . . . [for] producing chaos," while blaming the chaos on Black people and claiming that if they behaved better, success would come.[34]

These "cultural" framings were slippery because they focused on Black people's agency to change their situation. At the same time, they legitimated remedial and punitive responses. Because certain people's behaviors were the problem, if they proved unwilling to change, the solution was further order and control, thus legitimating the role of discipline and policing to maintain such control. More extreme forms of school punishment came to school districts including Los Angeles's in the wake of the *Brown* decision, as did more policing. As Northern liberals took pains to make clear, this policing was not like those racist Southern cops putting hoses on schoolchildren. It was modernized, targeted, and employed through rationalized systems because some people required more control; not all Black people, they made clear, just certain "dangerous" types who were menacing the good Black people.[35] Cultural framings provided a way to understand the kind of "help" and "protection" Black people needed and to provide further systems of control for those who continued on this dangerous path. As such, cultural approaches continued to dominate social science, by white and Black academics, in the 1980s and 1990s, and this narrative of Black urban pathology became a reigning national common sense.[36]

These "cultural" explanations then turned up in contemporary memorializations of the civil rights movement but were framed as a new problem—as a younger generation having gone astray from the strong values and behaviors of the civil rights generation. Bill Cosby's speech at the NAACP's fiftieth-anniversary commemoration of the *Brown* decision lambasted Black youth and their parents ("It's not what they're doing to us. It's what we're not doing."). And many of Obama's movement tributes, from his campaign speech in Selma in 2007 to his March on Washington fiftieth-anniversary speech, included exhortations about the need for Black people to change certain dysfunctional cultural practices that now held them back.[37]

As they functioned over the course of the twentieth century, these culture-of-poverty formulations absolved the nation of primary responsibility for the inequalities still rife in American society and put the responsibility back on the Black community to fix them. And as writers such as Ta-Nehisi Coates make clear, these formulations also accrued political benefits for Black leaders willing to talk tough to Black people.[38]

Seeing the ways "cultural" explanations were used to thwart demands for desegregation and explain inequity in the civil rights era, particularly by many Northerners seeking to distinguish their opposition from that of Southerners, provides a much different window on their contemporary use. Today, they are often employed in claims of a new "crisis in Black America"—that the current generation of Black youth has lost its way since the civil rights generation and needs to right itself. Seeing how these "cultural" explanations have been prevalent throughout the twentieth century as a way of explaining existing disparities reveals the lie in castigating this current generation of Black young people as so different from the civil rights generation, many of whom were similarly disparaged. Rather, this "cultural" explanation has recurred decade after decade to explain and justify disparity—and has proved disturbingly effective in disparaging Black demands for equity and justice by placing the solution on changing Black people's values and behaviors and deflecting public responsibility in ways palatable to liberal sensibilities.

Recognizing the centrality of polite racism—of silence, coded language, and the demonization of dissent; the leveraging of bureaucracy and political power; and the use of cultural explanations to account for disparities—also reveals the enduring use of these strategies in maintaining racial inequality from the civil rights era to the present. These methods are slippery; many who employ them will assert that they hate racism and fight hard against racial demagogues like Bull Connor or former Ku Klux Klan Wizard David Duke. The civil rights movement struggled with this over and over. Alone in a Birmingham jail in 1963, King noted that the "Negro's great stumbling block in the stride toward freedom" was not necessarily the Ku Klux Klan but the moderate who "is more devoted to 'order' than to justice . . . who constantly says: 'I agree with you in the goal you seek but I cannot agree with your methods.'" So too for us today: silence, disregard, political influence, and cultural explanations are key tools for maintaining racial injustice then and now. This history asks us to refuse the comfort redneck racism allows and confront the responsibility of a much broader swath of American society who continue to prefer "order" to justice.

CHAPTER FOUR

The Media Was Often an Obstacle to the Struggle for Racial Justice

"If you're not careful, the newspapers will have you hating the people who are being oppressed, and loving the people who are doing the oppressing."

—Malcolm X[1]

IN THE WAKE of the Watts uprising, the *Los Angeles Times* was shocked. Horrified by the events unfolding in the city, it minimized Black grievances: "What happened the other night may well have been symptomatic of more serious underlying conditions, which should and are being treated. . . . The police are doing their job and doing it well."[2] Later that week, the editors became even more agitated: "Terrorism is spreading."[3] Describing Los Angeles as a "civilized city," by the end of the week, the lesson the editors had drawn from the events was to call for "an increase in the size of the police force."[4] While the paper had covered a growing movement in Los Angeles over the decade that had repeatedly challenged school segregation, housing segregation, job discrimination, and police brutality, sometimes on the front page, it now conveniently forgot it.

Well-known political commentator Theodore White took to the opinion page and encapsulated the "surprise" at the riots: "One must start, of course, with the beginning mystery, the most puzzling of all—why Los Angeles? For, in Los Angeles, Negroes have lived better than in any other large American city, with the possible exception of Detroit . . . and, up to now, [have been] treated better by their white fellow citizens than in any other city in the nation."[5] White described the city's "open and easy tolerance," where Black people had made "spectacular" progress.[6] While endorsing dialogue between the Black community and the police department, a *Los Angeles Times* editorial similarly minimized Black concerns: "It is likely that Negro complaints hinge more around their resentment of alleged police attitudes and procedure, than outright brutality."[7] At the same time, the paper gave ample space to Police Chief William H. Parker and Mayor Sam Yorty, who claimed allegations of police brutality were "a big lie" and likened the rioters to "monkeys in a zoo."[8] Few Black activists were interviewed; the long movement challenging police brutality and calling for Parker's resignation was ignored. Nonetheless, the *Los Angeles Times* would win a Pulitzer Prize for its coverage of the uprising.

Similarly, as school was set to open in 1974, and white opposition to court-ordered desegregation mounted, the *Boston Globe* was shocked by events unfolding in the Cradle of Liberty. The paper cast federal judge W. Arthur Garrity's June decision ordering system-wide school desegregation in Boston as having come largely out of the blue. For twenty-five years, Black activists had organized meetings, organizations, rallies, boycotts, independent busing programs, independent schools, and candidacies for public office—all to draw attention to the inequalities endemic in BPS. And this decades-long struggle had encountered unyielding white resistance. A number of those actions had been covered by the *Globe*, occasionally on the front page. Yet, in its extensive coverage of school opening, the *Globe* framed the "crisis" around "busing," and refused to grapple with the long history of school segregation in the city, the three decades of Black activism challenging it, and the vehemence of white resistance that had brought the city to that juncture. Paralleling the ways Southern papers obscured civil rights issues in their own backyards, the *Boston Globe* had long enabled many white readers to feel like the racial politics of the city were good overall, and it had contributed to the gap between a growing Black protest movement and the soothed consciences of many white Bostonians who felt entitled to protect their "neighborhood schools."[9] From the *Globe*'s coverage, it would be impossible to understand that white disruption and the violence the city faced at the opening of school was due to a long-standing, intentionally segregated school system that Black people had challenged relentlessly for a quarter century and that white citizens and public officials had endeavored relentlessly to protect and defend. The fact that students had been taking school buses for years to segregated schools without complaint from white parents was completely left out of the *Globe*'s coverage. Nonetheless, the *Boston Globe* would win a Pulitzer Prize for its coverage of the start of school desegregation in 1974.

In Los Angeles and Boston, the media seemed to possess an endless capacity for surprise at these "crises": *How is this happening here? Why are they so angry?* It was a shock that stood in the way of a sober consideration of racial injustice in either city—a shock that ignored history and discriminatory city institutions and long-standing movements and instead legitimated the blinkered perspectives of many of its white readers. Looking at media coverage of the Black freedom struggle, particularly coverage of the movement outside the Deep South, reveals a sobering truth: the media often stood in the way of the struggle for racial justice.

In the national fable of the civil rights movement, the media gets a great deal of credit for the movement's success. Journalists show up as courageous heroes who braved the South's violent parochialism to shine a necessary light on the important struggle happening there. "If it hadn't been for the media," Congressman John Lewis extolled, "the civil rights movement would have been like a bird without wings, a choir without a song."[10] Thus, in popular understanding, journalists are the good guys who provided the needed amplification of the Southern struggle to force these places to change. "Sympathetic referees," as Lewis termed them, they forced the nation to see what it hadn't seen, and lifted up the work of Southern Black activists, offering a measure of protection to these struggles.

But while a number of journalists courageously left their homes to journey south to cover the "real struggle," as they saw it in the decade from 1955 to 1965, their newspapers took a different approach toward inequality and struggle in their own backyards.[11] They increasingly covered the Southern movement in serious, more righteous ways, while chiding local activists for not protesting in the right way, or they portrayed local movements as dangerous or disruptive. Using fewer photographs and often a paternalistic tone, these news outlets tended to treat local Black leaders as largely irrelevant or as troublemakers demanding too much too fast—functioning, as Stokely Carmichael put it, as "self-appointed white critics."[12] By covering local issues as individual protests or disturbances rather than as a movement, they devoted little space to what segregation looked like in their cities, how it functioned, and who the people who protected it were.

Southern Black people and the movements they built were increasingly covered as noble and necessary, while Northern Black people and the movements they built were deemed marginal, unreasonable, and disruptive. Or they were not pictured at all. Media historians Matthew Delmont and Mark Speltz both have found that coverage of race relations in

Northern cities tended to focus on white backlash rather than Black protests—and on riots.[13] As Speltz argues,

> Ironically, Americans today are more likely to see news photographs of
> riot-torn Chicago, Detroit, Philadelphia, or Los Angeles than pictures
> of the many preceding demonstrations against discrimination, police
> brutality, and unjust incarceration. . . . The photographs of peaceful
> protests decades before uprising took place lend clarity to the causes
> underlying the problem. In this light, the civil disturbances look less
> like senseless violence and more like the consequences of mounting
> frustration in the face of chronic inaction.[14]

There was little history on their pages or evidence of the long trails
of Black grievance that preceded them—these uprisings were pictured as
coming out of nowhere.

Southern white politicians who protected segregation came under
question on the pages of the nation's most important newspapers by the
1960s, while Northern politicians not only escaped scrutiny but were often
portrayed sympathetically for having to deal with these "unreasonable"
Black people. Northern newspapers increasingly criticized Southerners
for refusing to acknowledge their race problem but allowed Northerners
to talk about "busing" and "racial imbalance" and "law and order" to cover
up theirs. The nation's leading print newspapers enabled the framing of
civil rights and desegregation as Southern issues and helped to inoculate
polite racism across the country. Northern segregation was treated as less
systemic and more happenstance, and resistance to desegregation there as
different and *not as segregationist* as Southern resistance.

Because much of the national media was located in the North, their
myopia went largely unchecked. Black newspapers that covered these issues were regularly dismissed; Southern newspapers that highlighted
Northern hypocrisy were easily disregarded as deflecting their own racism; and international news sources were considered "red" for exposing
US race relations. Indeed, the myopia of the Northern press was often rewarded. In moments of crisis—such as the 1965 Watts uprising or court-
ordered school desegregation in Boston in 1974—a number of these news
outlets won awards for their coverage.

This celebration has continued, sewn into contemporary understandings of the civil rights movement in the scholarship and given epic weight in Gene Roberts and Hank Klibanoff's 2006 Pulitzer Prize–winning book, *The Race Beat: The Press, the Civil Rights Struggle, and the Awakening of a Nation*. Lionizing the role of the media, *The Race Beat* painstakingly detailed the process by which many Northern journalists came to see the importance of the Southern struggle and summoned the courage and resources to cover it. At the same time, Roberts, former managing editor of the *New York Times*, and Klibanoff, former managing editor of the *Atlanta Journal-Constitution*, overlooked entirely the role of the media in the North, which would have provided a less heroic narrative.[15] History as *ABC Afterschool Special*, their story of the scrappy journalists who helped push their news outlets to expose the South's intransigence is ultimately a feel-good one—of good people who do the right thing. To have examined how their colleagues disregarded and legitimated racism in their own cities and regions raises more disturbing questions.

In a 2013 NPR interview, Klibanoff explained the Southern media's reluctance to cover Black protest: "Publicly they would say . . . 'We can't be putting a lot of stories of ruffians on the street provoking violence.' . . . What I think they also were trying to say and acknowledge without being able to say it is they really didn't know how to cover the story. . . . Most news reporters at the time would not have had in their Rolodexes or address books the names of any African-Americans in town. They wouldn't know who to call, by and large. . . . There's no sense of 'let's live the lives of our readers.'"[16] But this exact point could be made about the *New York Times* or *Los Angeles Times* regarding coverage of Black life and struggle in their own cities. These newspapers, too, saw Black residents as problems to be studied, as strange people with unusual culture, had few local Black contacts in their Rolodexes, and tended not to portray "lives of our [Black] readers." When pressed by the NPR interviewer that many Southerners criticized the press for not covering the "race story" at home, Klibanoff acknowledged there was "some truth to it" but didn't elaborate, much less take stock of the ways his own book didn't cover the "race story" in the North either, and then returned to Watts as a signal moment.

While it is now generally accepted that Southern newspapers did not cover the civil rights movement fairly or accurately, there has been reluctance to examine the role that the national media, based largely in the North, played in struggles in its own backyard. With television news not yet fully dominant, these newspapers defined the important issues of the day. And editors invested fewer resources in investigating local racism than they had started to invest in the South. While a number of journalists showed real courage in the way they pushed for coverage of Southern struggles, by and large their newspapers were not necessarily equally courageous in questioning white prerogatives in their own cities (often using caveats to describe white families opposing desegregation like "however free from prejudice they might be").[17] When Northern papers did picture local racism, they typically did so by focusing on working-class whites, such as those in South Boston.[18] While there were some important exceptions, many Northern journalists accepted the terms of their middle-class white readers: they liked their "neighborhood schools" (a term that didn't arise till after *Brown*), didn't want "forced busing" (even though many of their children were being bused to maintain segregated schools), were concerned for their children's safety in "dangerous neighborhoods" (blaming Black communities for the conditions in schools), and had rights as "parents and taxpayers" (even though Blacks and Latinos were also parents and taxpayers with rights)—and this didn't make them racist like Southerners. These papers naturalized the shock and disgust of many whites at Northern uprisings and under-covered Black perspectives—regularly downgrading Black protest, interviewing few Black people, and devoting few resources to investigating the structures of racial inequality in their cities.[19] In so doing, the national press became another obstacle to racial justice, another form of protection for segregation and inequality in much of the country.

DISSEMBLING IN THE CRADLE OF LIBERTY

Boston was a case in point. While the *Boston Globe* covered many of the activities of Boston's freedom movement in the two decades before Garrity's decision, it tended to treat them as discrete and episodic protests—not a movement—that were at times problematic in their disruptiveness. Initially critical of the term *busing* when antidesegregation whites in the city first employed it, the *Globe*'s Robert Levey described busing as a "nonword that sets off flames of anger" and a "hobgoblin" because "of course the millions of children who take school buses every day as a matter of necessity are not considered to be in a 'busing' program."[20] Yet by the mid-1960s, the paper nonetheless took up the frame of "busing" to characterize

white Bostonians' opposition to school desegregation and, in part, to differentiate it from what was happening in the South.[21] For the next decade,
the *Globe* and other news outlets cast white opposition to Black demands
for school equity and desegregation as mere opposition to having their
kids "bused," thus helping to inoculate the racism and the hoarding of resources this opposition to desegregation actually evidenced. Black activists found it hard to get their issues taken seriously, not only by the Boston
School Committee but also by the *Boston Globe*. In 1966, troubled by the
"liberal use of stereotypes, i.e., culturally deprived, agitators, forced busing," by many Boston media outlets, Black leaders convened a roundtable
meeting with media representatives to try to change how racial issues were
covered.[22] But the meeting produced little change.

The *Globe* did not raise sufficient attention to the long-standing and
multivarious white resistance in the city that persistently sought to avoid
the requirements of *Brown*. Nor did the *New York Times*. In a lengthy 1973
article on the Boston schools entitled "More Segregated Than Ever," the
Times likewise cast a benign eye: "The Boston area can boast a long record of good race relations . . . a spirit of tolerance that can be traced as far
back as the eighteen-thirties, when the abolitionist movement took root
in Boston. . . . The effects of segregated schools can only be surmised. For
the most part, they [Black students] attend overcrowded and run-down
schools, but the sociological evidence suggests that the quality of school
buildings and facilities is not overly important to learning."[23] This culturalist explanation allowed the *Times* to frame the educational issues of
Black students in Boston as somehow different and outside the mandates
of *Brown*, which had decisively linked the quality of facilities to effective
learning and constitutional equality.

When two decades of frustrated Black struggle prompted the NAACP's
filing of a federal lawsuit, that history was largely forgotten. Following
Judge Garrity's June 1974 ruling that ordered comprehensive desegregation, the *Globe* wrote a positive editorial calling the decision "balanced"
and "like an operation to cure a long and crippling illness. The procedure
may be painful but at least it is definite and the chances of healing are
great."[24] But the frame of healing still sidestepped what was at stake: jobs,
resources, access, and control. And many, many white people in Boston
saw those stakes and objected. Leading up to the opening of school in 1974,
the *Globe* obsessed about safety while revealingly referring to Garrity's

desegregation plan in a first-day-of-school editorial as the "opening of racially balanced schools" (the preferred Northern euphemism for desegregation), rather than the dismantling of more than a century of segregated schools in the city.[25]

An editorial the next week referred to the large-scale white boycott of schools as "legitimate," never used the word "segregation" or "desegregation" in describing what was occurring in Boston, and called Boston a "city to be proud of."[26] Even as it prodigiously covered the violence and upheaval that occurred at the start of school in 1974, the *Globe* approached those resisting desegregation very gingerly. On September 27, it ran a fawning article on the antidesegregation group ROAR, entitled "Opposition to Busing Led by Publicity-Shy ROAR," legitimating the utter fabrication that ROAR was media-averse (as opposed to being partly fueled by the media over the years).[27] With the focus overwhelmingly on white resistance, the Black activists who had labored for decades to challenge the city's entrenched segregation—Ruth Batson, Ellen Jackson, Muriel and Otto Snowden, Mel King, Melnea Cass—barely warranted a mention in the drama that would unfold on pages of the city's most-regarded newspaper over the next months.

This fit with a broader pattern of coverage of school-desegregation issues. By the 1970s, television and newspapers dramatically overcovered white opposition to "busing." While "busing" dominated news coverage, it was a key strategic distortion. In most Northern and Western cities, busing itself had long been a tool of segregation; for years, busing enabled white students to go to "white schools," but that fact did not make it into the news stories. As Julian Bond would wryly note at a Boston rally: "It's not the bus, it's us."[28] If television news played an important role in framing Southern civil rights protests for a national audience in the 1950s and 1960s as righteous and necessary movements, according to historian Matthew Delmont, by the 1970s, television news offered frequent and sympathetic coverage of busing opponents in cities including Boston, Los Angeles, Denver, and Pontiac, Michigan.[29] When massive prodesegregation events were organized, as they were in Boston between 1974 and 1976, they received far less coverage than "antibusing" protests.[30] "We wanted to show that there are a number of people who have fought for busing, some for over 20 years," explained Boston organizer Ellen Jackson. "We hoped to express the concerns of many people who have not seen themselves, only seeing the anti-busing demonstrations in the media."[31] But the coverage of these demonstrations, including a massive one in Boston in May 1975 where forty thousand marched in support of desegregation, was much slimmer than "anti-busing" leaders and events received; Black organizers, parents, and leaders, interviewed far less frequently. Through this inaccurate framing of "busing," and by ignoring Black perspectives, journalists and political leaders succeeded in deeming system-wide desegregation a failed strategy in Northern cities.

ALL THE NEWS THAT'S COMFORTABLE TO PRINT

Similar to the *Globe*, the *New York Times* in the 1950s and 1960s provided coverage of the movement for school desegregation and equity in its own hometown that ran from lackluster to paternalistic to dismissive—that was far different from the multiple front-page stories it ran nearly simultaneously on the Southern struggle. While acknowledging "integration is a nation-wide problem not just one that belongs south of the Mason–Dixon line," the *New York Times* insisted in 1957, "there is of course no official segregation in the city," despite the fact that New York school officials produced zoning maps that rendered the city's schools segregated and hired few Black or Puerto Rican teachers.[32] Repeatedly, the *Times* cast school inequality and segregation in the Big Apple as "entirely different from that in the South . . . The root is not in any systematic exclusion fostered by law or administrative policy but in neighborhood population patterns."[33] And again in 1963: "The problem of 'desegregation' in New York City is entirely different from that in the South, despite efforts by some Southern segregationists and some Northern integrationists to equate them. The city's schools have always been integrated."[34]

Coverage of escalating Black protest was tepid. The paper briefly covered Mae Mallory's 1957 case against the New York City Board of Education (BOE), referring to it only as a case against a school-zoning system that is "now being attacked on the ground that the all-Negro schools in Harlem and elsewhere are inferior to the predominantly white schools"— as if the Supreme Court hadn't already settled that matter of separate facilities being unequal in *Brown v. Board*.[35] "If the zoning laws are declared unconstitutional," the *Times* opined, "the entire school pattern would have to be altered dramatically." While the *Times* understood that *Brown* would require dramatic changes for some school systems, the idea that New York school practices would also have to be altered dramatically seemed a bit absurd to the paper.

Echoing the New York Board of Education's position (which sought to evade responsibility by blaming the problem on housing patterns), the *Times*, in a big 1963 story, referred to segregated school patterns in the city as "de facto segregation that is the product of economic status and housing discrimination," though "the leaders of integration efforts say the effects are the same. They refer to it simply as segregation."[36] The coverage reified the idea of neighborhood schools as both true and naturally occurring. Referring to those pushing for school transfers as "militant groups," the paper again wrote dismissively: "The groups pressing most vigorously for desegregation of predominantly Negro and Puerto Rican schools appear to be convinced that the educational quality in them will never be raised until a full measure of physical integration is achieved." (As if the Supreme Court had not also said this.)

At the same time, few Black activists were pictured or quoted. Despite her many efforts around New York schools, Ella Baker did not make it into the pages of the *New York Times* till she died. The Reverend Milton Galamison made it into many stories, including a positive profile in 1963 that described him as "calm, reasoned" (and repeatedly as "urbane"). But in escalating negative terms, *Times* articles subsequently described him as possessing "unpardonable irresponsibility," said he was "callous, disgraceful and utterly illegitimate," and called his group "militant" and "insurgent."[37]

After nearly a decade without progress on school desegregation in the city, the *Times* took pains in 1963 to note that New York City school officials were "sympathetic" to Black demands but that Black people were "unlikely to be satisfied with the pace."[38] After years of parent organizing that got nowhere with the BOE, and with no progress toward transforming individual schools, activists called for a citywide school boycott. In the days before the February 1964 boycott, the *Times* repeatedly editorialized against it. It lambasted the protest as a "violent, illegal approach of adult-encouraged truancy," dismissed civil rights demands, including the expectation that the city should create a comprehensive desegregation plan, as "unreasonable and unjustified," and claimed that "few things could be more destructive to the welfare of all of the city's children."[39] Just as the *New York Times* condemned the proposed school boycott as "violent," other Northern media outlets often framed disruptive protests in their own cities and states as "violent," even when there was nothing violent about the intentions nor any damage to persons or property. Calling them "violent" legitimated public fear of disruptive Black protest while discrediting the protest before it even began.

In a scathing op-ed entitled "A Boycott Solves Nothing," the *Times* described the planned school action as "reckless" and "utterly unreasonable and unjustifiable," and referred to activists as possessing a "stubbornly closed mind."[40] The day after the boycott, while acknowledging the significant numbers of students who stayed out, the *Times* still called the boycott "misguided" and referred to Black students as "the socially and economically deprived."[41] The paper claimed school segregation resulted from "barriers of the housing pattern and composition of the population," but then suggested that money was the real barrier to systemic change. It instructed civil rights activists "who have been harassing and admonishing the school authorities [to] bend their energies to the search for the required dollars."[42] Like its Southern counterparts, the *Times* chided protest leaders for being impatient and overly demanding, and it sympathetically quoted city leaders: "We're asking them to wait a little longer."[43] The February school boycott was the largest civil rights demonstration of the era (the numbers far outstripping the March on Washington the previous August)—but you wouldn't have known it from the *Times*'s coverage.

Coverage of a much smaller protest of white mothers over the Brooklyn Bridge the following month amplified the perspectives of white parents opposing desegregation. In March 1964, more than ten thousand white New Yorkers, most of them mothers, marched over the bridge to protest very modest plans to desegregate forty elementary schools and twenty junior high schools by pairing schools. The *New York Times* did not call it what it was—a march to defend New York City's segregated schools. Under the headline "More Than 10,000 March in Protest of School Pairing," the opening sentence read: "Thousands of demonstrators, many of them homeowners from Brooklyn, the Bronx and Queens, marched on the Board of Education and City Hall yesterday, shouting that they wanted to preserve the tradition of neighborhood schools."[44] Conveniently forgetting that excusing segregation as "tradition" was a move out of the Southern newspaper playbook, the paper's reporting departed from the more critical tone it was using to cover white parents protesting in the South.[45]

In September of that year, when 275,000 white parents kept their kids home to protest limited plans for desegregation, the *New York Times* criticized the boycott timidly. It called for "neighborliness, for concern for those among us who for too long have been left back," and qualified its criticism of white parents who protested desegregation as "however free from prejudice they may be." Ten years after *Brown*, the *New York Times* treated the city's school segregation as unfortunate but not illegal or immoral, and it made even small efforts at desegregation seem like a favor, rather than the law of the land. In a move straight out of Montgomery (where city leadership had equated White Citizens' Councils with Black leadership organizing the bus boycott), it equated the white boycott with the February Black school boycott: "When this current demonstration is over we hope there will be no more of these boycotts, whether sponsored by white or Black. They succeed in nothing except to make a good many New Yorkers a little ashamed of their city."[46] How different the *Times*'s tone was here compared with the more sharply critical ways it covered the white protests—and George Wallace's actions—in Birmingham opposing school desegregation the year before.[47] How implicitly comfortable it was with New York's school segregation, as it wished for no more boycotts "white or black," feeling little responsibility to expose or change the deep inequities of the city's schools. Indeed, the nation's most prestigious newspaper covered the struggles in its own city very differently than it covered Southern ones, shining a light on Southern segregation and the noble movement that fought it while obscuring segregation at home and the movement within New York City that challenged it.

There is no way to understand how segregation endured across school systems in the "liberal" North and West without understanding the role the news media played. Had the media—from the outset—written stories that assumed the *Brown* decision applied to schools in their cities and exposed the effects of segregation in terms of school quality and the material benefits white families gained from such inequality, and treated those pressing for change as serious and their demands urgent, New York officials would have felt watched. Had these newspapers started to cover the movement in their own cities with similar methods and the same intrepidness and humility they brought to coverage of the Southern ones—understanding that equating positions of "both sides" benefits the status quo, that injustice requires exposure by bold reporters willing to question prevailing wisdom, that decent people do indecent things—the movement's wings would have had more power. Had they covered a growing Black movement in the city as a righteous movement, as they were increasingly doing in their coverage of the South, it would have increased the pressure on school officials to act. Instead, they let those officials off the hook.

This kind of coverage was not confined to school desegregation but characterized the coverage of other racial matters, particularly before the uprisings of the mid-1960s. As with school segregation, the *New York Times* did not take seriously the issue of police brutality in the city and rarely covered it. According to historian Clarence Taylor, the paper covered policing from the police point of view and rarely wrote about police brutality or took the point of view of the Black victim. As the *Times* relied on police and prosecutors for sources, perhaps it saw costs to the paper if its coverage was too critical. By the early 1960s, in places such as Birmingham, the *Times* was taking a more jaundiced view of what police and public officials were saying, in part because it came to see those sources as slanted and in part because it had less to lose by alienating Southern politicians or police departments.

The *New York Times* put a negative frame around growing protests over racial inequity in city life. By 1964, Brooklyn CORE had grown frustrated with the lack of change in the city. It had protested unequal sanitation services in the borough and been told Black people needed to learn to use trash cans; it had exposed housing segregation and the ways real estate agents steered away Black renters and buyers, with only modest change to the housing practices; it had protested businesses like Ebinger's Bakery, which didn't hire Black people (CORE managed to secure two jobs); and it had engaged in protests at Downstate Medical Center because of discrimination in the construction trades and come away with promises, rather than actual hiring. Frustrated with the lack of change in the city, Brooklyn CORE decided it needed to disrupt business as usual to force people to see what they refused to see. Fed up with "empty promises and pious pronouncements," it called for a stall-in on the first day of the 1964 New York World's Fair unless Governor Nelson Rockefeller formulated a "comprehensive plan . . . which will end police brutality, abolish slum housing, and provide integrated quality education for all."[48]

Describing the proposed stall-in as a "mischievous scheme," the *Times* decried: "The World's Fair has been discriminating against no one."

Ignoring how the fair was the brainchild of Robert Moses, the city public works czar and construction coordinator, whose policies had contributed to the neglect of Black neighborhoods across the city, the *Times* claimed it had "no authority to bring about civil rights reforms or correct wrongs in the social order [and] sympathy with the just aspirations of all peoples."[49] Moses had vetoed plans to extend the subway out to Flushing because the park, to him, was not designed for low-income people of color. The original plans for the stall-in focused on five roadways: the Grand Central Parkway, the Brooklyn-Queens Expressway, the Belt Parkway, the Interboro Parkway, and the Van Wyck Expressway—every one of them built or refurbished thanks to Moses's policies.[50]

Moses himself used his connections at various newspapers to persuade them to write editorials condemning the stall-in.[51] The city went to court, and a state supreme court judge issued an injunction against CORE. A number of protesters were arrested as some blocked subway entrances. "It is worth noting," historian Craig Wilder writes, "that the authority of the state could be marshaled so easily and effectively to stop a protest of racial inequalities but was not available to prevent those injustices . . . for, not only did white New Yorkers dominate social resources, they also determined the appropriate moments, venues and methods for the airing of grievances."[52] That included the *New York Times*.

AMNESIA AND BLAMING IN THE CITY OF ANGELS

Alongside the lackluster ways they covered Black protests were the ways these papers of record promptly forgot long-standing protests of racial inequality amidst crises like the Watts uprising. By dismissing Black grievances and disparaging Black protest, they had helped to maintain a segregated status quo in the North and a recurring "shock" about Black anger. Unwilling to hold politicians to account for ignoring these grievances, they didn't examine their own coverage (and lack of coverage) for answers about where these uprisings had come from. While challenging Southern surprise at the sit-ins and demonstrations rippling across the South, most media organizations proved unwilling to challenge this Northern shock and cloak of deniability. How different the understandings of the 1965 Watts and 1967 Detroit uprisings would have been if journalists had actually questioned public officials and local residents about the ways they had dismissed Black grievances and discredited movements in their cities for years—or even provided that broader context in their articles as essential background for understanding how long people had tried to raise these injustices to no avail.

The *Los Angeles Times* was a case in point in convenient amnesia. The paper had covered, however tepidly, the protest movement that emerged in 1962 after the police killing of Ronald Stokes, the unarmed secretary of the Nation of Islam whose death, as the *Los Angeles Times* reported, resulted in the creation of a blue ribbon committee. But that committee produced little change in police practices. In 1964, the *Times* noted growing Black calls, from CORE and the United Civil Rights Council, for Chief William H. Parker's resignation. Yet, despite years of activism and a six-day uprising, the *Times* was unwilling to acknowledge a pattern of police brutality in Los Angeles, let alone call the city to account for ignoring for so long Black grievances involving police misconduct. Instead, the paper continued to question the existence of LAPD brutality in the first place and called for the hiring of more police.

Similarly, in Detroit, the mainstream newspapers, the *Detroit News* and the *Detroit Free Press*, had refused to cover incidences of police brutality before 1967. While the city's Black newspaper, the *Michigan Chronicle*, detailed incident after incident, Detroit's major newspapers, according to NAACP Detroit branch leader Arthur Johnson, "had a standing agreement not to cover issues of police brutality."[53] Much like Southern newspapers, Detroit's major newspapers overwhelmingly kept coverage of police mistreatment of Black people out of the paper. Faced with exposure by the People's Tribunal of police brutality during the 1967 uprising, the papers again turned the other way. The *Detroit Free Press* had promised a big story and sent people to cover the tribunal. "That's another reason I wanted to do it," organizer Dan Aldridge explained, "because I was promised by the head of the *Free Press* to make it a big story." But nothing appeared in the paper. "I was so angry. I charged down to *Free Press* and got in [the reporter's] face and he told me, he said, 'Dan, the editors would not let us put it out there. I got the full story, had my full staff, and the editor said that they were going to squash the story,' and they did. There was nothing I could do about it."[54]

The surprise expressed by many white citizens and city officials should be understood in part as the surprise of intransigence—a willful shock nourished by the news media to deny the long-standing nature and significance of those grievances and obscure the history of a protracted struggle within the city. The framework of Southern exceptionalism, evident in the differential coverage between Los Angeles (or Detroit) and Birmingham, enabled this blind spot. The papers had refused to see years of protest in Los Angeles as a movement with authentic grievances, unlike the ways it had come to treat Black movements in the South. And like Southern newspapers, the *Los Angeles Times* took a measure of self-satisfaction in thinking Black Angelenos were largely content and white Angelenos largely open and fair. The news media did not force public officials to account for the fact that a decade-long civil rights movement in the city had produced little change in schools, housing, most job structures, or police practice (which certainly fueled the frustration that spurred the uprising) because it too had constructed Los Angeles's movement as different from the righteous Southern movement.

An examination of the Black newspapers the *Los Angeles Sentinel* and the *California Eagle* in the years leading up to the Watts uprising illuminates what the city's mainstream (white) newspapers refused to see: the variety of actions in the years before the uprising and the interconnections between various strands of the movement often viewed as divergent—for example, the NAACP and the Nation of Islam. Nearly every week, often on the front page, they detailed numerous grassroots actions happening within the city. By highlighting the systems of racial injustice in the city that people were contesting, this reporting disrupted the notion of Los Angeles's liberalism and challenged the ways Black people were blamed for conditions they faced in the city. But national news outlets preferred a different story, one that didn't highlight long-standing Black grievances but portrayed the rioters as riffraff, angry and alienated, and different from the good Black people in the South. As one *Times* staffer put it, "Ordinarily when there was trouble in the ghetto, the Times desk men downplayed it."[55] The *Los Angeles Times* didn't have a single Black reporter on staff before the uprising.[56]

When King came to town, even though he had been in Los Angeles multiple times before the uprising highlighting issues of racial inequality in the city, reporters made it seem like this was his first visit. They repeatedly highlighted an interaction between Martin Luther King and a young rioter who told him, "We won. . . . We made them pay attention to us," to highlight the disjuncture between the good civil rights leader and alienated ghetto youth. But the interaction reads much differently in the context of a protracted civil rights struggle in the city that had long been dismissed. In addition, nearly incessantly at first and for years following the uprising, journalists repeatedly asked King about Watts; highlighting his shock—in other words, working the frame that most journalists brought to the subject—gave King more room to expound on the racial problems endemic to American capitalism and democracy that he had been talking about before the uprising. These outlets had discovered the interlocking issues of racism, poverty, and state violence so they cast it as new, when in fact they hadn't been listening before.

And as King increasingly made connections between racism, war, and poverty, these news outlets grew increasingly critical, publishing editorials condemning him. After King was assassinated in 1968, singer and longtime civil rights supporter Harry Belafonte grew angry at a *New York Times* reporter standing next to him at the funeral: "I could not help but tell him that this grievous moment was in part the result of a climate of hate and distortion that the *New York Times* and other papers had helped create. . . . Just coming to grieve the loss was no cleansing of guilt."[57]

A new vein of reporting, intersecting with trends in urban social science, arose by the mid-1960s that furthered "cultural" explanations for inequality. Reporters journeyed to the "ghetto" to provide their readers a snapshot of "real" Black life—treating Black Angelenos (or Detroiters or Milwaukeeans) as some foreign culture to be observed, studied, and commented on. Their reporting could have taken Black life seriously, investigating the structures of segregation in the city and the community and religious organizations that had grown to challenge and survive it. But through the culture-of-poverty frame many employed, they portrayed Black people in these cities as a kind of foreign population possessing a distinct and often dysfunctional set of cultural practices. Such cultural framings corresponded to paradigms city officials and residents already employed to deflect Black demands for change. As poet and author Maya Angelou, living in Los Angeles at the time, observed, reporters who descended on Black Los Angeles after the riot maintained a familiar set of cultural stereotypes, noting that one journalist "wrote an account of the Watts riot allowing his readers to hold on to the stereotypes that made them comfortable while congratulating themselves on being in possession of some news."[58]

Renowned novelist Thomas Pynchon's much-vaunted 1966 article for the *New York Times Magazine*, "A Journey into the Mind of Watts," was a case in point. Pynchon traveled to "the heart of L.A.'s racial sickness . . . the coexistence of two very different cultures: one white and one black."[59] According to Pynchon, "Black culture is stuck pretty much with basic realities like disease, like failure, violence and death, which the whites have mostly chosen—and can afford—to ignore. " He claimed, "These kids are so tough you can pull slivers of [glass] out of them and never get a whimper. It's part of their landscape, both the real and the emotional one: busted glass, busted crockery, nails, tin cans, all kinds of scrap and waste"—missing all the joy, humor, care, and tenderness that characterized Black life in Watts. Making a nod to political struggles in a self-satisfied way, Pynchon observed: "The only illusion Watts ever allowed itself was to believe for a long time in the white version of what a Negro was supposed to be. But with the Muslim and civil-rights movements that went, too." Such a culturalist approach treated Black urban communities as a problem to be studied; portrayed urban Black kids as some sort of different, toughened kind of person; cast inequality through a lens of cultural difference; and disregarded the movement as made up of blustery illusion-breakers. Pieces like this provided a palatable way for liberal readers to make sense of visible disparities in the city without having to do anything about them.

The uprising did prompt the *Los Angeles Times* to run many more stories about poverty, racial injustice, housing and school inequality, and underserved neighborhoods. In certain ways, it discovered the problem of racial inequality in Los Angeles; in a 1967 article, it claimed that "the summer of 1965" was "when the white community abruptly discovered what Negroes already knew—that Negro area schools were less than equal."[60] While the *Times* had covered Black protests around school segregation in the early 1960s, it took the uprising for the paper to actually acknowledge it was a problem. In many ways, the *Los Angeles Times* would provide the template for covering the uprisings over the next few years: "surprise" at the uprising and alarm at Black anger, followed by discovery of patterns of inequality in the city (which had been pointed out for years), with little to no acknowledgment of the long history of organizing and Black grievances beforehand.

This was accompanied by mounting fear about Black Power and calls for more law and order. As historian Peter Levy has observed, "The national media not only helped undermine the struggle against [Northern] Jim Crow, it helped fuel the cry for 'law and order' and the politics of white resentment. . . . Disinclined to look for racism in their own backyard, the 'national' media, which was located in the North (and West) framed [Black Power] as an illegitimate offspring of the civil rights movement."[61] Indeed, because many of these news outlets discovered the problem only after the riots and conveniently dismissed any organizing beforehand, they framed Black Power as having come out of nowhere and were fearful of rising Black militancy. They wondered why people didn't go through the proper channels, even though had they looked back, even to their own pages, they would have seen how Black efforts to go through the proper channels had been dismissed and disparaged by local officials and their own reporters.

And these outlets embraced the need for more policing and continued to be reticent in covering police misconduct and violence. For instance, in the days and weeks after Chicano and Black high school students walked out of school in spring 1968, police attacked many of the Chicano students. But most of that footage did not make it into the news. Decades later, Moctesuma Esparza, who played a key role in the walkouts, explained:

> The coverage was extraordinarily censored, on a corporate level following the lead of the district attorney and the mayor and the power structure. They self-censored. . . . CBS and NBC and all of these corporate stations that had tremendous news coverage capability and were there, and all of these photographers that were there for the LA Times and the Herald, they did not publish or show or comment on the police violence. And the police violence was extreme.[62]

Because of these ongoing silences, Black activists increasingly pointed to the media as a key problem and highlighted the need for Black people to create their own media. The Black press had long covered issues in these cities far differently than white counterparts did. From Malcolm X's creation of Muhammad Speaks to the Black Panther newspaper to Reverend Cleage's Illustrated News to Richard and Milton Henry's Afro-American Broadcasting Company, Northern activists created new venues for even more hard-hitting and expansive coverage. Cleage had started the Illustrated News in 1961 as "a radical counterpart to Detroit's three black newsweeklies" and targeted Detroit's white liberals as part of the problem propping up system of segregation.[63] Taking its own pictures, framing its own stories, the *Black Panther* newspaper, started in 1967, published articles, photos, and art from branches around the country; it chronicled happenings both at home and abroad, according to historian Robyn Spencer. As one Panther put it, "The beautiful thing about it is that all you have to do is show it like it is."[64] It also documented police brutality and harassment of the Panthers and critiqued government policies.[65] In other words, it became an outlet to challenge the kind of reporting happening in the country's mainstream newspapers. The Black press had long played this role—and this new set of more revolutionary papers aimed to go further. Particularly given the conduct of law enforcement and the state, Black activists saw the need for new outlets that would take on this policing and the politics of law enforcement.

Fast-forward a half century, and a handful of Southern newspapers have reassessed their coverage of the civil rights movement. "40 Years Later Civil Rights Makes Page One," the *New York Times* headline read, detailing how the Lexington, Kentucky, *Herald-Leader* began a process of taking responsibility for its coverage (and lack thereof) of the movement, noting how in the 1990s the Jackson, Mississippi, *Clarion-Ledger* had acknowledged the bias of their coverage against the civil rights movement. But as the *Times* observed unselfconsciously, "Few newspapers, if any, have taken critical looks at what was the less egregious, but more common, practice of simply disregarding civil rights protests in their hometowns."[66]

The *New York Times* framed the need for others to do this kind of soul-searching but largely eschewed it for itself. In 2015, it broke a series of stories about battles relating to rezoning and desegregation in both the Dumbo neighborhood of Brooklyn and the Upper West Side of Manhattan. Its approach bore a sharp resemblance to the articles the *Times* published in the 1950s and 1960s. In a 2015 article, "Race and Class Collide in a Plan for Two Brooklyn Schools," the reporter acknowledged that "New York by some measures has one of the most segregated school systems in the country." Nonetheless, as it had done fifty years earlier, the newspaper's coverage naturalized the perspectives of upper-middle-class parents opposed to rezoning, who asserted their rights as homeowners and taxpayers and claimed they weren't racists. It quoted UCLA professor Gary Orfield stating that residents who opposed the rezoning "aren't

racists. . . . They just don't want to be in a ghetto."[67] Despite mentioning
school segregation, the article placed the issue outside of a long history
of inequality in the city and sixty years of white efforts to prevent desegregation and rezoning in the city. Similarly, it ignored equally long-
standing organizing by Black and Latino parents and community groups
in the city. This blinkered coverage was repeated in articles on zoning
struggles in District 3 in Manhattan, where long-standing organization
by immigrant and Black families through the Parent Leadership Project
barely drew a mention in the *Times*.[68] In a long story entitled "Harlem
Schools Are Left to Fail as Those Not Far Away Thrive," their organizing
was never mentioned.[69]

As Boston marked the fortieth anniversary of Garrity's decision, the
Boston Globe took a similar approach, framing the story largely around
"busing," not around segregation. It ran a piece entitled "Still Deciding
What Busing Gained and What It Cost," forgoing a more honest title like
"Still Deciding What Segregation Gained and What It Cost."[70] A lengthy
feature reflecting on the fortieth anniversary of court-ordered desegregation, "History Rolled In on a Yellow School Bus," began and ended the
story in 1974. It was framed singularly around the experiences and perspectives of person after person (Black student, white student, Black mother,
white mother, bus driver, cop) involved in busing between Roxbury and
South Boston in September 1974.[71] Another retrospective column, entitled "Did Busing Slow Boston's Desegregation?," examined lasting racism
in Boston but talked about racism largely in terms of personal relationships and maintained the myth that busing hadn't existed in the city for
years prior to 1974, with no objection from white parents.[72] Readers would
have gotten a much different sense of the city's history if the *Globe* had
detailed what segregation looked like in the decades before Garrity's decision (meager, overcrowded classrooms; racist textbooks; language exclusion; few teachers of color) and how the city used busing before 1974 to
maintain segregated schools. Had the newspaper included a section on
the various movements and tactics Black and Latino community leaders and parents employed to challenge Boston's segregated and unequal
schools, or examined the massive and unrelenting opposition they encountered that ultimately led to the federal lawsuit in 1972, its anniversary
coverage would have gone a lot further to grapple with the city's history.
Instead, it focused on the "busing crisis," and the upheaval that ensued in

the mid-1970s with court-ordered desegregation was treated as perhaps unnecessary, while the enduring educational inequity in the metro area was unfortunate but largely unchangeable.[73]

The few attempts by Northern outlets to go back and analyze their previous coverage have still tended to avoid the question of the Northern civil rights movement. In a lengthy and substantive fiftieth-anniversary piece reflecting on *Los Angeles Times* coverage of the Watts uprising, Doug Smith raised significant questions about the paper's handling of the events: "My first reaction was, 'How could this coverage have won a Pulitzer Prize?'"[74] Smith criticized how "a flurry of one-source stories failed to challenge Parker and Yorty's now obvious efforts to deflect responsibility for the continuing violence" but didn't investigate the coverage before 1965, when the paper had honed that style over a period of years. He claimed, with a similar myopia, that fifty years later, "it's unthinkable that reporters or editors would show such unskeptical deference to public officials." Smith praised how, two months later, the *Los Angeles Times* pledged an "open and frank communication with the people of Watts, not just its leaders but the people themselves, including the rioters . . . to explore the kind of thinking, the kind of passions, the kind of despair and apathy, that led to an explosion of hatred that rocked a great city and shocked the entire world," and how the paper began to explore "the resentment over lack of jobs, loan redlining, bungled anti-poverty programs and educational failures that fueled the rage."

But Smith did not critically examine the pathologizing tone often employed in these stories, and he included no analysis of how the *Times* had covered a growing protest movement in Los Angeles in the decade before the uprising that it promptly forgot when the upheaval happened. While Smith claimed "the riots made *The Times* a better newspaper—and . . . this journalistic evolution was good for Los Angeles, as well," he still replicated one of the most glaring omissions of its coverage: the absence of the fact of long-standing Black organizing and the ways that city had ignored and disparaged nonviolent Black protests for years prior to the uprising, as well as after.

A similar problem exists today. While uprisings in Cleveland, Baltimore, and Ferguson, Missouri, in 2014 and 2015 prompted much reporting on the nature of injustice in law enforcement, municipal policy, and court practices, few stories focused on the groups in these cities that had highlighted such problems *for years*. Such silences are comfortable. It is easier to castigate protesters as "thugs" unwilling to work through the proper processes than for media outlets to hold accountable neighbors and public officials who didn't listen when they had. It is easier to cast the people who rose up as the problem, rather than focus on the readers who stayed silent for years amidst police injustice after injustice.

The myth of the media as the good guys lets the role news outlets played as maintainers of injustice off the hook. It assumes that if you have a righteous struggle, news outlets will cover it, when they often didn't. Or that when people work through the "proper channels," the media would take note, which they often didn't. Many times, these news organizations treated nonviolent protests in their own backyards as silly, unreasonable, or even violent. Other times they ignored them. While they came to see Southern surprise at Black protest as contrived, they largely did not question white surprise at Black grievances in their own cities. The humility and bravery many journalists exhibited in covering the Southern struggle was fundamentally not replicated in the ways their news outlets covered racial issues in their cities. Largely, they proved unwilling to shine a significant light on the racial inequities embedded in their city's schools, policing, or municipal structures—or to challenge the "but I'm not a racist" claims of many middle- and upper-class Northerners who labored mightily to preserve segregated and unequal structures in their hometowns.

The media's willingness to name injustice when they saw it in the South—and the corresponding realization that simply covering both sides risked upholding inequality—proved easier there. At home, this would have required turning the light on the racial politics of their own communities and challenging the "fantasy of self-deception and comfortable vanity," as King put it in 1967, that most white Americans who "consider themselves sincerely committed to justice" lived within.[75] Unfortunately, it was easier for these papers of record to maintain the fantasy.

CHAPTER FIVE

Beyond a Bus Seat

The Movement Pressed for Desegregation, Criminal Justice, Economic Justice, and Global Justice

> *I have never been what you would call just an integrationist. I know I've been called that. . . . Integrating that bus wouldn't mean more equality. Even when there was segregation there was plenty of integration in the South, but it was for the benefit and convenience of the white person, not us. . . . [My aim was] to discontinue all forms of oppression.*
>
> —Rosa Parks[1]

ROSA PARKS HAS BEEN trapped on the bus. When she died in 2005, it was not enough to have her coffin lie in honor at the Capitol; the procession to and from the Capitol rotunda included an empty vintage 1957 bus dressed in black bunting. In 2013, when the statue for Rosa Parks was unveiled in the Capitol's Statuary Hall, the first full-size statue of a Black person to be installed there, Parks was rendered sitting. (Nearly all the other hundred statues are displayed in regal standing poses that typically have little to do with their historical accomplishments.) And at President Trump's inaugural lunch in January 2017, Missouri senator Roy Blunt kicked off the affair in Statuary Hall, noting the "important figures in national history" surrounding them and taking pains to mention a "new statue" installed since the last inauguration: "Rosa Parks is now in Statuary Hall and she is of course seated rather than standing, as she should be."

Parks's vision has been relegated to a bus seat, narrowing what she fought for her entire life and how she defined her bus stand. Indeed the movement itself has been constricted and diluted, framed narrowly around bus seats and lunch counters, rather than the equity, access, and justice these activists demanded. Tellingly, Parks and her comrades typically used the term "desegregation" rather than "integration" to signify that their struggle was not a matter of having a bus seat or a school desk next to a white person but of dismantling the apparatus of inequality. Parks was clear that there had long been integration, even in the South, but it was for the benefit of whites; for instance, Black women were allowed to ride in the white section of the bus if they were caring for white children. It wasn't some sort of osmosis that sitting next to a white person would lead to success—which is often the way integration is now portrayed. It was about access, equality, resource reallocation, political transformation, jobs, justice, and tying the futures of all families together, so that material advantages, opportunities, and expectations given to some would be available to all.

Narrowing the goal of civil rights activists to a seat diminishes the expansive vision of justice they fought for, making the movement smaller, more cloistered, and less relevant to where we are today. If the movement is reduced to a lunch counter seat, then the oppression it fought against can seem long ago and far away, and its happy ending celebrated: the bus is desegregated, the lunch counter opened, the Civil Rights and Voting Rights Acts passed. But those pieces of legislation were not the ends; they were momentous steps on a much longer road for social justice. Massive victories won through decades of pressing and struggling around voting rights and public desegregation were just a portion of the modern Black freedom movement's goals. Moreover, equating their vision simply with the *Brown* decision or passage of the 1965 Voting Rights Act misses the important questions of how these would—and would not—be substantively implemented, and how hard activists pressed for full and far-reaching implementation.

By missing how civil rights activists saw these as steps rather than the endgame, the goal of desegregation gets reduced to a seat next to a white person, rather than a fundamental reordering of the social, political, and economic landscape of the city and the nation. As Boston organizer Muriel Snowden elaborated, Black children "were not going to have a chance unless there is some kind of equity . . . something to bring them to the point where they start at the beginning line, unencumbered . . . [and then something to ensure] they don't get tripped up or rabbit punched or something along the way."[2] The goal necessitated transforming the structures of opportunity, not simply changing attitudes or seeing beyond color. As

Parks herself put it: "Desegregation proves itself by being put in action. Not changing attitudes, attitudes will change."[3]

In 1960, as students put their bodies on the line sitting-in to strike a blow at downtown segregation, organizer Ella Baker brought these young leaders together at a meeting at Shaw University, which led to the founding of SNCC. She made clear that they were "concerned with something much bigger than a hamburger." Their goals were "not limited to a drive for personal freedom, or even freedom for the Negro in the South . . . [but] the moral implications of racial discrimination for the 'whole world.'"[4] Because segregation was about material denial, resource hoarding, and restrictions on the terms of first-class citizenship, desegregation sought to disrupt those limitations, spread the resources around, and demand full social citizenship. From the outset, the movement had that comprehensive vision.

Activists sought substantive desegregation, massive transformation of the criminal justice system, antipoverty programs and welfare rights, school equity and the incorporation of Black history into the curriculum, jobs and union rights, anticolonialism, and an end to the United States involvement in Vietnam. Given the structures of white supremacy and interactions between social, economic, and political power, the stakes of desegregation and access to the vote were big, and activists were clear about that at the time. The vote, according to SNCC's Courtland Cox, was "necessary but not sufficient," a step toward securing and protecting other rights but nowhere near the end of the road. As SNCC built voter projects throughout Mississippi, Georgia, and Alabama in the early 1960s, attaining the vote was always understood as key to also securing economic power.[5]

In building its campaigns in the Deep South, SNCC sought real power for Black people to control their own economic and political lives. It established a research department because it was committed to understanding the breadth of the problem. As Julian Bond explained,

[SNCC] had the best research arm of any civil rights organization before or since. . . . "Power structure" was no abstract phrase for SNCC's band of brothers and sisters, but a real list with real people's names and addresses and descriptions of assets and interlocking directorships. . . . Knowledge of who owned what was crucial to SNCC's strategies. From it, we knew that Southern peonage was no accident, but rather the deliberate result of economic policies determined thousands of miles away from the cotton field.[6]

But this broader vision of human rights and economic justice does not often make it into popular fables of the civil rights movement, which often distort its goods into a narrow notion of personal freedom, seats next to white people, and color blindness. As the late historian Vincent Harding explained, "Our struggle was not just against something, but was trying to bring something into being."[7]

In the fable, honoring the civil rights movement often comes with a slight lurking shadow—the ghost of Black Power and the "times when some of us claiming to push for change lost our way," as President Obama put it in his March on Washington anniversary speech.[8] In this version, the movement went astray in the mid-1960s, abandoning its dream of Black and white together for anger and separatism. This "master narrative," as Julian Bond has termed it, has tremendous power over how the period is depicted: "Once Americans understood that discrimination was wrong, they quickly moved to remove racial prejudice and discrimination from American life, as evidenced by the Civil Rights Acts of 1964 and 1965. . . . Inexplicably, just as the civil rights victories were piling up, many African Americans, under the banner of Black Power, turned their backs on American society."[9] The turn to Black Power, as Bond observes, is thus framed as inexplicable and ungrateful—cast as the product of an alienated Black community unwilling to work through the proper channels and unappreciative of its white allies. As the previous chapters have shown, this narrative partly rests on forgetting the decades-long struggles in Northern cities that had been repeatedly dismissed, disparaged, and denied. But it also ignores the broad vision of justice the civil rights movement had across the South as well as the North in the period before 1965.

Lee Daniels's film The Butler trafficked heavily in this distorted narrative. Inspired by the true story of Eugene Allen—an African American who worked on the White House kitchen staff from Truman to Reagan—Daniels's widely acclaimed historical drama was applauded for its uncompromising look at race in America. As the world outside the White House is afire with lunch counter sit-ins, Freedom Rides, and urban riots, Cecil Gaines (played by Forest Whitaker) musters forward as the invisible Black servant to a succession of white presidents, while his family wrestles with the contradictions of the era. Gaines makes sure his wife, Gloria (played by Oprah Winfrey), doesn't have to work—and in the mode of the Betty Friedan housewife, she turns to alcohol and an affair. His two sons choose opposite paths: Louis rebels against his father to become a Freedom Rider and later a Black Panther, while Charlie enlists and dies in Vietnam. The movie touted itself as a true story. But, save the fact of there being an actual man, Eugene Allen, who did serve as a White House butler for eight presidents, most of the film does not resemble Allen's life. His wife was not an alcoholic. He had only one son, who went to Vietnam and came home. The older son-turned-activist is completely fictional.[10]

Entirely made up, Gaines's son's journey—and conflict with his father—becomes the film's comment on the arc of the Black Freedom movement, confirming a narrow Southernized version of the movement and an unflinching divide between the civil rights and Black Power movements. In *The Butler*, there are no protests of segregation in DC, no sense of Black poverty or police brutality, no systemic Northern racism, no movement for jobs, no school desegregation or open housing, welfare rights, or DC statehood—though all were occurring in the city in the 1950s and 1960s.[11] Black Power in the movie is equated solely with the Black Panthers, who are then reduced to Afros, black leather, and in-your-face attitude. Louis's girlfriend transforms from a well-mannered, feminine Freedom Bus Rider into a surly, unshaven Black Panther, whom Louis ultimately (and, in the movie's take, wisely) jettisons. By the film's end, Louis rejects the Panthers' "violence" for more "reasonable" electoral politics and "respectable" women. While Black Power is rendered as dangerous youthful naiveté, war is treated as patriotic. Charlie attends Howard University at a time when demonstrations for African American studies roiled that campus, and he enlists in the army at a time when a protest movement among Black soldiers was rising and Black anticolonialism was burgeoning—yet none of this is depicted. In excluding or belittling this broader history of activism, the movie forfeited the opportunity to portray a fuller, more accurate history of the 1960s and 1970s and rendered Black militancy as angry, ungrounded, and out of nowhere. In many ways, even though the film was praised for its boldness ("brilliantly truthful," the *New York Times* said), *The Butler*'s view of history was largely derivative, confirming the fable and obscuring the scope of what Black activists fought for and imagined.[12]

The mounting militancy of the later 1960s didn't come out of nowhere. It came from ignoring, denigrating, and rejecting the demands community organizers had made for years for real school desegregation and educational equity, open and affordable housing, jobs and a robust social safety net, equitable municipal services, and the transformation of the criminal justice system. That breadth of issues was there all along and ultimately took new forms in the Black Power movement. Too often reduced to slogans, guns, and leather jackets, the demand for Black Power was much broader than popularly portrayed. But there's a convenience in making Black radicalism all about the guns and leather jackets because it obscures the larger goals for social, political, and economic transformation that ran through the Black freedom struggle and the deep resistance Black activists encountered. "This distorted historical memory," according to historian Will Jones, "has reinforced the impression that the racially egalitarian politics of the civil rights movement were somehow incompatible with struggles for economic justice."[13]

Desegregation, criminal justice, economic justice, global justice—understanding the movement that activists built in the South and in the North in the 1950s, 1960s, and 1970s means seeing that these goals (as well as school equity, as we will see in the next chapter) were crucial from the outset. Understanding the way these goals were woven into the movement from its earliest days reveals civil rights activists' expansive "freedom dreams," as historian Robin Kelley has termed them, and the massive opposition activists encountered.[14] And when we see that one form white resistance took was the constant distortion and dilution of those goals, the political interests behind narrowing that vision in our popular memory today come into sharp relief.

BEYOND THE BUS: CRIMINAL JUSTICE WAS KEY

Criminal justice was a key through-line in movement efforts. Reckoning with this history shows us familiar moments of the movement anew. The Montgomery bus boycott was sparked in part by the recent acquittal of the two men who had lynched fourteen-year-old Emmett Till. In the decade before the boycott, Montgomery's small cadre of activists—including E. D. Nixon, Johnnie Carr, Irene West, Rufus Lewis, and Rosa Parks—targeted the criminal justice system as a key arena of injustice. They worked on two interrelated problems: the ways the justice system disproportionately and discriminatorily targeted Black people for policing and prosecution, and the ways that brutality, violence, and sexual aggression against Black people often went unaccounted for and unpunished. They pushed to get the law to be responsive to white brutality against Black people, particularly sexual violence against Black women; in cases such as those of Recy Taylor, who was raped by six white men, and Gertrude Perkins, who was raped by two police officers, they labored mightily to get justice for these women but ultimately the rapists went unpunished.[15]

And they sought to protect Black people—largely Black men—from wrongful charges and legal lynching. One particularly egregious case was that of teenager Jeremiah Reeves, who was having a consensual relationship with a young white woman, but when they were found out, she claimed rape. Fifteen-year-old Claudette Colvin, who would refuse to give up her seat on a bus in March 1955, remembers seeing the police arrest Reeves, whom she knew as a student at Booker T. Washington High School, and the impact his arrest had on her growing political consciousness.[16] The police beat the sixteen-year old Reeves and forced the teenager to sit in an electric chair until he confessed.[17] Reeves later retracted his admission of guilt but was convicted and sentenced to death. The Supreme Court in 1954 overturned his conviction because of biased jury composition. He was tried again in 1955 and a second all-white jury took only thirty-four minutes to restore his death penalty. Despite years of work by Montgomery activists to try to have him exonerated, when Reeves turned twenty-one in 1958, he was executed.[18]

Many in Montgomery had been devastated when the news came in August 1955 that Emmett Till, a teenager visiting from Chicago, had been lynched in Mississippi. Having known other cases like Till's that were swept under the rug, Rosa Parks and her comrades were heartened by national attention to the case. The difference in Till's case, according to Parks, was that Emmett Till came from the North and Till's mother's courageously decided to allow his brutalized body to be photographed by *Jet* magazine. Organizers such as T. R. M. Howard succeeded in getting news outlets to care. Montgomery activists were hopeful that finally—given the publicity around Till's murder—there might be justice when his two killers were put on trial in the fall of 1955.

Then, four days before she would make her historic stand, Parks, Nixon, and many of Montgomery's Black activists attended a packed mass meeting on the Till case at Martin Luther King's Dexter Avenue Baptist Church. The lead organizer, Howard had come to town to raise awareness of the recent acquittal of the two men, Roy Bryant and J. W. Milam, who had kidnapped and killed Till. Howard had also come to bring the news that two voting rights activists had recently been killed in Mississippi, and a third brutally beaten. He detailed Till's gruesome murder and the lack of justice—and exhorted Black Montgomerians to keep up the fight. Parks and Nixon had worked on such cases for years. The massive attention drawn to the Till case was far beyond anything activists had previously managed to secure. And yet Till's killers had now gone free. Angry and despairing, many of the Montgomery activists who would be key to organizing the boycott were at the breaking point.

Four days later, when bus driver James Blake told her to move, Rosa Parks thought about Emmett Till and—"pushed as far as she could be pushed"—refused.[19] "Let us look at Jim Crow for the Criminal he is," she thought.[20] Understanding that it was a system of white supremacy that countenanced segregation and allowed Till's murderers to walk free, Parks saw an opportunity to strike a blow at that system. Thus, her decision to remain sitting and get arrested and the boycott that ensued stemmed not only from resistance to bus segregation but also from outrage at systemic criminal injustice.

THE MOVEMENT WAS ALSO A FIGHT FOR
ECONOMIC JUSTICE AND WELFARE RIGHTS

Demands for jobs also ran through the movement and were a key, but now largely unrecognized, part of the Montgomery bus boycott. Bus segregation was a way to hoard jobs. Weeks before Parks's stand on the bus, activists had invited New York congressman Adam Clayton Powell down to Montgomery to speak about organizing in New York and a successful 1944 bus boycott Powell had helped spearhead to secure bus driving jobs for Black people. One of the Montgomery bus boycott's initial demands was the hiring of Black bus drivers, yet in our public retelling, that demand has completely dropped out of sight. It wasn't until 1962 that Montgomery finally hired its first two Black bus drivers.[21]

Demands for jobs and economic justice that ran through the civil rights movement, and King's work specifically, are regularly backgrounded, just as they are in recollections of the Montgomery bus boycott. While King's

speech at the 1963 March on Washington is now one of the most celebrated in American history, it is largely known for its ending. Forgotten is the beginning, where King laid out how America had given Black
people a "bad check." The country had "defaulted on this promissory note
insofar as her citizens of color are concerned," and so they had come
to Washington to collect on a debt stemming from generations of economic exploitation and rights abridgement.[22] Crucial to King's vision at
the march was the idea that Black people were owed restitution by the
nation and had come to claim their rightful payment; understanding that
dramatically shifts our view of the political vision of that day—the idea
of material redress as necessary to undo the debt the nation owed to
African Americans. March organizers A. Philip Randolph and Bayard
Rustin had from the outset framed the focus of the march as "jobs and
justice," and even when they abandoned plans for civil disobedience to
build a broad coalition of groups to join the march, that economic vision
was not lost. This was not some warm and fuzzy dream but one that demanded real material compensation. March leaders, according to historian Will Jones, "insisted that such racially egalitarian measures would be
ineffective unless coupled with a minimum wage increase, extension of
federal labor protections to workers in agriculture, domestic service, and
the public sector, and a 'massive federal program to train and place all
unemployed workers—Negro and white—on meaningful and dignified
jobs at decent wages.'"[23] From Cambridge, Maryland, to Ruleville, Mississippi, to Lowndes County, Alabama, SNCC married campaigns for public
desegregation and voting rights with the need for economic power, self-
determination, and public assistance.[24]

King's last campaign—taken up by Coretta Scott King, SCLC, and a
multiracial coalition of poor people after he was killed—was to build a
large-scale Poor People's Campaign (PPC), a multiracial group of poor
people from across the nation who would descend on the Capitol and stay
until their needs were addressed by Congress and the president. By 1967,
King and the SCLC had grown critical of Johnson's War on Poverty, which
claimed to prioritize "maximum feasible participation" by poor people but
did nothing to encourage (and at times discouraged) their political organization. Many in the Johnson administration subscribed to a cultural-
deficit model for understanding the problem of poverty and its solutions
(which held that the problems of the poor were located in behaviors that

needed altering), ignoring the structural racism that produced poverty in America. Moreover, the escalation of the war in Vietnam had caused cuts in funding to education, job training programs, and social services. A mass mobilization of poor people would force the interlocking issues of poverty, racism, and war into public consciousness and move Congress to action.

At a December 1967 press conference announcing the Poor People's Campaign, King zeroed in on the federal government's "primary responsibility for low minimum wages, for a degrading system of inadequate welfare, for subsidies to the rich and unemployment and underemployment of the poor." The nation had developed ways to ignore and hide the impacts of poverty—and part of the campaign's aim would be to force the country to "see the poor."[25] Poor people would come from across the nation to the Capitol to demand "$30 billion annual appropriation for a real war on poverty; congressional passage of full employment and guaranteed income legislation [a guaranteed annual wage]; and Construction of 500,000 low-cost housing units per year."[26] The PPC's first gathering took place in Atlanta in March 1968, a month before King's assassination, and brought together over fifty organizations representing poor African Americans, whites, Latinos, and Native Americans.[27] "It didn't cost the nation one penny to integrate lunch counters," King observed during a February 1968 trip to Mississippi, "but now we are dealing with issues that cannot be solved without the nation spending billions of dollars and undergoing a radical redistribution of economic power."[28]

When King was assassinated, the work did not stop. A month later, on May 12, 1968, organizers broke ground in Washington, DC, setting up a tent city of plywood shanties on the Mall named Resurrection City. Nine caravans of poor people of all races began making their way from across the country and people journeyed by bus, train, car, and mule train to DC. The most visible Black caravan—the Mule Train—with a hundred people and seventeen mule-drawn wagons, started out from Marks, Mississippi, the poorest county in the country, where King's idea for the PPC had crystallized in 1966. (Visiting Marks in 1966, King had surprisingly broken into tears seeing four kids eagerly awaiting lunch at a Head Start center—where they were each served a quarter of an apple.)[29] Two buses of poor whites came from Appalachia, while caravans of Latinos and Native Americans journeyed thousands of miles to the nation's capital.

A combination of local, state, and FBI officials kept the Mule Train under constant surveillance as it traveled the thousand miles to DC.[30] About 2,500 people stayed at Resurrection City, but heavy rain made the conditions of the tent city hazardous. Many poor people stayed elsewhere; an encampment of Chicanos led by Rodolfo Gonzales and Reies Tijerina set up at the Hawthorne School, and many Native Americans congregated at a nearby church.

The high point of the campaign came on June 19, Solidarity Day. Some fifty thousand to a hundred thousand gathered to hear Coretta Scott King, Rosa Parks, and others address the crowd. Scott King gave a powerful speech that day, calling on American women to "unite and form a solid block of women power" to fight racism, poverty, and war.[31] Despite its well-defined demands for full employment, a guaranteed annual income, and construction of more affordable housing, the Poor People's Campaign was criticized by many in Congress and the media as "unruly" and needing "clarity."[32] Resurrection City was torn down by police on June 24. It made poverty visible, but it did not succeed in getting Congress to act. It did, however, alter relations with local officials; Bertha Burres Johnson of Marks, Mississippi, explained how public officials were "very nice to me because I guess they were afraid not to because they thought I would call the SCLC." And access to social assistance opened up for many following the PPC.[33] But the PPC has been largely lost in our public memory because memorializing it, as Mule Train photographer Roland Freeman observed, requires acknowledging "the work that began then is still unfinished."[34]

Key to the vision of the PPC was the idea that people had the right to social assistance and that people were not the cause of their own poverty, an unjust and exploitative labor market and centuries of racial and gender injustice were. Activists began organizing nationally to demand public assistance and to challenge punitive and humiliating welfare policies. Beginning at kitchen tables and community centers across the country, local groups of welfare recipients had organized in the early 1960s. Growing directly out of the civil rights movement, the welfare rights movement was led by Black women, many of whom had been active in earlier desegregation and voting rights campaigns. In 1967, they coalesced to form the National Welfare Rights Organization, in part through the initiative of former CORE organizer George Wiley. The NWRO was largely Black but included whites, Latinas, and Native Americans. It framed welfare as a right and a matter of equality. The first battleground of local and national welfare rights organizing was access—taking on the exclusions embedded in the New Deal social citizenship.

Deriving from mothers' pension programs of the early twentieth century, welfare was nationalized through the 1935 Social Security Act, which created Aid to Dependent Children (changed to Aid to Families with Dependent Children, AFDC, in 1962) to provide cash assistance to women and children. Embedded in the legislation were "suitable home" provisions, giving case workers great discretion in determining who qualified for aid. Because welfare was administered by the states, and because white politicians feared losing African American and Latina women's agricultural and domestic labor, suitable home provisions were often enforced on a racial basis, and women of color gained little access to ADC in its first decades— they would be barred during the cotton harvesting season or intimidated from even applying.[35] This was not just a matter of Southern politicians' influence, as historian Mary Poole has shown; Northern politicians were invested in elevating white workers and mothers, and the shape of the Social Security Act reflected that.[36] Until the 1960s, Black and Latina workers were rendered ineligible for other wage and union protections as the New Deal created what historian Jill Quadagno calls a "racial welfare state" that denied people of color "the full perquisites of citizenship," while ensuring their availability as a flexible, low-wage workforce for US employers.[37] Excluded from their rights as workers, poor Black and Latina women were also cast as "bad mothers" and denied cash assistance for their children.

The NWRO and its local movement affiliates took its message on the rights of poor women to the streets, into welfare offices and courts, and before state legislatures. Challenging the stereotypes of poor women of color as lazy, promiscuous, and undeserving of full rights, they successfully fought to overturn "man of the house" rules, establish a right to due process to maintain or obtain welfare benefits, and ensure enforcement of little-known regulations outlining minimum standards for people on welfare. In their public campaigns, they sought to break the stigma of poverty and social assistance, reframing it as a matter of citizenship and self-determination. By 1968, NWRO membership numbered thirty thousand, with thousands more participating in actions across the country. Though it has received little attention, in many ways the NWRO constituted one of the most mass-based Black Power organizations of the era.

Other radical organizations, including the Black Panthers and Brown Berets, took up the call for welfare rights. The *Black Panther* newspaper, along with the Chicano movement newspaper *La Raza*, contained extensive coverage of welfare rights and the exclusions of Black and Latino families from social benefits. Panther artists Asali Dixon and Emory Douglass made poor mothers and the support they were demanding a visual motif in the paper. And the Panthers' survival programs, including the free breakfast, free food, and free shoe programs they built, free medical clinics they founded, and free ambulance services they started, were an active attempt to redress the material needs of Black people largely left out of the New Deal.[38]

The welfare rights movement exposed the racialized and gendered ideas undergirding the denial of social assistance to poor women and the public disgust expressed toward them. "There are a lot of other lies that male society tells about welfare mothers," Johnnie Tillmon, the first chairwoman of the NWRO and a Black welfare recipient herself, explained. "That AFDC mothers are immoral, that AFDC mothers are lazy, misuse their welfare checks, spend it all on booze and are stupid and incompetent. If people are willing to believe these lies, it's partly because they're just special versions of the lies that society tells about all women."[39] Tillmon had been born in Arkansas but moved to Los Angeles. Having worked all her life as a sharecropper and then as a shirt-line operator at a California laundry, when she got sick, she went on public assistance and was astonished by the dehumanizing treatment recipients received. In 1961, she formed Aid to Needy Children-Mothers Anonymous to bring together other welfare mothers in the Nickerson Gardens housing project where she lived in Watts.[40]

By 1967, Los Angeles had more than a dozen welfare rights groups. According to historian Alejandra Marchevsky, following the establishment of the NWRO, a coalition of welfare rights groups, which had grown out of collaborative efforts in the late 1950s and early 1960s by Mexican American and African American women in South Los Angeles to demand fair treatment from the California Department of Public Social Services (DPSS), formed the LA Welfare Rights Organization (LAWRO).[41] As LAWRO's African American president Catherine Jermany recalled, "We were loud. We were out there. And basically we wanted to be inclusive ... [and] attack the biggest offices of the welfare department."[42] Alicia Escalante, a single mother of five who became a leading Chicana welfare rights organizer, got involved with Tillmon and Jermany when then governor Ronald Reagan slashed the state's Medicaid benefits. Their protest caught the attention of *Jet* magazine, which reported that "the lame, blind, [and] poor" had marched for three hours carrying placards that read "Even Poor Children Have the Right to See a Dentist."[43]

Escalante began attending campaign meetings, and she recalled how "they asked if anyone was here to represent East L.A. and I was the only one who raised my hand."[44] She formed the East Los Angeles Chicana Welfare Rights Organization. By 1969, Escalante had emerged as a leader of the countywide welfare rights movement, frequently collaborating with Jermany in planning campaigns and negotiating with county welfare officials. In December of that year, Escalante and Jermany worked together on a campaign to protest the slashing by DPSS of funds for food, appliances, furniture, and other household items (labeled "special needs").[45] In a blistering article, "Are Welfare Recipients Human?," published in *La Raza* in 1968, Escalante zeroed in on the process of dehumanization:

> Notice to all welfare clients: You are not taxpayers; you don't support yourselves. You don't take good care of your kids; they are hungry, dirty, not clothed properly. [. . .] You are no good; you should be sterilized, your children put in homes; you should be forced to go to work; you should be ashamed of yourselves for living.

Casting public assistance as a form of dignity and independence, welfare rights activists challenged the stigma of public assistance and the various barriers and caseworker biases that made it difficult for Black, Chicana, and Puerto Rican women to access assistance. Locally, Escalante and other women with the Chicana Welfare Rights Organization pressed DPSS to hire Spanish-speaking social workers and make all forms and services available in Spanish—seeing this as crucial for full social citizenship.[46] Just as the Black Panther programs established school breakfast and health programs that are now widespread, the Chicana welfare rights activists' organizing resulted in multilingual access to social services taken for granted today.

Welfare rights campaigns, according to historian Premilla Nadasen, "sought to instill pride in welfare recipients by debunking the racial and sexual stereotypes of AFDC and affording recipients a degree of control and autonomy over their lives."[47] These grassroots organizing efforts, along with President Lyndon Johnson's War on Poverty, opened access to welfare; by 1971, over 90 percent of eligible families were receiving AFDC, up from less than 33 percent in 1960. With the mechanization of Southern agriculture and deindustrialization in Northern cities throwing more Americans into extreme poverty, the need for assistance also grew. By 1974, 10.8 million people were receiving AFDC, up from 3.1 million in 1961. This expansion of access to AFDC and the introduction of food stamp benefits began combating hunger and malnutrition in America.[48]

But even amidst this expansion, women of color were seen as unworthy, and escalating attacks on welfare in the 1970s, 1980s, and 1990s became a veiled but effective method of attacking Black and Latina women and the civil rights struggle more broadly and dismantling parts of the social safety net. By the time Bill Clinton rode into office in 1992 on his promise to "end welfare as we know it," the fact that welfare rights had been part of the civil rights movement had long since been repudiated and forgotten. The welfare rights movement may have been one of the era's most paradigm-shifting—but now it is one of its least known, despite a wealth of scholarship on it.[49] The profound challenge it raises to today's political assumptions, even among liberals, about the right to public assistance, and about the vision welfare-rights activists put forth of social assistance as self-determination, imagines a different possibility for the country today.

BEYOND AMERICAN EXCEPTIONALISM: JUSTICE AT HOME AND ABROAD

Civil rights leaders and organizers understood that fighting for economic justice was inseparable from global justice and that opposition to US involvement in Vietnam was part of a commitment to civil rights and economic justice. Vietnam has "played havoc with our domestic destinies," King explained at an address at the National Cathedral the week before he was assassinated, as he questioned the nation's priorities, noting that killing a single Viet Cong soldier cost "about five hundred thousand dollars while we spend only fifty-three dollars a year for every person characterized as poverty-stricken in the so-called poverty program, which is not even a good skirmish against poverty."[50] Racism and economic exploitation intertwined in "cruel manipulation of the poor" sent to fight other poor people in the Vietnam War. Four years earlier, SNCC's Bob Moses had observed that the kind of racism that killed the three young men during Freedom Summer in Mississippi "is going to kill a lot more people in Vietnam." The white supremacy at the core of American identity meant "the country [was] unable to see Vietnam for exactly the same reasons. . . . They didn't see us."[51]

The international vision of justice many activists possessed and their critique of the racial heart of American democracy disrupt the American exceptionalism that sits at the heart of the fable. While the civil rights movement is cast today as emblematic of the special power of American democracy, civil rights activists saw American racism at the heart of both its domestic and global projects. Lorraine Hansberry's play *A Raisin in the Sun* debuted on Broadway in 1959, the first play by an African American woman to do so. *Raisin* was based upon the Hansberry family's own struggle against restrictive covenants in Chicago. Her own life story was even more somber. Her father, with the NAACP's help, tried to challenge these neighborhood restrictions in court. In an unpublished 1964 letter to the *New York Times*, she highlighted the costs of "respectable" dissent in America: "My memories of that 'correct' way of fighting white supremacy in America include being spat on, cursed, and pummeled in the daily trek to and from school. And I also remember my desperate and courageous mother, patrolling our house all night with a loaded German luger, doggedly guarding her four children, while my father fought the respectable part of the battle in Washington court."[52] Despite his use of the proper channels to attack housing segregation, Hansberry's father would be forced into exile in Mexico "when he saw that after such sacrificial efforts the Negroes of Chicago are as ghetto-locked as ever." While *Raisin in the Sun* is a regular staple of the high school and college curriculum, the larger critique of American exceptionalism and Northern apartheid is often missed.

Their assessment that race was constitutive to American democracy moved beyond US borders. Many saw the Black freedom struggle as part of a larger global human rights struggle, understanding that the structures of white supremacy, segregation, and economic disfranchisement that characterized Black life in America were reflected in US practices, as well as other colonial enterprises, around the world.[53] And so, many activists made global connections, from ardent opposition to the Vietnam War and South African apartheid to building solidarity with anti-colonial and independence struggles in Africa and Asia and Palestinian self-determination. One of the very first American groups to condemn US involvement in Vietnam was none other than the Student Nonviolent Coordinating Committee. Its members understood the connection between the justice they sought in Mississippi and the injustice being meted out in Vietnam. Fannie Lou Hamer sent President Lyndon Johnson a telegram linking the expansion of US troops in Vietnam with the limits of Johnson's antipoverty approach: "If this society of yours is a 'Great Society,' God knows I'd hate to live in a bad one."[54]

And as SNCC activists began to speak out publicly against US intervention, they were resoundingly criticized for being outside the bounds of "civil rights." SNCC's Julian Bond was elected as a state representative in Georgia, but he was attacked for treason and Communist sympathies because of his public endorsement of SNCC's policy opposing the war. His antiwar views were widely condemned by white and Black Georgians, including by the Black press.[55] In January 1966, by a vote of 184 to 12, Georgia state representatives voted to deny Bond his seat, though Bond had won election through a massive grassroots campaign, garnering 82 percent of the vote. He took his case to regain his seat all the way to the Supreme Court, where he prevailed. Meanwhile, he wrote a comic book in 1967 to explain the parallels between the experiences of African Americans and the Vietnamese.[56] Also in 1967, SNCC, under its new chair, H. Rap Brown, began to call itself a "human rights organization," established an international affairs committee, and came under fire for its support of Palestinian rights.[57]

Civil rights activists were aggressively attacked for this global vision. When Martin Luther King took the pulpit of Riverside Church in 1967 to make public his criticism of US involvement in Vietnam, the *New York Times* criticized him in an editorial, headlined "Dr. King's Error." He was also criticized by the *Washington Post* and by the NAACP.[58] King had not stayed in his lane and was resoundingly chastised for it. Describing the United States as "the greatest purveyor of violence in the world today," King preached before a phalanx of reporters that April day to make public what had long been in his heart: "The world now demands a maturity of America ... that we admit we have been wrong from the beginning of our adventure in Vietnam ... [and] be ready to turn sharply from our present ways."[59] King decried the vast sums of money being spent on the war that could be spent on social programs at home, and the ways Black soldiers were serving alongside white soldiers, while at home, schools and housing and many jobs were still segregated. Highlighting the "giant triplets of racism, extreme materialism, and militarism," he continued to speak out after making this speech, intertwining his critique of war abroad with the need for social spending at home, even though he lost many friends, supporters, and donors.

Like King's, Rosa Parks's vision of justice was profoundly global. An early opponent of US intervention and war in Vietnam, she supported John Conyers's 1964 bid for Congress in part because he was too. Taking part in numerous rallies, meetings, mobilizations, and study groups, she was active in the antiwar movement in Detroit and nationally, and the anti-apartheid, prodivestment movement. At age seventy-one, Parks picketed the South African embassy; questioned by a reporter why she was there, she explained: "I am concerned about any discrimination or denial of any people regardless of their race."[60] Speaking out against US policy in Central America in the 1980s, she took part in a 1984 war crimes tribunal on US policies in Latin America, sponsored by the National Lawyers Guild. The tribunal heard testimony and sought to expose US military activities and covert operations in Central America and the Caribbean and helped spur antiwar activism against US military interventions across the Americas.[61] That global vision continued to the end of her life; eight days after 9/11, she joined Harry Belafonte, Danny Glover, and other civil rights activists in a public statement against a "military response" to the attacks and called on the United States to act "cooperatively as part of a community of nations within the framework of international law."[62]

But that international vision is often ignored in the public ways we have celebrated King and Parks of late, even though both were clear that the fight for racial justice at home was indivisible from the struggle for human rights abroad. Just as the Movement for Black Lives has been critiqued today for making common cause with Palestinian struggles, these activists were criticized for mixing the cause of civil rights with global justice and anticolonialism.

Their expansive vision of racial justice—of fulsome desegregation, criminal justice, economic justice, and global justice—has largely been removed from our public celebration of the movement; their "freedom dreams," shrunk and disfigured to make the civil rights story one that ends in the celebration of the greatness of American democracy. In diluting it to a bus seat—to something palatable, narrow, and finished—the fable conveniently makes the movement less relevant for where we are today and misses its far-reaching challenge. Grappling with civil rights activists' internationalist, anti-imperial vision and their critiques of the injustices embedded in the US economy and criminal justice system raises questions about the United States' role in the world today and foregrounds the enduring need "to turn sharply from our present ways."

CHAPTER SIX

The Great Man View of History, Part I

Where Are the Young People?

We waited a long time for those folks to do something to improve our schools, but they let us down and so we have decided to do the job ourselves.

—Jefferson High School student, March 1968[1]

The most important learning I do at this age in my life is learning from young people.

—Angela Davis, 2017[2]

EVEN THOUGH MANY civil rights memorials are aimed at "uplifting youth," the central role young people played in the Black freedom struggle, from *Brown* to Birmingham to the Los Angeles blowouts, is often omitted. Indeed, the civil rights movement is often misused to tell young people today that they are not living up to its legacy. At the same time, contemporary inequities are blamed partly on Black and Latinx youth who are cast as having lost their way from the civil rights generation. But high school students blazed the trail in many crucial battles of the Black freedom struggle, often against the wishes and "better judgment" of their parents and other adults in the community. Their vision and resolve proved crucial at key moments in breaking through stasis and fear and moving the community to bolder action. And their willingness to push the envelope and be more confrontational than their elders is all but absent in understandings of the movement's successes. The activism of young people sixty years ago—like the activism of young people today—inspired many but also provoked much consternation from parents, teachers, and older activists, who saw them as too reckless or confrontational. But they pressed forth anyway, and the country is better for it.

In 1951, sixteen-year-old high school junior Barbara Johns organized a strike with her classmates at the all-Black Robert Russa Moton High School in Prince Edward County, Virginia. Students refused to go to class to protest the school's unwillingness to respond to Black demands that the school's poor conditions and overcrowding be addressed. "We had talents and abilities here that weren't really being realized," Johns explained.[3] Twice the number of students were attending Moton High School than the school was built for, and classes were being held in school buses, the auditorium, and hastily constructed tar-paper shacks, which often were very cold. The school lacked a cafeteria and a gym, had limited science labs, and did not offer physics, world history, or Latin. Teachers were underpaid and had to do jobs reserved for janitors in other schools.

Johns decided to organize the student strike in 1951 after some of her male classmates, who worked at the white high school after school, told Johns and her friends how nice the white school was. "I remember thinking how unfair it was." Students assembled to hear Johns speak. She told her classmates that "it was time that Negroes were treated equally with whites, time that they had a decent high school, time for the students themselves to do something about it."[4]

A classmate recalled Johns saying, "Our parents ask us to follow them but in some instances . . . a little child shall lead them."[5] Johns and her classmates also called the NAACP to ask for their assistance. The national office sent lawyers Oliver Hill and Spottswood Robinson to Virginia to caution the students against their action, seeing it as too dangerous and foolhardy given white resistance in the area. But Johns and her band of 114 striking students persisted and eventually won the lawyers over. Hill recalled: "Their morale was so high that we didn't have the heart to say no."[6] Hill and Robinson agreed to represent them as long as their parents agreed to support a legal case that attacked segregation head-on. These students had blazed the way and ultimately brought the adults along with them. Their initial case was lost in federal district court in 1952, but the NAACP appealed to the US Supreme Court, making it one of the five cases that formed the basis of the historic 1954 *Brown v. Board of Education* decision.

Worried for her safety, Johns's parents sent her to live in Montgomery with her uncle Vernon Johns, the activist pastor of Dexter Avenue Baptist Church, who preceded Martin Luther King Jr. But as historian Taylor Branch notes, "The case remained muffled in white consciousness, and the schoolchild origins of the lawsuit were lost as well on nearly all Negroes outside Prince Edward County. . . . The idea that non-adults of any race might play a leading role in political events had simply failed to register on anyone—except perhaps the Klansmen who burned a cross in the Johns' yard one night, and even then people thought their target might not have been Barbara but her notorious firebrand uncle."[7]

The *Brown* decision is one of the most well-known moments of the civil rights movement, but the driving role a group of high school students played in it is much less recognized. Prince Edward County teenagers weren't the only courageous ones. Indeed, in 1955, months before Rosa Parks made her stand, two teenagers—Claudette Colvin and Mary Louise Smith—refused to give up their seats on the bus and were arrested. The Black community was outraged, particularly following Colvin's arrest, but a mass movement did not develop, in part because Colvin and Smith were young and adults did not fully trust them. But both cases, particularly Colvin's, caused rising indignation within Montgomery's Black community and contributed to the decision, when Rosa Parks was arrested, to call for a boycott. If these young women had not done what they did, it is unlikely people would have taken the action they did after Parks's arrest.

Both Colvin and Smith became plaintiffs in *Browder v. Gayle*, the federal case that Montgomery activists, with lawyer Fred Gray, proactively filed three months into the boycott. These two young women agreed to take part in the case when most adults did not have the courage to do so. Gray could not find a minister or other male leader to serve as one of the plaintiffs—and one of the original plaintiffs, Jeanetta Reese, pulled out a day later when she and her husband were threatened. These two teenagers paved the way for the movement that emerged after Rosa Parks's bus stand, and then went the distance in signing on to the federal case. In May 1956, three judges of the Middle District of Alabama heard the case. Both Colvin and Smith testified. "Our leaders is just we, ourselves," Colvin explained.[8] Colvin and Smith met for the first time at the hearing. "I was proud" Colvin recalled, "that two teenaged girls had stood up."[9] The case ultimately went to the US Supreme Court and led to the desegregation of Montgomery's buses. Again, teenagers played a decisive role in that victory.

High school and college students led sit-ins that swept the country in 1960 to protest downtown business segregation and job exclusion in

Southern cities. As one student explained, "I myself desegregated a lunch counter, not somebody else, not some big man, some powerful man, but little me. I walked the picket line and I sat in and the walls of segregation toppled. Now all people can eat there."[10] Many of their parents did not approve, warning them, like Greenwood SNCC activist Endesha Ida Mae Holland's mother did, to stay away from those troublemakers. Many adults and school administrators tried to discipline and control this new youth militancy, disapproving and fearful of their civil disobedience.

But some elders, such as Rosa Parks, rejoiced in this youth militancy. Ella Baker, who helped form SNCC, insisted that young people establish their own separate group, rather than become a youth wing of SCLC or the NAACP, which wanted to subsume them. "There comes a new and young fresh group of people," Parks observed months into the sit-ins, "who have taken this action in the sit-in demonstrations . . . [and] put more pressure to bear than many of us have done in the past."[11]

And it was teenagers in Birmingham in 1962 and 1963 who formed the backbone of the Southern Christian Leadership Conference's Project C, bringing new momentum to the downtown protests and filling Birmingham's jails in order to bring the city to its knees. As SCLC's campaign to challenge Birmingham's downtown segregation in spring of 1963 stretched on, there were not enough adults willing to get arrested—and so the SCLC made a daring decision, one that was criticized by many at the time, to draw on the energy and fierce determination of these young protesters.[12] Through their sustained courage in facing police chief Bull Connor's firehoses, dogs, and jails, these junior high and high school students captured the attention of the nation and underscored the need for a federal civil rights act. While the Birmingham movement and the visuals of young people being sprayed by firehoses is much-remembered, the students whose actions gained that attention are not taken seriously as actors, but are often assumed to have been puppets of King. Part of the reason the SCLC turned to young people was that these young people were ready and organized, and insistent on taking part.

In the late 1960s, students walked out of high schools across the North, Midwest, and West. Schools in most cities in those regions were still segregated (despite movements challenging them for years). They had biased and often racist curricula, few Black and Latino teachers and administrators, and often criminalized young people through suspensions and expulsions. Black and Latino high school students had had enough and decided more militant action was needed.

Yet while high school students provided crucial vision and action, in the history books and in our public conversation, they often function as walk-on players, visible in the pictures but not treated as serious political players. The brief glimpses of high school activism in the Black Power era that do appear often focus on angry slogans, dashikis, and fists in the air—in short, on the appearance of Black Power. But that appearance was undergirded by these students' demands for educational equity and respect (which included changes in dress codes, curriculum, facilities, and teaching staff, and increased access to college). They walked out to demand resource equality and teacher and administrator hiring, an increase in the number of guidance counselors, and Black and Latino studies. An examination of these student walkouts challenges the prevalent picture of urban Black teenagers, particularly those living in large Northern cities, as angry, antithetical to the spirit of the civil rights movement, and at fault for their own educational failures.

Looking carefully at these protests reveals that many young people were thoughtful and organized in their politics and saw their demonstrations picking up from earlier civil rights activism that had produced little change in their schools. While some of these protests devolved into disarray, or their participants engaged in unplanned acts of sabotage, most of these walkouts were not simply spontaneous eruptions but actions that were months in the making. Aware of the kind of schooling they were receiving, many students objected to the ways they were characterized as anti-intellectual, "problem students" or criminalized in school. Attempting to voice their grievances, they were ignored or treated like troublemakers (as their parents had been), and then moved to more confrontational action.

Fears of juvenile delinquency and the rise of more extreme forms of school discipline drastically escalated in the mid- to late-1950s in many school districts across the United States.[13] That shift took place in the decade after *Brown*, often alongside protests for comprehensive desegregation in cities. Many districts, from New York to Los Angeles, cast Black and Latino students as "problem students," invested in new modes of punishment, and poured large amounts of money into new rehabilitation programs to address juvenile delinquency, in part to deflect calls for desegregation. At the same time, many Northern and Western cities were seeing a great deal of Black migration from the South, Mexican migration to the Southwest, and Puerto Rican migration to the Northeast. The children of migrants were channeled into increasingly overcrowded, segregated, punitive schools. Resources were limited and buildings were often decrepit. Even working bathrooms were in short supply. Parents were treated as part of the problem—and weren't taken seriously when they tried to intervene on behalf of their children's educations and protested repeatedly, as earlier chapters demonstrate, about the state of their children's schools. By the late 1960s, young people took up the fight.

During the first week of March 1968, high school students staged a five-day walkout at six Los Angeles high schools—Garfield, Roosevelt, Lincoln, Wilson, and Belmont, all predominantly Chicano schools in East Los Angeles, and at Jefferson High School, a Black school in South Los Angeles. These dramatic school walkouts drew attention to curriculum and dress code issues and dramatized the lack of resources and inferior schooling conditions where Black and Chicano children were educated. Students pressed for college-prep courses, more Black and Chicano teachers and administrators, and community control of schools. The LA walkouts show commonalities in the types of discrimination Black and Chicano students faced in city schools, and in the ways Black and Chicano young people together took the lead, highlighting their willingness to take dramatic action and engage in the planning to make it happen.[14] In doing so, they forced their parents and other adults in the community to action as well.

In 1966, young people, including a number of Chicano college students who would play an important role assisting the East LA walkouts, organized the reform-oriented Young Citizens for Community Action; by 1968, inspired in part by the Black Panther Party, the YCCA reformulated to call itself the Brown Berets. With the help of a local priest, YCCA opened La Piranya in 1966, an East LA coffeehouse where young people could meet, discuss, and hang out. Many Chicano high school students congregated there; some Black young people came as well. Prominent radicals such as Cesar Chavez, Reies Lopez Tijerina, H. Rap Brown, Stokely Carmichael, and Ron Karenga all visited La Piranya. According to historian Ernesto Chavez, "The coffeehouse remained, however, a gathering place for young people run by young people, with little and only nominal supervision."[15] Police would often harass the young patrons of La Piranya, claiming that it was a hangout for hoodlums. La Piranya was forced to close in March 1968, just days before students walked out.

By early spring 1968, according to legal historian Ian Haney Lopez, plans for mass walkouts in the Chicano high schools in East LA were in place. Strike committees were organized at each high school and a central committee formulated a list of demands, which included "reduced class size, more teachers and counselors, expanded library facilities, and an end of the requirement that students contribute janitorial services. By and large, however, the demands focused on community control of the schools: the students called for bilingual education, more Mexican teachers, the implementation of a citizen review board and the establishment of a Parents' Council."[16] Part of the issue was the high dropout rate, as students were being suspended or forced out of school, as well as the tracking of Black and Latino young people into vocational classes.

As was the case with Barbara Johns, rising student anger was driven in part by having seen how their schools differed from those educating white students in the city. "Our schools on the Eastside," Chicana student Paula Crisostomo explained,

> were in such poor condition as compared to others schools. We had taken this [trip] to . . . Paley High. And just the physical appearance was appalling to all of us. And I know for myself, never having ventured very far from my own neighborhood . . . just traveling out and seeing how other people lived and how other kinds went to school . . . The building of the new high school, Wilson [in East Los Angeles] was taking an awfully long time. . . . And again schools in the Valley and West LA, brand-new schools were being put up right away with swimming pools."[17]

On Friday, March 1, to protest the cancellation of the school play, students staged an impromptu walkout at Wilson High School in East Los Angeles. The Wilson students had jumped the gun on the strike plans students were making, but once they had walked out, students at the other schools were committed to following. On Tuesday, March 5, thousands of students at Garfield High School (in predominantly Chicano East LA) and Jefferson High School (in predominantly Black South LA) stayed out of their afternoon classes "in orderly fashion."[18] The next day, thousands of students at Lincoln and Roosevelt High Schools walked out as well. Simultaneously, four hundred Jefferson students congregated on the bleachers instead of going to classes. Jefferson students initially walked out to draw attention to conditions in the cafeteria, but their grievances included dress code and hairstyle restrictions, lack of Black history in the curriculum, teacher insensitivity, poor guidance counseling, lack of college preparation, and the need for more Black administrators. (Black students were required to wear their natural hair no longer than two inches. Homeroom and physical education teachers would measure students' hair with a ruler, and students were sent home if their hair was too long. The physical inspection and monitoring were deeply violating to students.)

Two student leaders at Jefferson, Brenda Holcomb and Larry Bible, told the *LA Sentinel* that dissatisfaction about conditions at the school had been building for a while but students' grievances hadn't been taken seriously. Students were frustrated with the ways their concerns had been brushed aside and decided to take measures into their own hands. Issues of class size, curriculum, hiring, and college preparation had been long-standing grievances that community activists had been pressing for years. Bible explained: "We picked up on what was already started." Students had formed a Black Student Union in 1966 and looked to Malcolm X as an inspiration. At four Black high schools—Fremont, Jordan, Washington, and Jefferson—students boycotted school in May 1967 to honor Malcolm X's birthday.

Moreover, like their Chicano peers across town, students at Jefferson noted that LAUSD's curriculum almost completely ignored the literatures, histories, and experiences of Blacks and Latinos. According to Bible, those Blacks who did appear in the curriculum were "yes sir, no sir" types, rather than rebels. Students had taken steps to educate themselves, drawing on the resources of the public library and the advice of a handful of sympathetic teachers, and had organized in study groups the previous year. "We were coming with action," Bible explained, referring to the walkouts as the "accumulation of a year and a half" of growing frustration and unanswered Black grievances around the kind of education Black students were receiving.[19] The criminalization of Black and Chicano youth in the city's schools was staggering. Over 50 percent of Chicano high school students were forced to drop out, according to historian Ernesto Chavez, "either because of expulsion and transfers to other schools or because they had not been taught to read and thus failed their classes."[20] A star track athlete at Jefferson, Bible believed he was made an example of because of his activism, suspended from school and followed home by the police.[21]

The walkouts also stemmed from the lack of guidance counselors and college-prep classes at Black and Chicano high schools. Many students getting As were not being properly prepared for college and were unable to pass college entrance exams, while others were tracked out of college courses altogether. Jefferson had only one counselor for every five hundred students. Most of the student organizers at Jefferson were student leaders in the academic tracks. As they prepared to go to college, these students felt the inadequacies of the education they were receiving at Jefferson—and objected to the ways they were not expected to be college material and how a diploma from a school like Jefferson was looked down upon in the city.[22] Thus, contrary to the popular notion of Black Power appealing to troublemakers turned off on school, the protests at Jefferson reveal the ways successful students—indeed student leaders—turned to militancy as a way of demanding a quality education. According to Larry Bible, Black Power movements in Los Angeles—and the walkout at Jefferson in particular—were, in part, intended to show "the intellectual side of Black people."[23]

One reason they turned to walkouts was that they had had little success getting their concerns addressed by other means. Holcomb explained: "Too often teachers and administrators shrugged off student complaints or branded students who differed with them as 'troublemakers.'"[24] As Floyd Benton, a sixteen-year old Jefferson High School student, explained: "The news media, instead of dealing with the causes, jumped on our backs. We were very orderly."[25]

On Thursday, the LA Board of Education (BOE) met and one Jefferson student testified to "set the record straight that there were no outside influences in control of the students. The students wanted black studies and other things to solve their problems."[26] On Friday, teachers walked out of Jefferson, saying they "could no longer hold classes under prevailing conditions." According to the *Los Angeles Times*, the teachers initially left in protest of the latitude being shown toward students and the way they felt the school had allowed "student militants" to control the campus.[27] Many adults (parents, teachers, and some community leaders) were scared and disapproved of the walkouts. Roosevelt High teacher Carmen Terrazas urged the administration to punish the student strikers.

Still, echoing one of the students' demands, the teachers also called for more Black administrators at the school. The school shut down Friday and did not reopen until the following Wednesday. School board president Georgiana Hardy and board members Ralph Richardson and the Reverend James Jones met with students in the cafeteria and library to discuss the core issues of the walkout. With Jefferson closed and the teachers supporting student demands for Black administrators, the board bowed to the pressure and three Black administrators were reassigned to Jefferson High School. The BOE acted differently and moved more quickly at Jefferson than it did at the East Los Angeles schools. This likely stemmed in part from the teachers' protest at Jefferson, but all must be seen in the context of a visible Black militancy in the city and the specter of the Watts riot three years earlier and Martin Luther King Jr.'s assassination a month earlier. The three administrators brought to Jefferson were not new hires but Black people already in other administrative positions in LAUSD who were then promoted to Jefferson. Lewis Johnson Jr. (formerly the vice principal at the new Locke High School) was appointed to be principal of Jefferson, along with a new Black vice principal and guidance counselor.

The BOE also offered amnesty to boycotting students at all six high schools, a move that, although more practical than expelling thousands of students, also implicitly legitimated students' grievances. The board made a commitment to teaching Black history, and human relations meetings were to be held to improve communication between teachers and students. Students were "jubilant," and the *Sentinel* ran a front-page banner headline trumpeting "Jefferson High Gets Negro Principal." The paper called the board's proposal a "victory" in which "virtually all their [the students'] demands" had been met."[28]

On Monday, March 11, students presented thirty-nine demands to the LAUSD Board of Education. Protests also spread to George Washington Carver and Edison Junior High Schools, both predominantly Black junior high schools. At a meeting later that month at Lincoln High School, attended by 1,200 people, the board agreed with many of the students' demands but cited a lack of funding. At the end of March, Principal Johnson spoke publicly about the problems facing Jefferson, including school debt because of a lack of support for its athletic programs and a need for more guidance counselors (particularly to work on college scholarships). But even though some changes were made, such as an end to hair restrictions, "it wasn't resolved. Just talk," as Bible explained later.[29]

The city moved to criminalize the East Los Angeles students. These Chicano students were also met with police violence (which was filmed by many news stations and photographed by the *Los Angeles Times* but, under pressure from the city, none aired).[30] Then on May 31, thirteen individuals connected to the East Los Angeles walkouts—including activist teacher Sal Castro, editors of *La Raza*, and five leaders of the Brown Berets—were arrested on felony charges for criminally conspiring to create riots, disrupt the functioning of public schools, and disturb the peace.[31] That the city went after an emerging Chicano leadership and sought to paint the walkouts as having been engineered by militants reveal how it sought to break the momentum of a growing Chicano movement in the city. In doing so, it mired the Chicano movement in years of legal defense (a tactic used at other junctures with groups like the Black Panther Party). After two years of legal battles, the charges ultimately would be dropped.

School protests would continue over the following years in South and East Los Angeles. In December 1968, students, along with a number of Black teachers, walked out of Fremont High School (which was 95 percent Black), demanding the removal of (white) principal Robert Malcolm, the hiring of more Black teachers and administrators, and the creation of Black studies courses. While the protests succeeded in prompting changes in teaching and administrative personnel, the BOE capitulated to the demands of teachers for more security personnel on campus. Increased security measures and police presence were the targets of student protests the following spring. In March 1969, eleven Black junior high schools and seven Black high schools walked out to demand the police leave campus.[32] And again in the fall of 1969, students walked out of Jefferson to protest overpolicing at school. Policing—and the disproportionate security forces at schools serving students of color—would continue to be a significant grievance of Black and Latino community activists and young people in years to come. Many of the high school student organizers went on to be leading educators, artists, politicians, journalists, and scholars in the city.

Similar walkouts occurred across the country. As in Los Angeles, students picked up the struggle for educational equity, hiring, and desegregation they had seen parents or community members engage in for years and injected it with new militancy. Thousands of students in Boston walked out of school and organized protests calling for more Black studies—"culturally relevant education"—and desegregation. Growing frustration about the lack of change in Boston had led them to form a Black Student Union and, in January and February 1971, to call for a citywide boycott. The organization of Black teachers endorsed the student strikes. Student leader Anthony Banks, speaking to Boston school officials in 1971, explained: "We are fighting for the same things our parents fought for over 10 years ago right here in Boston but we will not bow down to the threats from the mayor or the School Committee. . . . We intend to fight on until schools change to meet the needs of the students they are supposed to educate."[33] Similar to their LA counterparts, these young people challenged the ways they were often cast as the problem and blamed for the inadequacies of their own educations. As one young woman said, "Juvenile delinquent youth they called us. But we were simply trying to make a statement." They had five demands: recruit Black teachers, recruit Black guidance counselors, end harassment of Black students, grant amnesty to all striking students, and commission an independent study of racial patterns in the city's schools. Many of their demands were similar to those that the NAACP had presented to the School Committee eight years earlier.

Foregrounding the history of high school activism shows the powerful organizing and leadership roles young people played. Directly challenging the idea that they were at fault for their educations, these young people put forth a vision of the kind of education they deserved but weren't getting. A record of their actions provides, as LA walkout organizer Moctezuma Esparza explained decades later, a "manual on how to organize, you know, what the risks are, what has to be thought of, and what could happen, and what needs to be done."[34] The power of this history lies in what high school students accomplished and envisioned, often over the objections of many adults. But that may be what leads to the backgrounding of this history as well. These young people demonstrated that they and their families were committed to educational excellence, but city leadership continued to provide them with a separate and unequal education and treat them as "problem students." Students fought back to show that they were not the problem but that the education they were being provided was—a lesson this country still wants to ignore.

CHAPTER SEVEN

The Great Man View of History, Part II

Where Are the Women?

MUCH OF THE national memorialization of the civil rights movement maintains a "great man" version of history. Women regularly appear in tributes to the movement, but a clear sense of their leadership, lives, and organizing efforts is often missing. The women who are celebrated, such as Rosa Parks and Coretta Scott King, are too often shrunken versions of themselves, and these limited images at times reproduce gendered silences in the movement itself. When Parks died in 2005, she was eulogized as the "accidental matriarch of the civil rights movement" and incessantly referred to as "quiet," "soft-spoken," and "not-angry."[1]

A similar phenomenon occurred three months later when Coretta Scott King died. As flags flew at half-mast, Scott King's body lay in honor in the Georgia state capitol (a far cry from thirty-eight years earlier, when then governor Lester Maddox refused to close state offices and stationed state troopers outside to make sure the capitol wouldn't be contaminated by her husband and prevent mourners from storming the capitol). Scott King was praised as "kind and gentle," "obedient," and "beautiful," and defined principally as her husband's "helpmate," rather than as the peace and economic justice activist she was for her entire life.[2] President George W. Bush journeyed to Georgia for her funeral, where he praised her strength and her beauty: "In all her years, Coretta Scott King showed that a person of conviction and strength could also be a beautiful soul."[3] When Bush decided to attend the funeral, longtime King family friend and Bush critic Harry Belafonte, who'd been scheduled to give a eulogy, was disinvited—perhaps because he would serve as a potent reminder of Scott King's enduring critique of US racism and war making.

Through such two-dimensional renderings, much of the national memorializing and eulogies to Parks and Scott King implicitly prescribe the right way to be a woman activist. By rendering Parks and Scott King as passive and meek, they neuter them for a new generation of freedom fighters. Stripped of their long histories of activism and continuing critique of American injustice, both become self-sacrificing mother figures for a nation who would use their deaths for a ritual of national redemption. Celebrating these women's "quiet" and "unassuming" natures also erases gender issues within the movement, along with government interests, that often sought to keep these women quiet. By casting them as gentle, beautiful, and accidental, these tributes obscure their substantial leadership roles and those played by many other women, ignore the marginalization women at times experienced, and implicitly castigate most other women as too poor or loud or angry—and therefore not worthy for national recognition. By honoring these individual women outside the broad networks of women they worked within, they miss the collective power of women's organizing and strategic action that were brought to bear in the movement.

Too often when sexism in the civil rights movement is acknowledged, it becomes another blinder to the leadership, vision, and organizing skill of a broad group of Black women in the struggle, as if gender inequity and women's leadership could not exist in tension and in tandem.[4] In other words, sexism in the movement and in American society more broadly did not prevent women from organizing, envisioning, prodding, and leading. There were numerous barriers, and yet a variety of women led, organized, agitated, fund-raised, and showed up anyway. They played myriad roles, and many critiqued and challenged the gender roles they were, at times, placed into during the movement. Civil rights women were charismatic leaders and behind-the-scenes organizers, visionary thinkers, and pragmatic doers. In challenging the great man view of the movement, we need to both examine and critique the gender roles and assumptions that were embedded in it and to grapple with the full expanse of women's organizing efforts, leadership, and intersectional vision within the struggle itself.

"ALWAYS MORE THAN A LABEL":
CORETTA SCOTT KING'S LIFE OF ACTIVISM

An interesting thing happened a few weeks into the Trump presidency. Attempting to read a 1986 letter by Coretta Scott King opposing the nomination of Jeff Sessions to a federal judgeship, Massachusetts senator Elizabeth Warren was silenced by the Senate. According to Scott King, Sessions had used "the awesome power of his office to chill the free exercise of the vote by black citizens."[5] Citing these words and a rule that senators must not impugn colleagues, Senate Majority Leader Mitch McConnell interrupted Warren, and Senate Republicans voted to prohibit her from speaking for the remainder of debate on Sessions's nomination for attorney general. Leaving aside the differential and gendered treatment of Warren (Senator Tom Udall read Scott King's entire letter into the record the next day without censure), part of what was interesting about the episode was how McConnell and his fellow Republicans recognized the power of Coretta Scott King's words.

Many expressed shock that Republican leaders would treat Scott King like that. Former presidential candidate Bernie Sanders proclaimed on the Senate floor the next day, "The idea that a letter and a statement made by Coretta Scott King, the widow of Martin Luther King Jr. . . . could not be presented and spoken about here on the floor of the Senate is, to me, incomprehensible."[6] But elevating her to some sort of sainthood as the widow of Martin Luther King, hasn't necessarily meant Scott King has been taken seriously as a political thinker in her own right. As horrifying as it was, the censoring of Warren backhandedly acknowledged the substance of Scott King's letter—not to mention that it brought the letter to the attention of millions more Americans than would have heard it if Warren had simply read it on the Senate floor.[7]

During her life, Coretta Scott King lamented how she was too often seen but not heard, admired but not considered in her substance. "I am made to sound like an attachment to a vacuum cleaner," she explained, "the wife of Martin, then the widow of Martin, all of which I was proud to be. But I was never just a wife, nor a widow. I was always more than a label."[8] Her memorialization as wife and helpmate, and the corresponding backgrounding of her lifelong commitments, misses the wider critique of social injustice that underlay her life's work. Not simply an accessory of her husband's, Coretta's activism complemented and at times led Martin's politics. Active in racial-justice politics and the peace movement *before* marrying King, she spoke up earlier and more forcefully against American involvement in Vietnam than her husband did, and her critique of American economics and war making continued for decades after his death. An examination of her political commitments highlights the international dimensions of the Black freedom struggle and the long-standing commitment to nonviolence, anticolonialism, and human rights around the world held by her and many civil rights activists. And it returns a much fuller and more militant picture of her husband's activism to public view, particularly the ways Coretta Scott King helped shape his antipoverty work and his opposition to the war in Vietnam.

Born on April 27, 1927, in Marion, Alabama, Coretta Scott graduated valedictorian from Lincoln High School. Her childhood was marked by racial violence: as a teenager, her home and her father's sawmill were burned down. Attending Antioch College, she became politically involved in the campus NAACP, the Race Relations and Civil Liberties Committees, and various peace activities.[9] Majoring in music and elementary education, she encountered discrimination at Antioch when the college sided with the local school system's decision not to allow her (or any Black person) to student-teach in the city's schools. "This . . . made me determined to become more involved in addressing issues of social and political injustice."[10] A strong supporter of racial progressive Henry Wallace's 1948 third-party bid for the presidency, she attended the Progressive Party convention, one of 150 Black people in attendance.

An accomplished singer, she earned a scholarship to the New England Conservatory of Music, where she received her bachelor of music degree. It was in Boston where she met Martin Luther King Jr., who was working on his doctorate at Boston University. Scott, according to King biographer Clayborne Carson, "was more politically active at the time they met than Martin was."[11] Independent and "ferociously informal," according to James Baldwin, Scott worried about how "circumscribed" her life might become if she married a pastor.[12]

Part of the attraction between Coretta and Martin was political, as letters between the two of them reveal. While they were courting, Coretta sent Martin a copy of Edward Bellamy's socialist utopian novel, *Looking Backward*, with the note: "I shall be interested to know your reactions to Bellamy's predictions about our future." She later told Baldwin that her emerging relationship came to feel "somehow, preordained." And she made clear, "The media never understood Martin so they will never understand Coretta. I didn't learn my commitment from Martin, we just converged at a certain time."[13] They married in June 1953, Coretta insisting that "obey" be removed from their wedding vows.

In September 1954, they moved to Montgomery, where Martin had received his first pastorship at Dexter Avenue Baptist Church. Montgomery would be where Martin's civil rights commitment first caught national attention, when he emerged as the young leader and spokesman of the Montgomery bus boycott. But Coretta played a decisive role there as well. Seven weeks into the boycott, the Kings' house was bombed. Coretta and ten-week-old baby daughter Yolanda were at home when the bomb went off, but they escaped uninjured. Terrified by this violence, both Martin and Coretta's fathers traveled to Montgomery to pressure the family—or at least Coretta and baby Yolanda—to leave. She refused. As she explained later, "This was a very trying time, when everyone seemed frightened. I realized how important it was for me to stand with Martin. And the next morning at breakfast he said, 'Coretta, you have been a real soldier. You were the only one who stood with me.'"[14] Had Coretta flinched in this moment, the trajectory of the bus boycott and the emerging civil rights movement might have been very different.

While the Montgomery bus boycott is customarily seen as the advent of Martin Luther King's leadership, Coretta was vital to its emergence. "During the bus boycott I was tested by fire and I came to understand that I was not a breakable crystal figurine," she said. "I found I became stronger in a crisis."[15] During the year of the boycott, their phone rang incessantly with hate calls, and Coretta often had to answer them. She took to quipping, "My husband is asleep. . . . He told me to write the name and number of anyone who called to threaten his life so that he could return the call and receive the threat in the morning when he wakes up and is fresh."[16]

Coretta Scott King's peace activism and global vision continued after her marriage as well. In many ways, her commitments to global peacemaking helped inspire Martin's, since he had not been active on these issues before meeting her. In 1957, she was one of the founders of the Committee for a Sane Nuclear Policy. In 1958, Scott King spoke on her husband's behalf at the Youth March for Integrated Schools. Drawing inspiration from India's march to the sea, led by Mohandas Gandhi, and from the Underground Railroad, she praised the young people for "proving that the so-called 'silent generation' is not so silent." In 1959, she and her husband traveled to India for five weeks to learn from Gandhi's work, meeting with India's prime minister, Jawaharlal Nehru, and dozens of local leaders and activists. In 1962, she was a delegate for the Women's Strike for Peace to the seventeen-nation Disarmament Conference in Geneva, Switzerland.[17] Joining the Women's International League for Peace and Freedom, she became even more vocal on peace issues as US involvement in Vietnam escalated in the early 1960s.

With four kids, Scott King had to contend with her husband's contradictory beliefs on women's roles—his appreciation of her politics and his conviction that she should stay home to raise the children. Forced to scale back her singing, she continued to do benefit concerts for the movement: "I once told Martin that although I loved being his wife and a mother, if that was all I did I would have gone crazy. I felt a calling on my life from an early age. I knew I had something to contribute to the world."[18] After he received the Nobel Peace Prize in 1964, she stressed to him "the role you must play in achieving world peace, and I will be so glad when the time comes when you can assume that role."[19] Following the award, she pressed him to make the international dimension of the philosophy of nonviolence more prominent; their belief in nonviolence and commitment to human rights necessitated speaking out on global human rights as well as domestic ones. The work and responsibility that came with the award were clear to her: "I felt pride and joy and pain too, when I thought of the added responsibilities my husband must bear and it was my burden too."[20]

The death threats and continued harassment took their toll. In 1966, she explained the effect of John F. Kennedy's assassination to reporter Trina Grillo: "It seemed worse than seeing a member of my own family dying . . . a feeling of complete despair. After that, Malcolm X's assassination disturbed me more than anything else. I was depressed for several days."[21]

While her husband wavered in publicly speaking out against the Vietnam War, having been attacked severely for his early criticisms of US military escalation, Coretta Scott King remained steadfast in her public opposition to the war. In 1965, two years before her husband's famous sermon against the war at Riverside Church, she addressed an antiwar rally at New York's Madison Square Garden, the only woman to address the crowd. Late in 1965, when her husband backed out of an address to a Washington, DC, peace rally, she kept her commitment to speak.[22] Following her appearance, a reporter asked Martin if he had educated his wife on these issues. He replied: "She educated me."[23]

Coretta continued to push her husband to take a stronger public stand against the war.[24] In April 1967, Martin Luther King made his public declaration against the war at Riverside Church, decrying the resources being diverted from the War on Poverty to wage war in Vietnam, and the deployment of Black soldiers to a conflict thousands of miles away when their rights were not guaranteed at home—and was lambasted for it. When Martin spoke in New York at the Spring Mobilization to End the War in Vietnam, Coretta flew to San Francisco to speak at a peace demonstration attended by sixty thousand. In January 1968, missing celebrations of her husband's birthday in Atlanta, she joined five thousand women in the Jeanette Rankin Brigade in Washington, DC, to protest the war. At the end of March, she presided over a conference in Washington, DC, organized by the Women's International League for Peace and Freedom, where she called for a cease-fire in Vietnam.[25]

Along with peace activism, issues of poverty and economic justice motivated both Coretta and Martin. After her husband's assassination in Memphis, where he had gone to take part in a sanitation workers' strike, Coretta Scott King stepped in to fill the political void and lead the march he was supposed to have headed. "I gave a speech from the heart and some people 'saw' me for the first time," she recalled.[26] As historian Michael Honey observes,

> [Coretta and Martin's] partnership came not only from personal love but also from a joint political commitment. . . . True to the patriarchal society in which they had been raised, Martin felt she should devote herself primarily to making a home and raising the children. She did that, but she did it in the context of two lives absolutely committed to changing the world. . . . Now, as the King family reeled from tragedy, Coretta began to demonstrate her own quiet and steely commitment to nonviolence.[27]

Understanding the tremendous work to be done in the wake of Martin's assassination, she committed to carrying on the fight for racial and economic justice, making clear that this was how his death was to be honored: "The day that Negro people and others in bondage are truly free, on the day want is abolished, on the day wars are no more, on that day I know my husband will rest in a long-deserved peace."[28]

Her leadership was not always recognized. According to biographer Barbara Reynolds, after Martin's assassination, "Many of the men told her she should step aside, and let them run things" but she refused.[29] Four days after her husband's assassination, she traveled to Memphis to continue the planned march on behalf of the striking workers, stressing, "Every man deserves a right to a job or an income so that he can pursue liberty life, and happiness."[30] Indeed, Scott King was resolute that an appropriate memorial for her husband's death was to continue the struggle they had both committed their lives to.

And for the next four decades, that is exactly what she did. On April 27, 1968, Coretta Scott King delivered a speech at an antiwar demonstration in Central Park that Martin was supposed to have given. She linked her opposition to the war to antipoverty activism at home, drawing out what would be a persistent theme of hers on the multiple manifestations of violence in American politics. She saw the war abroad and economic injustice at home as "two sides of the same coin."

> Our policy at home is to try to solve social problems through military means, just as we have done abroad. The bombs we drop on the people of Vietnam continue to explode at home with all of their devastating potential. There is no reason why a nation as rich as ours should be blighted by poverty, disease and illiteracy. It is plain that we don't care about our poor people, except to exploit them as cheap labor and victimize them through excessive rents and consumer prices.[31]

She ended her speech with a call to the power of women to "heal the broken community now so shattered by war and poverty and racism."

Even though her husband had kept a distance from welfare rights, Coretta linked the struggle for economic justice to the need for a real safety net for poor families. She decried a proposal before Congress to cut welfare benefits as misguided and un-American: "It forces mothers to leave their children and accept work or training, leaving their children to grow up in the streets as tomorrow's social problems." She called for a guaranteed annual income for all Americans as a moral imperative—and encouraged people to join welfare mothers for Mother's Day at the nation's capital to "call upon Congress to establish a guaranteed annual income instead of these racist and archaic measures, these measures which dehumanize God's children and create more social problems than they solve."[32]

Coretta Scott King helped kick off the Poor People's Campaign the month after her husband's death. Martin had been working to build a poor people's movement to descend on Washington and engage in massive civil disobedience to make poor people unignorable and force Congress and the president to action. But it was Coretta Scott King, Ralph Abernathy, and a host of other antipoverty activists across the country who took up the task of actually enacting the plans. On May 1, Scott King launched the southern caravan of the Poor People's Campaign from the balcony of the Lorraine Motel in Memphis, singing "Sweet Little Jesus Boy." She declared her own dream, "where not some but all of God's children have food, where not some but all of God's children have decent housing, where not some but all of God's children have a guaranteed annual income in keeping with the principles of liberty and grace."[33] Coretta Scott King's dream was not ephemeral but one rooted in economic justice. Her Christianity was not an otherworldly religion but a living theology that understood Jesus as an advocate for the poor and oppressed.

On May 12, she joined seven thousand welfare recipients and their allies from twenty cities at Cardozo High School in Washington, DC, to decry the violence of poverty, call for the fulfillment of the spirit of the original 1935 Social Security Act, and kick off the events in the city. The next month, on Solidarity Day, June 19, 1968, in the midst of the Poor People's encampment on the National Mall, she gave a powerful speech to fifty thousand people at the Lincoln Memorial calling on American women to "unite and form a solid block of women power" to fight racism, poverty, and war.[34]

The stand-by-your-man image of Coretta Scott King thus misses the extended critique of injustice that underlined her political work before and during her marriage, and long after her husband's assassination. "I am not a ceremonial symbol," Scott King made clear. "I am an activist. I didn't just emerge after Martin died—I was always there and involved."[35] At both the Mother's Day March and then again on Solidarity Day, she criticized the hypocrisy of a society "where violence against poor people and minority groups is routine." She reminded the nation of its own acts of violence: "Neglecting school children is violence. Punishing a mother and her family is violence. . . . Ignoring medical needs is violence. Contempt for poverty is violence. Even the lack of will power to help humanity is a sick and sinister form of violence."[36] Coretta reframed the political language of the time, foregrounding issues of economic violence that were prevalent in American society. "More forcefully than her husband had articulated," King biographer Thomas Jackson explained, "Coretta King connected poverty and policy neglect to systemic social violence."[37] She critiqued the stereotypes of poor Black women as lazy, loud, castrating figures as a way to further disfigure women who advocated for themselves and their families and to take attention away from the structural causes of Black poverty. Indeed, Coretta Scott King's analysis of poverty highlighted the intersections of race and gender that often kept Black women poor and disregarded.

Her activism did not simply uphold her husband's legacy but expanded it. Scott King understood the need for a unified Black power and, according to historian Komozi Woodard, was a key driving force behind the 1972 National Black Political Convention in Gary, Indiana. She struggled with being marginalized in SCLC, in part because she was a "strong woman, not one to be pushed aside. . . . Most thought that women should stay in the shadows; however I felt that as women, we had much to contribute. In fact for the longest time, way before I married Martin, I had believed that women should allow our essence and presence to shine, rather than letting ourselves be buried or shunted to the sidelines."[38]

In a way similar to how she was treated in those years, there has been a tendency in popular histories of the movement to marginalize her work and focus only on her efforts to preserve her husband's legacy. Books allude to the fact Coretta Scott King spoke at a rally against Nixon's Family Assistance Plan in 1972; attended the National Black Political Convention; and joined marchers in Boston in 1975 to support school desegregation. In descriptions of those events, Scott King's attendance is mentioned but not elaborated on, as it would have been for other activists who were keeping the kind of political schedule that she was and building the kinds of connections between movements and issues that she did. Indeed, in 1976, she told a friend, "Sometimes I wish I could get at least four hours of sleep a day."[39]

As historian David Stein documents, Scott King played a pivotal role in the push for governmental guarantees relating to full employment in the 1970s.[40] Alongside her commitment to welfare rights, Scott King stressed unemployment as a crucial issue to be addressed: "if we could solve the unemployment problem most of the social problems we have could be solved. In fact, most of the social problems stem from unemployment."[41] Guaranteed jobs, Scott King believed, was a way to link the needs of Black and white workers, who were often pitted against each other. In 1974, she founded the National Committee for Full Employment/Full Employment Action Council, which, according to Stein, "was the energetic lobbying force behind the Humphrey-Hawkins Full Employment Act of 1978. The law set the goal of getting the country down to 3% unemployment within five years and attempted to hold the monetary policy of the Federal Reserve accountable to elected officials."[42] Their efforts did not succeed.

In the 1980s, she took an active role in the anti-apartheid movement and in 1984 was arrested outside the South African embassy. She traveled to South Africa, and subsequently met with President Reagan to urge divestment. To the end of her life, she continued her international peace work. In the months leading up to the second Iraq War, Scott King came out against the invasion: "A war with Iraq will increase anti-American sentiment, create more terrorists, and drain as much as 200 billion taxpayer dollars, which should be invested in human development here in America."[43]

She also became a vocal advocate of gay rights and a supporter of same-sex marriage. In the late 1990s, despite criticisms from civil rights leaders and her own children, she reminded the nation that "Martin Luther King Jr. said, 'Injustice anywhere is a threat to justice everywhere.' I appeal to everyone who believes in Martin Luther King Jr.'s dream to make room at the table of brotherhood and sisterhood for lesbian and gay people."[44] Scott King saw the struggle for gay rights as intimately connected to the one for racial justice and stood firm against those who would cast the battle for gay rights as dishonoring the spirit of the civil rights movement. In 2001, at the SCLC convention, she highlighted the threat of AIDS as "one of the most deadly killers of African-Americans. And I think anyone who sincerely cares about the future of black America had better be speaking out."[45] Decrying the dangers of legalized injustice, she opposed a constitutional amendment banning same-sex marriage and reminded

Americans that "gay and lesbian people have families, and their families should have legal protection, whether by marriage or civil unions."[46]

Coretta Scott King's political commitments and activism around international peace, economic justice, and human rights extended past her husband's and far beyond the 1960s, yet many of the memorials continue to place her in Martin Luther King's shadow. The erasures of Coretta Scott King's broader life and activism dovetail with public erasures of Black women's leadership at the time. While women took on key roles in the Black freedom struggle, there were numerous moments when their contributions were marginalized. Scott King herself had noted these gender inequalities in a 1966 article in *New Lady*:

> Not enough attention has been focused on the roles played by women in the struggle. By and large, men have formed the leadership in the civil rights struggle but there have been many women in leading roles and many women in the background. Women have been the backbone of the whole civil rights movement. . . . Women have been the ones who have made it possible for the movement to be a mass movement. In Montgomery, it was mostly women who rode the buses because most domestic workers were women. If a boycott is employed, women are the ones who must stop buying.[47]

In this 1966 piece, she highlighted a problem that had run through the movement: while women played crucial leadership and organizing roles throughout, at points that leadership was denied or dismissed by men in the movement. In other words, it wasn't that women weren't leading, organizing, and strategizing; it was that their work wasn't always recognized or respected.

"JANE CROW" AND THE MARCH ON WASHINGTON

One key example of that marginalization took place at the 1963 March on Washington. The crucial roles Black women played and the ways they were sidelined at the march have received limited mention in the ways the march has been memorialized. Martin Luther King, A. Philip Randolph, Bayard Rustin, John Lewis—these names rang out in fiftieth-anniversary celebrations for their significant roles in the march. In August 2013, the White House announced a posthumous award for Bayard Rustin, largely for his key role in organizing the March on Washington. But where were the women? What about Anna Arnold Hedgeman, the only woman on the march committee, who was largely responsible for the significant presence of white Christians at the march?

Raised in Minnesota and a graduate of Hamline University, Hedgeman worked for the YWCA and then the National Council for a Permanent Fair Employment Practices Commission. In 1954, she became the first Black woman to hold a cabinet position in New York City government before taking a job with the National Council of Churches. That role led to her inclusion on the march organizing committee, the only woman on it. With King and Randolph initially planning two separate events, Hedgeman arranged the meeting where the two civil rights leaders sat down and patched their differences and agreed to press forward with a March on Washington for Jobs and Freedom.[48]

As coordinator for special events for the Commission on Religion and Race, Hedgeman played a determining role in getting large numbers of white Christians to the march. Indeed, as Hedgeman's biographer Jennifer Scanlon notes, the interracialism of the march wasn't happenstance—Hedgeman organized to make the sizeable presence of white Protestants a reality.[49] This was not a given; white Christian support of civil rights had been limited up to this point and needed to be shamed, cultivated, and brought out. Part of Hedgeman's organizing genius was the way she managed to bring many white Christian leaders and laypeople into the civil rights struggle. The March on Washington would be the first mass civil rights event with a large percentage of whites (estimated at 25 percent of the marchers). Hedgeman also facilitated many of the day's logistics, including Operation Sandwich, in which she commanded a massive volunteer effort to produce eighty thousand box lunches for marchers.[50]

From the outset, Hedgeman pushed for the inclusion of women on the organizing committee and in the program itself; however, no women were slated to speak. Increasingly frustrated at the last organizing committee meeting in Harlem, she read aloud a letter she had written Randolph, saying that it was "incredible" that not a single woman was slated to speak. National Council of Negro Women (NCNW) president Dorothy Height was not given a formal role in the events. Nor was she included in descriptions of the march leadership, despite NCNW's considerable fund-raising for the march and Height's having met with all the other leaders for more than a year as part of the Council for United Civil Rights Leadership.

Height, along with Hedgeman, pressed for more substantive inclusion of women in the program. According to Height, Rustin responded, "Women are included. Every group has women in it." Height later observed: "Clearly there was a low tolerance level for anyone raising the questions about the women's participation."[51]

Angered at these oversights, civil rights activist lawyer Pauli Murray wrote A. Philip Randolph:

> I have been increasingly perturbed over the blatant disparity between the major role which Negro women have played and are playing in the crucial grass-roots levels of our struggle and the minor role of leadership they have been assigned in the national policy-making decisions. . . . The time has come to say to you quite candidly, Mr. Randolph, that "tokenism" is as offensive when applied to women as when applied to Negroes.[52]

Murray was dismayed that Randolph was willing to speak at the gender-segregated National Press Club and that no woman was part of the delegation to the White House after the march.[53] Graduating as valedictorian from Howard Law School in 1944, Murray had been a trailblazer for years in highlighting the twin harms of racial and gender injustice. Murray "coined the term 'Jane Crow,'" according to historian Brittney Cooper, "to name the forms of sexist derision she encountered during her time at Howard" and afterward.[54] Part of Murray's work would be used by Thurgood Marshall and Spottswood Robinson in their legal brief in *Brown*. Indeed, it was as a law student at Howard that she made a bet with Robinson, her law professor, that *Plessy* would be overturned within the next quarter century and wrote a paper on how to do it.

In 1940, Murray had been thrown off a train when she refused to sit in the back; like Ida B. Wells, she hated—and challenged—bus segregation because it "permitted the public humiliation of black people to be carried out in the presence of privileged white spectators, who witnessed our shame in silence or indifference."[55] In the 1960s, Murray was one of the first to argue that the equal protection clause could be used for gender as well as race, but when she had brought up this legal reasoning at Howard, many laughed.

Over and over, Murray pushed against societal boundaries of race and gender that prevented Black women's advancement, even in the plans for the march. Murray's close friend Maida Springer allowed Murray to stay at her apartment and organize from there—but refused to take part in Murray's protest, worrying that it would take away from the larger goals of what the march sought to accomplish.[56] Murray had considered picketing the National Press Club, where Randolph was speaking, because of its prohibition against women sitting on the first floor.[57] But Dorothy Height persuaded Murray not to do it.[58]

Hedgeman continued to object within the committee, asserting the march should really be called "Rosa Parks Day," since Parks had started it all. Yet all their criticisms were treated as demands for inappropriate recognition, at odds with the spirit of the event. March organizers worried about how to pick one woman to speak, even though Hedgeman had offered to caucus and come up with a selection. (The idea that multiple women might speak was too far-fetched to contemplate.) Randolph and Rustin then circulated a memo with their proposed resolution to the problem:

> The difficulty of finding a single woman to speak without causing serious problems vis-à-vis other women and women's groups suggest[s] the following is the best way to utilize these women: That the Chairman would introduce these women, telling of their role in the struggle. . . . As each one is introduced, she would stand for applause, and after the last one has been introduced and the Chairman has called for general applause, they would sit.[59]

This "Tribute to Women" was slated to highlight six women—Rosa Parks, Gloria Richardson, Diane Nash, Myrlie Evers, Prince Lee (the wife of slain civil rights activist Herbert Lee), and Daisy Bates—who would be asked to stand up and be recognized. No woman would formally address the crowd. The wives of civil rights leaders would be allowed to sit on stage with their husbands.[60]

On August 28, 1963, the main march, led by men—with Randolph at the head and King and others a few paces behind—proceeded down

Constitution Avenue to the Lincoln Memorial. The wives of the leaders were not allowed to march with their husbands. Scott King later wrote that she was "not pleased"[61] but "had to accede to their wishes. . . . I felt that the involvement in the Movement of some of the wives had been so extensive that they should have been granted the privilege of marching with their husbands and of sharing this experience together, as they had shared the dangers and the hardships."[62]

The women to be honored led a small, separate side march along Independence Avenue to the Lincoln Memorial. Cambridge Movement leader Gloria Richardson recalled that gendered treatment began even before the event started. The NAACP had called her beforehand, instructing her to not wear jeans but instead a hat, gloves, and a dress. Richardson did not appreciate the dress code requirements and scoured the Eastern Shore of Maryland till she found a jeans skirt.

Richardson had long refused the roles assigned to her. Born of a middle-class family, she attended Howard University and returned to Cambridge, Maryland, chafing under the racial restrictions of her hometown. The movement Richardson led in Cambridge had been inspired by SNCC. Richardson herself had joined initially because her daughter was involved. The movement she helped build married economic demands with calls for desegregation—they had surveyed the community for priorities and found housing and jobs were key needs for Black Cambridge. Using nonviolent civil disobedience, and with the participation of students and many working-class community members, they began conducting regular protests and sit-ins in 1963, employing personal self-defense when whites reacted violently to their activism. In response to the escalating situation, the governor ordered the Maryland National Guard into Cambridge, where it remained for nearly a year.[63]

This upheaval in Cambridge led US attorney general Robert Kennedy to convene a meeting with Richardson and other political figures in Cambridge. Richardson was able to negotiate an historic agreement, the "Treaty of Cambridge," with him, which included implementation of federally funded job training, acceleration of public-housing construction, school desegregation, and an amendment to the city charter prohibiting racial discrimination in public accommodations. When whites reacted badly to that amendment and put a referendum on the ballot to change it, Richardson called for a boycott of the election. "A first-class citizen does not beg for freedom," she said. "A first-class citizen does not plead to the white power structure to give him something that the whites have no power to give or take away. Human rights are human rights, not white rights."[64] Many civil rights leaders were aghast at her decision not to participate in the election.

That August day, these women of courage—Bates, Parks, Richardson, and Lee—sat silently on the dais. (Myrlie Evers wasn't there—she was in Detroit for a previous engagement—nor was Diane Nash.[65]) "This was very upsetting to me, especially when there were so many battle-weary female veterans who deserved to speak. . . . But that's how chauvinistic the leadership was at that time," Coretta Scott King later observed.[66] Dorothy Height later surmised that the more-feisty SNCC students got speaking roles even when no woman did: "They knew that the women were not going to turn over the Lincoln Memorial, but the students might."[67]

Little Rock NAACP organizer Daisy Bates introduced the Tribute to Women—a 142-word introduction written for her by NAACP assistant executive director John Morsell: "Mr. Randolph, the women of this country pledge to you, Mr. Randolph, to Martin Luther King, to Roy Wilkins, and all of you fighting for civil liberties, that we will join hands with you, as women of this country." Indeed, the only words spoken to acknowledge the role of women were written for Bates by a man and contained a pledge that women would support the men of the movement, despite the fact that the women on the dais and in the crowd that day had risked their lives for years—some even decades—to press for civil rights.[68]

Randolph himself seemed flummoxed during this portion of the program, at one point forgetting which women were actually being recognized.

"Uh, who else? Will the . . ."
[Someone behind him says: "Rosa Parks."]
"Miss Rosa Parks . . . will they all stand."[69]

Parks stood up and offered eight words of acknowledgment: "Hello, friends of freedom, it's a wonderful day." Richardson managed to get out a "hello" before the microphone was snatched from her.[70] Hedgeman, on the dais that day, described the feeling of listening to the tribute: "We grinned; some of us, as we recognized anew that Negro women are second-class citizens in the same way that white women are in our culture." Hedgeman was frustrated that Parks (or any other woman) was not invited to the meeting at the White House that followed the events.[71]

Right before Martin Luther King Jr. was to speak, Richardson found herself being put in a cab along with Lena Horne and sent back to her hotel. March organizers claimed that they were worried the two would get mobbed and crushed, yet no one else was sent back to the hotel. "They did this," Richardson believed, "because Lena Horne had had Rosa Parks by the hand and had been taking her to satellite broadcasts, saying, 'This is who started the civil rights movement, not Martin Luther King. This is the woman you need to interview.'" Richardson had helped her. "We got several people to interview Rosa Parks. The march organizers must have found that out." Richardson also fought the pressure being put on SNCC chair John Lewis to tone down his speech.[72] Also, Richardson's politics were viewed as dangerous by some civil rights leaders and members of the Kennedy administration, who called Richardson "a whore" and said she "would find a way to disrupt the march and turn it violent."[73]

After the rally, no women were part of a delegation of ten leaders who met with President Kennedy. Dorothy Height observed, "I've never seen a more immovable force. We could not get women's participation taken seriously." Rosa Parks was dumbfounded by the treatment of women that day, telling Daisy Bates she hoped for a "better day coming." Awed by the assembled crowd, Hedgeman nonetheless reflected, "in front of 250,000 people who had come to Washington because they had a dream, and in the face of all the men and women of the past who had dreamed in vain, I wished very much that Martin had said, 'We have a dream.'"[74]

Defying Randolph's request for marchers to leave the city upon the march's completion, Height convened an interracial gathering of women the next day to raise the interlocking issues of race and gender and women's participation in the struggle.[75] The dual experiences of the march—the power of the experience and the marginalization of women—stayed with many women activists. Pauli Murray addressed Height's National Council of Negro Women in November 1963, where she noted the "deliberate" omission of women at the march. Her speech and the continuing outrage around the treatment of women at the march, and in the movement more broadly, formed the bedrock of a rising determination. Black women activists, according to Height, became "much more aware and much more aggressive" in calling out the sexism of the male leadership

of the movement. While white women are often credited with the flow-
ering of the feminist movement of the mid-1960s, Black women sowed
these seeds in the civil rights movement and in the wake of the March
on Washington.

But this history of women's leadership and marginalization is largely
absent from many movement memorials. John Lewis was repeatedly described as the only living speaker during the fiftieth-anniversary celebrations—even though Gloria Richardson was alive and well in New York
City.[76] The public memorialization of the march, in many ways, has repeated the marginalization of women of fifty years ago, with little mention of Anna Arnold Hedgeman, Dorothy Height, Pauli Murray, and
Gloria Richardson—despite the important roles Black women played in
the march's organization and their attempts to challenge their marginalization at the event.

Leadership, vision, marginalization, contention, and challenge all
characterized the experiences of women in the movement. Rethinking
the Black freedom struggle thus requires interrogating a narrative of the
movement that casts women in supporting roles. There was sexism, but
women played crucial leadership, organizational, and intellectual roles in
the struggle, and challenged sexism at the time. Recognizing this means
jettisoning the tendency to cast the fight for gender justice as occurring
largely outside of the Black freedom struggle, rather than as interwoven
in it. And it demands moving women out of the background of civil rights
history and into the center.

CHAPTER EIGHT

Extremists, Troublemakers, and National Security Threats

The Public Demonization of Rebels, the Toll It Took, and Government Repression of the Movement

> *White America came to embrace King in the same way that most white South Africans came to accept Nelson Mandela—grudgingly and gratefully, retrospectively, selectively, without grace but with considerable guile. By the time they realised that their dislike of him was spent and futile, he had created a world in which admiring him was in their own self-interest. Because, in short, they had no choice.*
>
> —Gary Younge[1]

IN SCHOOLS AND NATIONAL TRIBUTES, the March on Washington is now pictured as one of the most American events of the twentieth century—the power of US democracy made real in the quarter of a million people who gathered on the National Mall that day. In 1963, however, most Americans disapproved of it, many congressmen saw it as potentially "seditious," and law enforcement from local police to the FBI monitored it intensively.

The popular fable of the movement makes it seem like most decent people were in favor of the movement. They were not. The civil rights movement was deeply unpopular and most Americans did not support it. They thought it was going too far, that movement activists were being too extreme. Some thought its goals were wrong; others, that activists were going about it the wrong way—and most white Americans were content with the status quo. And so they criticized, monitored, demonized, and at times criminalized those who challenged it, making dissent very costly.

Most contemporary tributes to the movement, however, paper over the decades when activists such as Martin Luther King Jr., Coretta Scott

King, and Rosa Parks, along with scores of their comrades, were criticized by fellow citizens and targeted as "un-American," not just by Southern politicians but by the federal government. And when they do acknowledge it, they make it seem like the targeting and surveillance of activists by the federal government was the result of one terrible man, FBI director J. Edgar Hoover, not the work of a legion of people who red-baited, collaborated, and looked the other way to make the widespread repression of the civil rights movement possible.

Most popular renderings of the movement miss how the very people we celebrate today were viewed as scary or crazy or unwelcome in their own day. And they sidestep the kinds of reckoning this history demands: how people who questioned the racial practices of the status quo and refused to live by them were treated as "radicals, sore heads, agitators, trouble makers, to name just a few terms given them," as Rosa Parks put it.[2] This meant the civil rights movement was built painstakingly and often at great cost to people's mental health and community relationships. By portraying these activists as consummate Americans, contemporary memorials gloss over the role local, state, and federal officials, as well as their fellow citizens, played in demonizing them as threats to the nation. Looking closely at this history, then, shines a different light on criticisms of "reckless" and "dangerous" activists today—and how fears of national security and public safety have long been used to rationalize political repression and justify the monitoring of "extremists."

Though the righteousness of Rosa Parks's actions may seem self-evident today, at the time, those who challenged segregation were often treated as unstable, unruly, and potentially dangerous by many white people and some Black people. Parks spent decades grappling with how hard it was to be a "troublemaker" and with the pressure on Black people to conform—"we perform to their satisfaction or suffer the consequence if we get out of line." She found it demoralizing, if understandable, that in the decade before the boycott, "the masses seemed not to put forth too much effort to struggle against the status quo."[3] This climate took its toll. Describing the "dark closet of my mind," her personal writings reveal how she struggled with feeling "alone and desolate as if I was descending in a black and bottomless chasm."[4]

It is striking how much Rosa Parks wrote about the difficulty of dissent—how much she pinpointed the effort and ostracism of being a rebel and the ways the system was designed to prevent it. "Such a good job of brain washing was done on the Negro," Parks observed, "that a militant Negro was almost a freak of nature to them, many times ridiculed by others of his own group."[5] Struggling with this hostile environment for more than a decade before the bus boycott began, she despaired, along with comrades like E. D. Nixon, that despite their efforts, no mass movement was emerging. Repeatedly, she underscored the difficulties in mobilizing people in the years before her bus stand: "People blamed [the] NAACP for not winning cases when they did not support it and give strength enough."[6] Her writings show how hard it was to be a person who couldn't conform to societal norms: "There is just so much hurt, disappointment and oppression one can take. . . . The line between reason and madness grows thinner." Those who thought and acted outside the norms of society were made to feel crazy.

Parks's writings about her loneliness also reveal what being a longtime freedom fighter entailed: the ability to act and persevere, even amidst her fears and sense of desolation. She continued to act, holding tight to a larger vision of justice and deep Christian faith but having no indication change would occur in her lifetime. Highlighting the untenability of negotiating this racial system, she observed that it was "not easy to remain rational and normal mentally in such a setting."[7] Her personal notes reveal she had reached her limit that December evening on the bus: "I had been pushed around all my life and felt at this moment that I couldn't take it any more."[8]

Parks well understood the impact that years of pressing for change with little result can have on a person. Like many young radicals, she had grown impatient with the pace of change and vehemence of white resistance by the mid-1960s. "Dr. King was criticized because he tried to bring about change through the nonviolent movement. It didn't accomplish what it should have because the white establishment would not accept his philosophy of nonviolence and respond to it positively. When the resistance grew, it created a hostility and bitterness among younger people."[9] She was insistent that people not comment from the sidelines but take "a critical honest look at ourselves in regards to the contribution we are making."[10] Critiquing the idea that people can possess endless forbearance, she noted the effect years of white intransigence had on young people: "The attempt to solve our racial problems nonviolently was discredited in the eyes of many by the hard-core segregationists who met peaceful demonstrations with countless acts of violence and bloodshed. Time is running out for a peaceful solution."[11]

As Rosa Parks's writings poignantly reveal, being an activist was lonely, and the Black community was not unified around rebellion. Punishment, both physical and economic, against those who challenged the system was all too real—as were people's fears of the costs of disrupting the status quo. Many civil rights activists, such as Septima Clark, Gwendolyn Zoharah Simmons, and Endesha Ida Mae Holland, faced criticism from their own families.[12] Clark had been a teacher in South Carolina for nearly forty years when, in the wake of the *Brown* decision, the state legislature passed a law that no city or state employee could be a member of the NAACP, asserting it was a "foreign" (read, Communist-linked) organization. Clark refused to give up her membership in the NAACP, which "bothered my family. . . . They weren't fighters. They didn't feel as if they could fight for freedom or for justice."[13] Clark also ended up feeling like her attempts to get other teachers to resist were largely futile: "I don't know why I felt that the black teachers would stand up for their rights. . . . Most of them were afraid and became hostile."[14] When the members of Clark's sorority, Alpha Kappa Alpha, gave her a testimonial, her sorority sisters still wouldn't have their picture taken with her, out of fear of being seen consorting together.[15] They admired her but didn't want to risk being associated with her in a photograph.

Many SNCC students, such as Simmons, faced discipline from their colleges for their activism, including from Black colleges, and disapproval from their parents. Simmons grew increasingly interested in the struggle as a student at Spelman College. At first, she tried to hide her activities from her family, who was extremely proud she was attending Spelman and didn't want her to do anything to mess up her scholarship. Her mother wouldn't let her attend the March on Washington. When she was arrested at a sit-in and the school called her mother, her mother then scolded her. "I had disgraced the family and [she] reminded me that I was the first person in our family ever to be arrested," Simmons recalled. "She told me that if the school didn't kick me out and send me home in disgrace, I had better mend my ways and stay clear of those marches."[16] Simmons continued with the sit-ins and was arrested again. Spelman accused her of being a Communist and suspended her scholarship. Only because of student protest was she reinstated.

Many local families told their kids to stay away from SNCC organizers. Endesha Ida Mae Holland was forbidden by her mother from associating with SNCC activists who had come to Greenwood, Mississippi, where they lived. She went anyway and became deeply involved with SNCC's efforts in Greenwood; local backlash was severe, and her home was firebombed, killing her mother.[17] Holland's activism continued, and she was jailed repeatedly for her civil rights work. But the costs of activism were significant. Indeed, there was much disagreement within the Black community about appropriate tactics and the best way forward, given the fearsome climate. Black clergy aligned with the movement were in the minority of Black ministers. As the Reverend Osagyefo Sekou notes, "in Montgomery there are about a hundred or so Black churches—less than a dozen participated in the bus boycott. In Birmingham, there are upward of 500, and less than a dozen participated in the marches."[18] The young activists of the Student Nonviolent Coordinating Committee did not just face pressure from their own families or schools but also from other civil rights activists who saw them as too "confrontational." Young people with SNCC criticized King's approach for not developing local leadership and not being bold enough—but so did the NAACP, which saw King's belief in mass protest as ineffective and inefficient. So, there was not a single "unified" approach in the movement.

If Black people were not of one mind in terms of the best strategy forward, the vast majority of white people, South and North, were against the movement. White religious leaders, beginning with the Montgomery boycott, criticized King's actions as unbiblical and morally indefensible. King was repeatedly called "anti-Christian," "pro-Communist," and "extremist" by white ministers, who questioned his sincerity and his intentions.[19] Civil rights activists received scores of hate calls, death threats, and public heckling for years. And while most Americans did not make hate calls to activists' homes, the majority of the American public did *not* support the civil rights movement while it was happening. In a May 1961 Gallup survey, only 22 percent of Americans approved of what the Freedom Riders were doing, and 57 percent of Americans said that the sit-ins at lunch counters, freedom buses, and other demonstrations by Negroes were hurting the Negro's chances of being integrated in the South. Just before the March on Washington, Gallup found only 23 percent of Americans had favorable opinions of the proposed civil rights rally.[20]

Lest we see this as Southerners skewing the national sample, in 1964 (a year before the passage of the Voting Rights Act), a *New York Times* poll found a majority (57 percent) of New Yorkers said the civil rights movement had gone too far. "While denying any deep-seated prejudice," the *Times* reported, "a large number of those questioned used the same terms to express their feelings. They spoke of Negroes' receiving 'everything on a silver platter' and 'reverse discrimination' against whites." Fifty-four percent of those surveyed felt the movement was going "too fast."[21] Nearly half said that picketing and demonstrations hurt the Negro cause, and 80 percent opposed school pairings to promote school desegregation in New York City public schools.

Nationally, white people's support of the civil rights movement continued to be low across the 1960s. In 1966, a year after Selma and the passage of the Voting Rights Act, only 36 percent of white people said King was helping the cause. Eighty-five percent of white people said that demonstrations by Negroes on civil rights hurt the advancement of civil rights, while 30 percent of Black people felt they hurt.[22] Seventy-two percent of Americans had an unfavorable view of King.[23] In a 1968 Gallup poll taken shortly after King's assassination, 73 percent of whites said that Blacks in their community were treated the same as whites. While many people of all races admired King and Parks in the 1960s, the majority of Americans did not and found the civil rights movement both wrong and unnecessary.

Today, many people tell current activists to be more like King and Parks, but King and Parks were reviled, red-baited, and called extremists at the time. On the Selma-to-Montgomery march, in 1965, White Citizens' Councils had plastered huge billboards along the route with King and Parks pictured attending a "Communist training school" (actually Highlander Folk School). When newly elected congressman John Conyers decided to hire Rosa Parks to work in his Detroit office in 1965, the office was deluged with hate mail, threatening calls, watermelons, voodoo dolls, and other racist trinkets, informing Parks and Conyers that she was not wanted in the North. The last time King and Parks saw each other was at a speech King gave in Grosse Pointe, Michigan, a month before he was assassinated. King said it was the most disruption he had ever faced in an indoor meeting.[24] He was called a traitor so many times that night he finally interjected, "We're going to have a question and answer period, and . . . if you think I'm a traitor, then you'll have an opportunity to ask me about my traitorness."[25] But in the national fable of the civil rights movement, this relentless opposition prevalent across the country is often left out.

The national fable also erases how much and how long federal and state governments targeted the Black freedom struggle as dangerous. Rampant government harassment and the FBI's monitoring of now-beloved figures are treated as unfortunate mistakes, rather than as a systematic strategy. Former president Jimmy Carter drew some controversy when at Coretta Scott King's funeral he mentioned the FBI's massive surveillance of the King family: "The efforts of Martin and Coretta to change America were not appreciated even at the highest level of our government . . . they became the targets of secret government wiretapping, other surveillance, and, as you know, harassment from the FBI."[26]

The history of the March on Washington reveals how the federal government approached the civil rights movement. Numerous congressmen condemned the August demonstration as decidedly "un-American." Extensive FBI surveillance in the months leading up to the March on Washington and the outsized police presence there dovetailed with public fears of civil rights activism. The Kennedy administration had rigged the microphone so it could be turned off if it was deemed necessary.[27] Every cop was on duty that day—and 150 FBI agents were on hand to monitor the crowd.[28]

King's influence and eloquent power alarmed the federal government. In the wake of the march and King's growing national stature, the FBI described him as "demagogic" and "the most dangerous . . . to the Nation . . . from the standpoint . . . of national security" and pursued greater surveillance of him.[29] Worried about King's growing reach and possible ties to Communists, Attorney General Robert Kennedy signed off on intrusive surveillance of his living quarters, offices, phones, and hotel rooms and those of his associates. FBI surveillance of King thus *expanded* after the march and further under the Johnson administration, particularly after King denounced US policy in Vietnam, and it continued until King's assassination in 1968.

The FBI monitored many other civil rights activists and nonviolent protests as well. Historian Barbara Ransby explains that longtime organizer Ella Baker "was under FBI surveillance off and on from the 1940s through the 1970s. . . . Even though at certain points agents reported her to be a 'non-threat' her files were repeatedly closed only to be reopened."[30] Also monitored were the Harlem Nine in their challenge to New York City school segregation in the late 1950s. And so was the Mississippi Freedom Democratic Party (MFDP), which SNCC built to challenge the regular Democratic Party's systematic disfranchisement of Black people.

In 1964, following three years of voter registration efforts met with much violence, harassment, and economic reprisals, but few actual registrations, SNCC turned its attention to taking the MFDP challenge to the 1964 Democratic National Convention to contest the seating of the regular Mississippi delegation and press for the seating of the MFDP. President Johnson found this threatening. According to historian John Dittmer, Johnson "turned to J. Edgar Hoover to provide his own 'coverage' of the convention."[31] Johnson ordered the bureau to spy on the MFDP and on Martin Luther King's hotel room at the Atlantic City convention, and he asked for background checks on all the participants. The 1976 Church Committee would later reveal the full extent of the spying on the MFDP: "Approximately 30 Special Agents . . . 'were able to keep the White House fully apprised of all major developments during the Convention's course' by means of 'information coverage, by use of various confidential techniques, by infiltration of key groups through use of undercover agents, and through utilization of agents using appropriate cover as reporters.'"[32]

FBI agents posed as NBC reporters (with full support of the network) to solicit information from the MFDP delegates, including the identities of those who supported their efforts on the credentials committee. Bill Moyers, who was a special assistant to Johnson at the time, served as a key player, and the president's ledger notes a number of calls from Johnson to Moyers at the convention to provide the FBI's information to be used by Johnson's operatives on the floor to pressure delegates to withhold support from the MFDP challenge.[33] Four years later, when Humphrey wanted the FBI's assistance at the Chicago Democratic Convention, Humphrey said Johnson told him that "the FBI had been of great service to him and he had been given considerable information on a timely basis throughout the entire [Atlantic City] convention."[34] Many critics slammed Ava Duvernay's movie *Selma* for portraying Johnson in league with J. Edgar Hoover, markedly overlooking the tremendous collusion between Johnson and Hoover over the MFDP. The idea that the FBI was completely rogue, or that Johnson's work on behalf of civil rights meant that he didn't also consider the movement a threat and endorse FBI surveillance at certain points, are convenient fictions.

The FBI's actions perpetuated twin harms. The agency surveilled, monitored, and at times tried to disrupt the civil rights movement, particularly through its COINTELPRO (short for Counterintelligence Program), which was begun in the 1950s to disrupt Communist-related groups and reformulated in 1967 to "disrupt, misdirect, discredit, or otherwise neutralize the activities of black nationalist hate type organizations."[35] Equally important, it stood aside amidst escalating violence on Black people, and Black activists in particular. The FBI regularly cast white racist violence as outside its jurisdiction, even when agents witnessed it or had inside information about it. It monitored the Montgomery bus boycott but was unconcerned with the bombing of boycott leaders' homes.[36] It had early knowledge of incoming violence against the Freedom Rides but stood aside and let it happen. It had an informant in the car used in the attack on Viola Liuzzo, the white Detroit woman killed following the 1965 Selma-to-Montgomery march; rather than risk bad publicity, the agency scuttled investigations of her murder.[37] In many ways, FBI inaction sanctioned violence against civil rights workers.

The agency considered the movement's growing power a threat. From ordering the intrusive wall-to-wall surveillance of Martin Luther King Jr. beginning in 1963 to the surveillance of Coretta Scott King for years after her husband's assassination, the bureau targeted the King family relentlessly. It sent Martin a letter urging him to commit suicide and mailed to Coretta a tape of Martin's sexual indiscretions. Two days before King's assassination, Hoover leaked a story that King was planning to stay at the Holiday Inn, at the time considered too "fancy" for a Black person; King changed to the Lorraine Motel, where on the evening of April 4, he would be assassinated coming out of his room.[38] And the FBI stepped up its surveillance of Coretta after King's death, worried that she might attempt "to tie the anti-Vietnam movement to the civil rights movement," and it closely monitored her travel and read her personal letters.[39] Lest we write this off as Hoover's obsession with the Kings, the Nixon administration and Secretary of State Henry Kissinger were kept in the loop on the "nearly constant" surveillance of Coretta in the years following Martin's death.[40]

From World War II on, the FBI also took aim at the Nation of Islam. FBI agents visited Elijah Muhammad's home in 1942, investigating him for sedition and draft evasion, and confiscating sixteen boxes of files on the

Nation of Islam.[41] Muhammad served four years in prison. Heavily monitoring Malcolm X from 1950 until his death in 1965, the FBI relished the growing rift between Malcolm X and Elijah Muhammad in the mid-1960s and sought to widen it, sending fake letters and disseminating information to keep it in motion.[42] On June 5, 1964, Hoover sent the FBI's New York office a telegram: "Do something about Malcolm X enough of this black violence in NY."[43]

The FBI initiated many efforts that targeted Black activists or civil rights organizations. In addition to its revisal of the COINTELPRO, in 1968, it introduced the Ghetto Informant Program, and with Project Z (a program to "prevent the rise of a Black Messiah"), the bureau took special measures to combat the rising Black Power movement.[44] The agency worked in collusion with the Chicago police in the raid that killed Black Panther leaders Fred Hampton and Mark Clark, and it spread misinformation and secret letters to spark rivalries and violent reprisals between Black groups.

As the bureau sent an army of Black informants into groups like the Black Panther Party, it finally desegregated its own ranks. Hoover had resisted hiring Black people except for menial jobs. In 1962, under pressure from Attorney General Robert Kennedy, the FBI hired two Black special agents. But as the FBI's surveillance of the Black struggle expanded rapidly, it was forced into more hiring—and into developing a wide cadre of Black informants, in essence weaponizing members of the Black community against the freedom struggle. The FBI also surveilled the burgeoning women's movement, and by the 1970s took aim at growing militant indigenous rights activism, particularly the American Indian Movement organization. Yet these uncomfortable truths find little place in our public celebrations of the civil rights movement.

While the FBI could find no proof of Communist influence on Martin Luther King (its alleged justification for wall-to-wall surveillance of him), it did gather evidence of his adultery, which it passed along to journalists and other government officials, hoping to discredit King's leadership. The FBI sent the anonymous letter urging King to commit suicide, hoping to destabilize the civil rights leader. No government official ever intervened to halt or divulge the surveillance. No journalist ever exposed the monitoring of King, though many knew at the time. The surveillance

of the civil rights movement only began to be revealed to the public after activists broke into an FBI office in Media, Pennsylvania, in March
1971, took records, and sent them to three news outlets. Under pressure
from the government not to publish, the *New York Times* and *Los Angeles Times* promptly returned the files to the FBI, but the *Washington Post*
courageously went ahead and reported the story. (Once the *Post* took the
risk, the *New York Times* and *Los Angeles Times* quickly followed with
their own stories.)

As Betty Medsger, the *Post* reporter who broke the initial story, details,
the Media files revealed the extent of surveillance of the Black community:

> To become targets of the FBI it wasn't necessary for African Ameri-
> cans to engage in violent behavior. It wasn't necessary for them to be
> radical or subversive. Being black was enough. The overall impression
> in directives written by Hoover, other headquarters officials, and local
> FBI officials was that the FBI thought of black Americans as falling into
> two categories—black people who should be spied on by the FBI and
> black people who should spy on other black people for the FBI. The lat-
> ter group was to be recruited by the bureau to become part of its vast
> network of untrained informers.[45]

FBI agents were *required* to develop informants in the Black community. Even if an agent was in charge of an overwhelmingly white area, the
agent was still expected to have a Black informant and "a fairly elaborate
bureaucratic process was required to assure that an agent who worked in a
white area was not penalized for not having black informers."[46] There was
a pervasive assumption of foreign influence on Black people, though most
Black people would have considered this a "joke," according to Medsger.
Students and campus Black organizations were targeted especially. A 1970
memo by Hoover noted, "Increased campus disorders involving black students pose a definite threat to the Nation's stability and security."[47] Hoover
then "required agents to investigate and, if possible, infiltrate every black
student organization at two-year and four-year colleges and universities,
and to do so without regard for whether there had been disturbances on
campus."[48] Every Black student organization was a threat; in other words,
it wasn't about what these students were doing, but who they were.

The government's reaction to the leak of the Media files demonstrates its willingness to claim "national security" to protect its dirty laundry. Attorney General John Mitchell called the *Post* twice to say that reporting on the files would endanger national security and the lives of federal agents and would reveal national defense secrets, though "he had neither read the documents nor had been briefed on them."[49] What the files did contain, as Mitchell knew, was some suggestion of the extent of the secret policies and surveillance practiced by the FBI. In other words, they would embarrass the government.

The histories of these movements reveal the contingent and political definitions of "national security" and of those viewed as "troublemakers" and "extremists," who bore the brunt of such targeting. Those individuals considered threats to national security have long included people who criticize the government and members of minority groups who are viewed as suspicious or un-American for asserting their racial pride and rights, and feared as potentially aiding the enemy in their criticisms. Such targeting was done not just by "bad guys" like Richard Nixon and J. Edgar Hoover but by "good guys" like Robert Kennedy and Lyndon Johnson, who saw a need to impose special measures to control these dangerous individuals.

When Muhammad Ali died in 2016, there was wall-to-wall celebration of his life, but as Medsger notes, there was little acknowledgment of the years of relentless surveillance of Ali "beginning with [the FBI's] investigation of his Selective Service case. Some of his phone conversations were tapped, and FBI informers gained access to, of all things, his elementary school records in Louisville."[50] Given public suspicion of the Nation of Islam, FBI informants closely monitored Ali's connections with the group, the proceedings of his divorce from his first wife, and his traffic tickets.[51] His bold, poetic voice and deep courage of conviction; his decision to join the Nation of Islam and change his name in 1964; and his subsequent refusal to be drafted to serve in Vietnam in 1967—all made the government and many Americans consider him dangerous and in need of extensive monitoring. It was only when Ali was beset by Parkinson's in the 1980s, according to biographer Mike Marqusee—when his public persona was stripped of his powerful and beautiful voice—that the boxer became fit for national honors.[52]

Ali's funeral became an occasion for a huge swath of Americans to celebrate a Muslim hero secure in their own liberalness. "Muhammad Ali became the 'brave American' who stood up for a cause," according to anthropologist Su'ad Abdul Khabeer, "rather than the 'black Muslim' who stood for his religious convictions . . . a kind of religious whitewashing that matches a broader tendency to dilute the radical politics of most figures of the era."[53] Little connection was made to the treatment and monitoring of politically active Black Muslims today—or to the way Ali's proud Muslim faith and criticism of US imperialism in post-9/11 America would have been treated by the federal government, if his voice still rang out.

This history of demonizing racial dissent shows the interconnections between the practices of surveillance and repression, then and now. It provides a caution to the massive surveillance state created in the wake of the 9/11 attacks and contemporary justifications that, if you're doing nothing wrong, you have nothing to worry about. By illuminating the ways full-throated dissent from nonwhite communities has long been regarded as "extremist" and "dangerous," this history demonstrates that claims of "new urgency" and "imperiled times" used today to justify surveillance and monitoring are similar to the rationales used fifty years ago against the civil rights movement. Fears of Communist subversion that provided justification for mass surveillance of Black communities are replicated in the fears of terrorism that justify counter-radicalization theories and the widespread monitoring of Muslim communities today.[54] Moreover, what the government had to keep somewhat hidden in its surveillance of King or through its COINTELPRO program fifty years ago has been largely legalized in measures like the USA PATRIOT Act. The tools of secrecy are now even more robust, making government overreach even harder to expose and root out.

The mass targeting of Black student groups and the development of tens of thousands of Black informants in the 1960s bear a sobering resemblance to the mass targeting of Muslim student groups and development of tens of thousands of FBI informants in Muslim communities in post-9/11 America.[55] The surveillance, harassment, and targeting of Muslims, particularly Muslims who express dissenting views, in post-9/11 America, have uncomfortable parallels in the civil rights era, as the intimacies of Muslim life—from worship to family time to community organization to student activities—have come under persistent scrutiny. Added to this is the particular targeting of activists of color. Growing reports attest to FBI and local police monitoring of movements such as Black Lives Matter and Standing Rock, and revelations from a leaked FBI counterterrorism memo claiming "Black Identity Extremists" are a rising threat.[56]

As part of their training, FBI agents now take a trip to the King memorial in Washington, DC, and pick a favorite King quote to discuss.[57] Former FBI director James Comey started this practice in 2014 to "provide a lesson on what happens when power is abused." But such an exercise misses what is to be learned through this history and the connections that need to be made. To take seriously how "power is abused" requires looking more soberly at our fears and who we monitor today. It necessitates identifying new forms of political repression, rethinking the ways we have conducted a domestic War on Terror over the past two decades, and seeing the ways present-day fears have countenanced a vast apparatus of surveillance and targeting of Muslim Americans and Black activists with eerie parallels to the civil rights era.

It is easier to be aghast at how unpopular the civil rights movement was and how surveilled Black activists were than to reconsider whom we fear and monitor today. It is easier to celebrate the civil rights movement against the "extremism" of Black Lives Matter than to see the historical continuities in the ways Black critics have been treated then and now. While the fables gloss over it, these histories demonstrate how critics of color have long been unpopular with the public and targeted by the government—often because they refused to accept the terms of American domestic and foreign policy. Over time, many of yesterday's "extremists" have been revealed to be not so much threats to national security, but deep critics of US policies.

CHAPTER NINE

Learning to Play
on Locked Pianos

The Movement Was Persevering, Organized,
Disruptive, and Disparaged, and Other Lessons
from the Montgomery Bus Boycott

*If we lock up Martin Luther King, and make him unavailable for where
we are now so we can keep ourselves comfortably distant from the realities
he was trying to grapple with, we waste King. All of us are being called beyond those comfortable places. . . . We can learn to play on locked pianos
and to dream of worlds that do not yet exist.*

—Vincent Harding[1]

PERHAPS THE MOST depoliticizing aspect of the national fable is the way it
removes the organizing from the struggle. It makes it seem like the movement happens naturally, taking the power and the difficulty, the messiness
and the magnificence out of it. In James Baldwin's words that began this
book, the civil rights movement was longer, larger, more various, more
beautiful and more terrible than it has been remembered. And in omit-
ting the work and the collectivity of it, these national fables take the movement away from the people who built it and make it much more difficult
to imagine how to construct webs of struggle today.

The Montgomery bus boycott occupies a central place in the fable—
the origin story where we meet its two most iconic figures, Rosa Parks and
Martin Luther King Jr. But what it took and how it happened is far different than we know—and this fuller story offers much for thinking about
social change today. In the fable, the Montgomery bus boycott just seems
to happen. Rosa Parks is arrested, and the community is galvanized to action. "By refusing to give in," President George W. Bush celebrated, "Rosa

Parks showed that one candle can light the darkness. . . . Like so many institutionalized evils, once the ugliness of these laws was held up to the light, they could not stand." Parks is cast as the candle that can destroy the darkness. A massive, yearlong community boycott follows naturally and inevitably. The action of one right individual becomes the key, not the collective effort that turned her act into a movement nor the vast groundwork that had been laid in the decade preceding her stand nor the accumulation of anger, sorrow, and indignation that pushed people past fear to act. In newer versions of the fable, the community's rejection of fifteen-year-old Claudette Colvin is noted, and Parks becomes the "right one," as if one respectable individual is all it takes to carry a movement. King and Parks are put on pedestals, furthering a Horatio Alger mythology that, without preparation, an American can make great change with a single act, and making it difficult for people today to imagine being like either of them. The hard and repeated choices people made to push forward and the collective action required are glossed over.

The how of it—the fact that the Montgomery movement began much earlier, took much longer, was fraught with tension and conflict, and was unbearably difficult and only possible because a few, then some, then many more people joined together—is secondary to the much neater story of the accidental respectable heroine and the movement she helped birth. Today, the injustice seems so clear, the activists so righteous, that their victory seems inevitable—which of course is implicitly contrasted with contemporary struggles, which seem longer, harder, less clear, and less righteous. But, in fact, the movement's righteousness was made through the conviction, imagination, sacrifice, and decades of struggle and tenacity of the Montgomerians who built it. There was nothing natural and preordained about it. People chose, amidst searing conditions, amidst threats to their person and their livelihood, to make it happen.

Looking at a fuller history of the Montgomery bus boycott reveals the work, sacrifice, perseverance, coalition-building, disappointment, disruptiveness, and collective action it took to imagine, build, and sustain it. It wasn't just a matter of shining a light on injustice; it required shining a light over and over and over, often in people's eyes, until the force of that collective pressure became undeniable. Parks and King didn't make the movement; the Black community of Montgomery, including Parks and King, did. There weren't direct roads forward or clear things to do, but as movement historian Vincent Harding reminds us, community activists "learn[ed] to play on locked pianos." One caveat: the Montgomery bus boycott was a Black, community-wide mass movement; many of the most successful struggles of the 1950s, 1960s, and 1970s were not community-wide but undertaken by relatively small groups of Black people that grew over time. It certainly didn't take a fully unified community for a movement to begin or be successful.

To see how they did it—what it actually took to spark, organize, and maintain a mass boycott—returns the movement to us and makes it possible to imagine how it could be done again. Looking at ten lessons of the Montgomery bus boycott demonstrates the power of local communities—what they imagined, struggled with, organized, and built—and suggests ways to move forward today.

The first and perhaps most important lesson is the role of perseverance—the decade of largely unsuccessful struggle that preceded the Montgomery bus boycott, the small band of people who pushed forward regardless, and how essential that relentlessness was to the emerging boycott. While the boycott was sparked by Rosa Parks's arrest for refusing to give up her seat, a number of acts of bus resistance—as well as the ongoing humiliation on the bus, years of organizing, and growing ties among key Black organizers in Montgomery—turned it into a movement. "I have told the press time after time," longtime organizer E. D. Nixon explained, "that we were doing these things before December 1955, but all they want to do is start at December 1 and forget about what happened . . . over a long period of time to set the stage."[2]

In the decade before Rosa Parks's bus stand, a small cadre of NAACP activists, including Parks, Nixon, and Johnnie Carr, struggled with how difficult it was to move people to action. Parks joined the NAACP in 1943, in part because she wanted to register to vote; to her it was galling that Black people were serving in World War II but were unable to register to vote at home. Carr and Parks had attended middle school together at Miss White's Industrial School for Girls. Like Parks, Carr had become active around the Scottsboro case. Seeing a picture of Carr in a photo of the Montgomery NAACP convinced Parks that women could be part of the branch, prompting her to attend her first meeting in 1943. E. D. Nixon, a Pullman porter and longtime organizer in the Brotherhood of Sleeping

Car Porters, was spearheading the branch's voter registration efforts and came by Parks's home with materials for voter registration. Here began a partnership that would change the course of American history—Nixon, Parks, Carr, and a small group of NAACP members would spend the next decade transforming the Montgomery NAACP into a more activist branch.

In 1944, Nixon, Parks, and Carr organized around the case of Recy Taylor, a Black woman who had been gang-raped by six white men. They tried unsuccessfully to get an indictment.[3] In 1945, Nixon won the presidency of the NAACP branch, opposing its more middle-class leadership and seeking to make the branch more political. Middle-class members of the branch were unhappy with his "politicking" and appealed to the national NAACP to intervene, but Nixon was reelected president (and Parks secretary) in 1946.[4] This small cadre of activists faced fearsome resistance from Montgomery whites and trepidation from some Black people about what rocking the boat might mean. "The Negroes here are slipping and sliding," one friend wrote Parks in 1948. "I guess it would take an atom bomb to jar them out of their complacency and into action."[5] This was dangerous work, as Parks traveled through Alabama taking down people's stories of rape and white brutality, hoping to file affidavits with the Department of Justice (DOJ). Most of their efforts produced little change. Parks explained: "It was more a matter of trying to challenge the powers that be and let it be known that we did not wish to continue being treated as second class citizens."[6] The work was discouraging—the DOJ looked the other way, and many Black people who had been willing to talk to Parks were unwilling to put their name on affidavits or testify publicly. "It was very difficult to keep going," Parks admitted, "when all our work seemed to be in vain."[7]

A small trickle of people stood up to bus segregation in Montgomery in the decade before Rosa Parks's stand. Viola White was arrested in 1944 for refusing to give up her seat; she filed a case against bus segregation and in retaliation, police raped her daughter. The state then tied up her case in court, and she died before anything happened with it. In 1950, veteran Hilliard Brooks (who was Rosa Parks's neighbor at the Cleveland Courts projects), refused to reboard from the back of the bus after paying his fare; the bus driver called the police and the police killed Brooks. Parks herself had been thrown off the bus for refusing this demand by some bus drivers that Black people pay in front but reboard from the back. Many in Montgomery, including Martin Luther King, Jo Ann Robinson, and Rosa Parks's mother, Leona McCauley, had also had humiliating experiences on the bus.[8]

When the Supreme Court handed down its decision in *Brown v. Board* outlawing school segregation, a legal challenge to bus segregation seemed more possible. The Women's Political Council wrote the mayor saying bus segregation needed to change or there would be a boycott. In March 1955, Claudette Colvin was arrested for resisting on the bus. Colvin's arrest outraged Montgomery's Black community and many stopped riding the buses temporarily. But a mass movement did not result, in part because the city and bus company made promises to change that they did not keep, and in part because many adults saw Colvin as too young, poor, and feisty to rally behind.[9] Parks fund-raised for Colvin's case and encouraged her to take a leadership role in her NAACP Youth Council—the only adult, according to Colvin, who kept in touch with her that summer of 1955.[10] (Despite popular belief, Colvin was *not* pregnant when community leaders decided not to pursue her case; she got pregnant later that summer.)[11]

In October, eighteen-year-old Mary Louise Smith was arrested, but again no mass movement emerged. Both arrests brought the community to a breaking point. Much has been made about the respectability politics that led community leaders to deem neither of these young women suitable to organize a mass movement around.[12] And certainly their youth, feistiness, and class status were factors that led adults to not rally behind them. But there is a danger in minimizing the impact of these young women's actions. Had Colvin and Smith not done what they did, adding to the weight of community outrage and growing frustration, it is unlikely Parks's arrest would have galvanized people the way it did. Movements do not result from the first or second outrage but from an accumulation of injustice that brings people to a breaking point.

"Over the years I have been rebelling against second-class citizenship. It didn't begin when I was arrested," Parks explained to a reporter during the boycott.[13] Part of what made Rosa Parks's bus stand so courageous was that there was nothing to suggest that taking a stand on that day would change anything. For two decades before she refused to give up her seat on the bus, she had made stands, other people she knew had made stands, and by and large nothing had changed—except that people had been ostracized, hurt, or killed for these actions. This was not Parks's first act of bus resistance. She had been thrown off the bus for refusing the practice some bus drivers insisted on, that Black people pay in the front but reboard in the back. In fact, by that December evening, she had grown quite bitter and pessimistic about the possibility of change.

Four months earlier, she had attended a two-week workshop at Highlander Folk School, an organizer training school started in the 1930s to encourage local leadership development, on implementing school desegregation. Parks found the workshop tremendously inspiring; nonetheless, in the closing session—which focused on what participants would do when they returned home—she told those gathered that "Montgomery was the Cradle of the Confederacy, that nothing would happen there because blacks wouldn't stick together. But she promised to work with those kids."[14] In other words, Rosa Parks left Highlander not holding out much hope in her generation and placing her hope for change with the young people she was mentoring in the NAACP Youth Council.

On December 1, coming home from work, Parks refused bus driver James Blake's order to move. Parks didn't see her bus stand ushering in a new chapter in American history but felt adults in the community "had failed our young people."[15] Parks had had enough: "I had been pushed around all my life and felt at this moment that I couldn't take it anymore. . . . We soothe ourselves with the salve of attempted indifference accepting the false pattern set up by the horrible restriction of Jim Crow laws."[16] One of Parks's most valued traits was the ability to be "stout-hearted," because she understood how difficult it was to keep on in the face of pressure. Well aware of the dangers Black women faced in getting arrested, she was "resigned to the fact that I had to express my unwillingness to be humiliated in this moment."[17] But perseverance finds little place in the fable; the fact that activists did things over and over, for years and then decades without success, is a crucial lesson that these memorials do not teach.

The second lesson is the role of anger and the ways people fashion that anger into action. Black anger finds little place in these fables, as seen in the ways King and Parks are regularly cast as "not-angry." When Colvin was arrested in March 1955, the community was outraged. The city promised change—but gave them "the run-around" as Parks called it. In fact, at the second meeting with city officials the summer after Colvin's arrest, Parks refused to join a group of Black community leaders taking a petition to the city that called for more courteous treatment on the bus and an end to visible signs of segregation: "I had decided I would not go anywhere with a piece of paper in my hand asking white folks for any favors."[18] Anger was mounting.

Four nights before her bus stand, Parks attended a packed mass meeting at King's Dexter Avenue Baptist Church to hear organizer T. R. M. Howard talk about the recent acquittal of the two men, Roy Bryant and J. W. Milam, who had lynched Emmett Till. Despite national attention to the case, the two men had still walked free. Like many of her friends and neighbors, Parks left the meeting deeply angry and despairing. Days later, in the moment when the bus driver told her to move, she thought of Emmett Till and, "pushed as far as she could be pushed," refused. When the cops boarded the bus, one officer questioned why she did not get up when instructed to. She was *not* quiet in that moment but coolly spoke back: "Why do you push us around?" The officer answered back: "I don't know. The law is the law and you're under arrest."[19] Parks thought to herself, "Let us look at Jim Crow for the criminal he is and what he had done to one life multiplied millions of times over these United States." Anger transformed into action.

As Reverend Vernon Johns, who had preceded King as the pastor at Dexter Avenue Baptist Church, explained, Parks "caught a vision"—she was able to see an opportunity to strike a blow at the system of white supremacy.[20] Late that night, after talking with Nixon, white allies Clifford and Virginia Durr, her husband, and her mother, Rosa decided to pursue her case in court, calling upon attorney Fred Gray for help. Knowing how outrage had been percolating, Gray called Jo Ann Robinson, head of the Women's Political Council, to let her know that Parks was pressing forward with a legal case. The WPC decided late on the night after Parks's arrest to call for a one-day boycott on the Monday when Parks would be arraigned in court. The boycott thus was the result of an accumulation of perseverance, anger, and relationships built over years.

The third lesson is how the sense of possibility grows by being in action. In the middle of the night, Robinson snuck into Alabama State College, and with the help of two students and a colleague, ran off thirty-five thousand leaflets on the mimeograph machine. (Robinson later got in trouble with the college for doing this.)[21] The leaflet began, "Another woman has been arrested on the bus."

In the middle of the night, Robinson called Nixon to advise him of the plans. She did not call Parks—in fact, Robinson claims that after talking to Fred Gray on the phone, she jotted some notes on the back of an envelope, including "The Women's Political Council will not wait for Mrs. Parks' consent to call for a boycott of city buses."[22] Robinson's belief that she didn't need to get Parks's consent or even apprise her of the one-day boycott likely stemmed in part from the WPC's determination to act quickly (and avoid what happened with Colvin), as well as class differences between the more middle-class Robinson and working-class Rosa Parks (who lived at the Cleveland Courts projects). So, Rosa Parks did not find out till the middle of the next day that a boycott had been called in her name.[23]

People galvanized behind Parks for a number of reasons. Solidly working-class, Parks was known to many in Montgomery's working-class Black west side for her community and church work, and for her steadfastness. She was forty-two the day of her arrest, married, active in her church and the NAACP, and known to be brave—so people trusted she wouldn't flinch under the pressure. And many in Montgomery's Black community across class lines saw themselves in her arrest.

In newer versions of the fable, Parks's respectability is cast as the key, as if by picking the right person, grievances will be recognized. This misses the incredible, harrowing, tedious work that went into the yearlong boycott, and the belief in things unseen. And it distorts the actual experiences of Rosa Parks—who was not middle class and whose bus stand would plunge her family into economic trouble. Moreover, Parks was not viewed as respectable by white people at the time. In the first weeks of the boycott, rumors snaked through Montgomery's white community about her. Most white people thought Parks's action had been cooked up by the NAACP, others claimed it was a Communist plot, still others believed the NAACP and Communist Party were in league together. Some whites believed Parks had only been in Montgomery for two weeks, a few going so far as to claim that Rosa Parks was not even her real name, and that she was actually Mexican and had a car.[24] The vast majority of white Montgomerians made her a pawn of larger agents and outside agitation—and certainly did not regard her as an upstanding figure.

Early the next morning Nixon, began calling Montgomery's political ministers to get them on board. About 6 a.m., Nixon called twenty-six-year-old Martin Luther King, who'd been in Montgomery for about a year and was active with the NAACP. Nixon wanted to use King's church for a meeting of the ministers; it was centrally located and King was new in town and didn't have enemies. Nixon woke King up. The Kings had a baby only three weeks old and King hesitated: "Let me think about it awhile and call me back."[25] There was nothing destined about this, no lightning bolt. Like all of Montgomery's activists, King would have to step into this action. When Nixon called back in a few hours, King agreed. In the days and months ahead, King would assume an important leadership role. But there was nothing easy about it.

Nixon also savvily used the media to get attention for the upcoming boycott, calling *Montgomery Advertiser* reporter Joe Azbell. Azbell was no liberal but Nixon knew to give him the "scoop." Azbell took the bait and published the story on the front page, ensuring that many who had not known about the Monday boycott now did. "We couldn't have paid for the free publicity white folks gave our boycott," Nixon noted.[26]

At first, many of Montgomery's longtime activists worried about whether people would support the boycott. Having struggled for years to bridge class lines, many feared that Black people wouldn't stand together, and the community would be humiliated. Reverend Vernon Johns often had chastised his middle-class congregation for its complacency; King too had criticized "tacit acceptance of things as they were."[27] People's reluctance to act was rooted largely in fear—in fear of being publicly singled out, of economic retaliation, of imprisonment, and of retaliatory violence, all part of the arsenal of weapons whites used well to maintain the racial status quo. Amidst that fearsome climate, Johnnie Carr noted, "many Negroes lost faith in themselves."[28]

The surprise and delight that rippled through Montgomery's Black community that first day was palpable. Martin and Coretta Scott King got up at 5:30 on the first morning of the boycott to see what would happen when the buses began their routes at 6 a.m. Coretta recalled shouting at Martin, "Come quickly. . . . There was not one person on that usually crowded bus! We stood together waiting for the next bus. It was empty too, and this was the most heavily traveled line in the whole city. . . . We were so excited we could hardly speak coherently."[29] Rosa Parks found the community's reaction to her arrest "gratifying" and "unbelievable" but also wondered why "we had waited so long to make this protest."[30] In speeches during the boycott she explained the power the organized protest held for the participants themselves: "We surprised the world and ourselves at the success of the protest."[31]

Buoyed by the power of the one-day stand, the community voted that night in a packed and overflowing mass meeting at Holt Street Baptist Church to continue on with the boycott. The power of collective protest changed the participants—from a one-day boycott to a long-term one, from the initial demand for courteous, first-come, first-served seating to full desegregation of the bus.

The fourth lesson is the power of collective organizing, which created a carpool system that sustained the thirteen-month bus boycott. The boycott didn't just succeed naturally. In our popular imagination inspired by Hollywood, the Montgomery bus boycott was all about walking. But what actually enabled a community-wide boycott for more than a year was a massively well-organized car-pool system built by the newly created Montgomery Improvement Association (MIA). Built through existing Black community structures, including churches and political groups, it was accomplished through Black organization. As Alabama State professor Reverend Ben Simms, who became the MIA's transportation coordinator, explained, "Of course we had white support but this was a black movement, planned and run by blacks."[32] Simms estimated they arranged fifteen thousand to twenty thousand rides per day.[33]

The MIA set up forty stations across town, and three hundred people volunteered their cars. People would use the "V for victory" sign to identify themselves to riders and drivers. As the boycott went along, using money donated by churches, organizers were able to buy fifteen station wagons to supplement the volunteer cars. The MIA's elaborately organized car pool required tremendous effort and resolve, and considerable fund-raising. Working-class organizers, such as Nixon, were amazed at the cross-class solidarity of the car pool—middle-class people were willing to take poor people in their cars and have their cars driven by others. Over time, the MIA hired fifteen dispatchers and twenty full-time drivers, all coordinated from a building, known as the Citizens Club, at the edge of Montgomery. Parks briefly served as a dispatcher for the car pool;

her instructions to riders and drivers reveal the effort, patience, and determination the car pool required of both riders and drivers. Reminding riders "how long some of us had to wait when the buses passed us without stopping in the morning and evening," she instructed drivers to "be careful," given the harassment the car pools were enduring at the hands of the police.[34] As the boycott continued beyond the first month, the MIA realized—given the scope of the car-pool system it had created—it would need to fund-raise across the country and sent King, Ralph Abernathy, Parks, and others across the country.

Despite popular focus on the ministers involved, women played foundational roles in maintaining and sustaining the boycott. Two groups of women—one calling itself the Club from Nowhere, led by cook and midwife Georgia Gilmore and her friends, and the Friendly Club, headed by Inez Ricks—spearheaded fund-raising and engaged in friendly competition to see who could raise more. None of the women in these groups had much money, but they knew how to fund-raise and began selling sandwiches, dinners, pies, and cakes to raise money each week. Every Monday evening at the weekly mass meeting, they would present their fund-raising accomplishments to a standing ovation. Women also provided the backbone of the boycott as walkers, car-pool riders, drivers, and organizers. The boycott, according to Jo Ann Robinson, had a transformative power, for it allowed people "to retaliate directly for the pain, humiliation, and embarrassment they had endured over the years."[35]

While the organizational capacity came from the Black community, there were a handful of key white allies: Clifford and Virginia Durr, the Reverend Robert and Jeannie Graetz, Aubrey Williams (publisher of *Southern Farmer*), and librarian Juliette Morgan all lent key support to the movement. The Durrs provided critical legal help, particularly the first night in getting Parks out of jail (Nixon had tried to call but the police station wouldn't give information to a Black person, so lawyer Clifford Durr called to figure out what happened). Virginia Durr, who had become friendly with Rosa Parks years earlier when she hired Parks to do sewing for her, realized the economic trouble the Parkses were in after both Rosa and Raymond lost their jobs because of the boycott. So she raised money for them from friends around the country. Williams provided crucial financial and logistical support, including money for Parks to attend Highlander. The Graetzes and Morgan became particular

targets of incessant white harassment and violence because of their steadfast support of the boycott. The Graetzes' home was bombed twice, and
Morgan was so harassed after she wrote a letter to the *Montgomery Advertiser* sympathetic to the boycott (and unsupported, even by her own
family), that she ultimately took her own life.[36] (Black Montgomerians
were forbidden to attend her funeral.) This white support was crucial because it provided an especially potent reminder of the unnaturalness of
white supremacist politics.

While typically known only for her role in galvanizing the boycott,
Parks played a key role sustaining it, spending much of the year on the
road from Los Angeles to Seattle, Detroit to Pittsburgh, raising attention
and money for the movement at home. She became one of the MIA's most
successful fund-raisers. It wasn't inevitable that the Montgomery bus boycott would become nationally known—people had to work and travel to
make sure it was seen, thus turning a local struggle into a national one.

Certainly, the galvanizing leadership of Martin Luther King Jr. proved
important. But transcripts from meetings and interviews with boycotters
make clear that, alongside his eloquence and charisma, an essential aspect
of his leadership was how King's courage made possible other people's sustained courage. When white people went after King during the boycott,
Black protectiveness of the young leader bubbled forth. In interviews with
Fisk researchers during the boycott, many female Black domestic workers
recounted confronting their employers when the people they worked for
began to attack King; these women could deal with the slurs of the boycott, but when white people started making stuff up about King—this was
a bridge too far.[37] When the city indicted King and other boycott leaders,
people were determined they would not feel alone. A crowd grew outside
the police station. "Black women with bandannas on, wearing men's hats
with their dresses rolled up. From the alleys they came," Reverend Simms
recalled. "One of the police hollered, 'All right you women get back.' These
great big old women with their dresses rolled up told him and I never will
forget their language, 'Us ain't going nowhere. You done arrest us preach-
ers and we ain't moving.'"[38]

The fifth lesson is the power of disruptiveness. The Montgomery bus boycott was a disruptive consumer boycott that used the power of Black con-
sumers to change public transportation policy and force the city to address

Black demands. It worked, and the bus company lost a great deal of money, prompting scaled-back routes and a fare increase. The MIA was accused of being just like the white supremacist White Citizens' Council in using economic means to advance racial issues. Coretta Scott King described how Martin struggled with these very criticisms but decided that such tactics were necessary to increase pressure to get the bus company to change. As Rosa Parks observed, "If you are mistreated when you ride and intimidated when you walk, why not do what hurts them most—walk and let them find $3000 per day to pay for it . . . until they learn [how] to treat us."[39] Seeing the power of the Black community's boycott, white citizens created a counter-campaign, calling on white people to ride the buses to try to reduce the impact of the bus boycott.

The MIA sought to unsettle the status quo, disrupting the order of segregation. To increase the pressure on the city, it called on Black people to boycott downtown businesses and forsake Christmas shopping to underscore Black economic clout in the city and the unacceptability of segregation. It was meant to be disruptive to Montgomery life and economic well-being.

There was nothing passive about this nonviolent direct action. The city, and its white citizens, recognized this—and massively harassed the car pool that sustained the boycott. Police gave out hundreds of tickets to drivers. They staked out the pickup stations to scare riders, and the MIA was regularly forced to change locations. White citizens attacked the cars.

Montgomery's main newspaper, the *Montgomery Advertiser*, steadfastly opposed the boycott, calling it a "dangerous weapon," and refused to print positive letters about the boycott because it did "more harm than good."[40] In an angry interview that reporter Joe Azbell gave to a Fisk researcher three months into the boycott, Azbell called the boycott "stupid" and the work of a "small proportion" of "big operators" who "have their own cars and they feel important driving a few people around in them."[41]

The national NAACP kept the disruptive protest at arm's length, not agreeing with its direct-action tactics, though it did provide support for the legal strategy. Throughout the boycott year, there was much disagreement and tension between the MIA and the national NAACP.

The sixth lesson is the cost and sacrifice activism entails. The activism took a considerable toll. On January 30, 1956, the Kings' house was bombed.

Coretta and the couple's tiny baby, who were both home, managed to escape unscathed. The police commissioner and mayor, curiously among the first people on the scene, seemed disappointed by King's and the assembled crowd's decision not to meet this shocking act of violence with violence. The next day, Nixon's house was bombed.[42]

Many boycotters saw the nonviolent action and refusal to retaliate after the bombings as a repudiation of assumptions by Montgomery's white leaders and citizens about how Black people would act. At the same time, most boycotters saw no contradiction in their embrace of organized nonviolence and long-standing belief in the right of self-defense. Many Black people in Montgomery, including the Parks family, Jo Ann Robinson, and E. D. Nixon, owned guns. A number of drivers in the car pool were Korean War veterans who carried their guns with them to safely ferry their passengers from one side of town to another.[43] At the same time, they relished the power of collective nonviolence to engage on their own terms and disrupt white people's ideas of Black people.

The toll on boycotters was severe. During the first month, Rosa Parks's coworkers "refused to have a conversation or to speak to me at all."[44] She lost her job five weeks into the boycott. Her husband was forced to give up his job when his employer, Maxwell Air Force Base, prohibited talk of the boycott or "that woman" in the barber shop where he worked. The Parkses never found steady work in Montgomery again. Raymond, angry at their situation, drank heavily as the death threats to their home mounted; he was "furious" at many things during the boycott year, according to Rosa: furious at himself "for being a financial failure," at the bus driver "for causing my arrest," at the Black community for not standing up before this, and at his wife for being a "goat head" and "at least getting off the bus."[45] Midway through the boycott, he suffered a nervous breakdown. Rosa developed ulcers and chronic insomnia. Even after the boycott's success, the Parks family continued to receive death threats, as did many other boycott leaders, and they still couldn't find work. Eight months later, they were forced to leave Montgomery for Detroit, where Rosa's brother and cousins lived. They continued to struggle to find work in Detroit; it was not until 1966—eleven years after her arrest—that the Parkses registered an annual income on their income tax forms ($4,026) comparable to what they made the year of her bus arrest ($3,749 combined annual income).[46]

The stress also took its toll on many other activists. Nixon developed high blood pressure. Many took to drinking, according to Parks, "to be able to sleep at night." Robinson slept with her gun. Over the course of his life, Martin Luther King Jr. grew deeply depressed. Even after the boycott's successful end, the violence continued. King's house was shot at; the Graetzes' and Abernathys' houses were bombed, as were four Baptist churches in Montgomery. Random violence occurred against Black people waiting at bus stops.

The seventh lesson is the importance of mentoring and building a community of support. Activists need other activists, and mentoring matters. In the years before the boycott, Rosa Parks found mentors in Ella Baker and Septima Clark, who served as models of women in the struggle and talented organizers who persisted amidst deep setbacks. They helped train Parks in the decade before the boycott in developing her own voice and organizing skills. Parks and Baker met in the mid-1940s, when Baker organized an NAACP leadership training event for local organizers that Parks and Nixon attended. Parks and Baker kept in touch, and Baker often stayed with her when she came to Montgomery. During the boycott, Baker provided key support when she helped organize a massive rally at Madison Square Garden in May 1956, with the help of the Brotherhood of Sleeping Car Porters, to raise money for the Montgomery movement. Sixteen thousand people packed the Garden to hear E. D. Nixon and Rosa Parks, along with Roy Wilkins, Adam Clayton Powell, Eleanor Roosevelt, and celebrities Sammy Davis Jr. and Tallulah Bankhead. The event raised six thousand dollars.[47]

When Parks met Septima Clark at Highlander Folk School the summer before her bus stand, she marveled at Clark's calm strength. Parks felt "tense" and "nervous" from years of unsuccessful struggle. Clark, who led the workshop, had recently been fired from her teaching job because she refused to give up her NAACP membership but was undeterred in her actions. Parks at one point said she hoped some of Clark's "great courage and dignity and wisdom has rubbed off on me."[48] Clark and Myles Horton, Highlander Folk School's founder, understood that leadership and vision come in different packages, and so they created spaces to enable and nourish them. According to Horton, Parks was the "quietest participant" in the workshop that summer: "If you judge by the conventional standards she would have been the least promising probably. We don't use conventional standards, so we had high hopes for her."⁴⁹ Despite her reticence, those two weeks at Highlander were transformative ones for Parks, and Clark encouraged her to share more of her experiences organizing in Montgomery with the interracial group at the workshop. "Rosa Parks was afraid for white people to know that she was as militant as she was," Septima Clark recalled.⁵⁰ When Clark heard that Rosa Parks had refused to give up her seat five months after returning from the workshop, she thought to herself, "Rosa? She was so shy when she came to Highlander, but she got up enough courage to do that."⁵¹ Clark and Horton provided key solidarity and material support during the boycott. Parks journeyed back to Highlander a number of times during the boycott to share what was happening in Montgomery, and to be rejuvenated by the Highlander spirit. In turn, Parks would provide crucial support and solidarity in the years to come when Highlander increasingly was red-baited by Tennessee authorities who wanted to put the organizing center out of business.⁵²

Parks mentored others, including twenty-five-year-old lawyer Fred Gray and the young people in her local NAACP Youth Council. The year before the boycott, when Gray returned to Montgomery after finishing at Western Reserve University School of Law (he had been forced to go out of state since no law schools in Alabama admitted Black people), she would often walk from her job at Montgomery Fair department store to Gray's new law office, and the two would have lunch together. According to Gray, Parks helped him "get on his feet" in the early days when he had little business, and she encouraged him to pursue issues of racial justice through his law practice: "She gave me the feeling that I was the Moses that God had sent Pharaoh and commanded to him to 'Let My People Go.'"⁵³ When she decided to pursue her bus case late the night she was arrested, she called him to represent her.

Parks had re-founded the NAACP Youth Council in 1954 and encouraged the small group of young people to take greater stands against segregation, including a read-in at the downtown library, which refused to serve Black patrons. (Most parents didn't want their kids to have anything to do with the dangerous work of the NAACP.) The weekend following her bus arrest, Parks had organized a workshop, but most of her young charges didn't show up. She was extremely discouraged, having spent weeks organizing it, only later learning they had been passing out leaflets about the upcoming boycott. "They were wise enough to see . . . it was more important to stand on the street corners and pass these papers out to everyone who passed than to sit in a meeting and listen to someone speak."[54] They had learned her lessons well.

The eighth lesson is the importance of learning. People learned from each other, from their own political experiences, and from previous bus boycotts. In early November 1955, a month before Parks's arrest, E. D. Nixon invited New York congressman Adam Clayton Powell to speak to the Progressive Democratic Association in Montgomery. Many people key to the boycott, including Parks, attended. Powell had helped lead a successful bus boycott in New York in 1941 that resulted in the hiring of two hundred Black bus drivers. In his Montgomery speech, Powell noted that the economic tactics of the White Citizens' Council "can be counter met with our own economic pressure."[55] Montgomery activists had also watched and been inspired by a successful bus boycott in Baton Rouge in 1953. Parks's trip to Highlander and the comrades she met there, meanwhile, provided additional ideas and support. Following events around the country, Montgomery's activists read, and shared newspaper clippings (Parks read multiple newspapers a day). They had also learned from the way Viola White's case had been tied up in state court in the 1940s and consequently made the proactive decision to file a separate case in federal court in February 1956. They continued to subscribe to the *Montgomery Advertiser*, despite its segregationist politics, to understand what white people were thinking in order to figure out their next moves.[56]

The ninth lesson is the multiple ways that white people in Montgomery tried to thwart the protest and how activists coped and strategized against this opposition. In our public imagination, Montgomery racism is typically portrayed in violence and epithets, which were certainly a fearsome part of white opposition. A number of homes of boycott leaders were bombed, and many received constant death threats. Car-pool drivers had their vehicles pelted with urine, rocks, and rotten food. But the opposition to the boycott wasn't all bombing homes and tossing urine. A much wider variety of tactics and approaches was employed by white citizens and political leaders to squash the boycott. In many ways, whites who opposed it also took up discourses and tactics familiar to us today. One of the first tactics city leaders employed was to assert that the bus problem was the fault of "a few bad apple" bus drivers or "rough bus drivers"—the problem was not segregation but "rude" drivers who needed to be disciplined.[57] City leaders then claimed they wished Black people had brought matters to their attention earlier (even though there had been numerous meetings in which Black citizens had raised concerns, particularly after Colvin's arrest, but Parks said they were "always brushed off and given the runaround."[58]).

Many white people sought to discredit Parks and King. Rumors swirled through Montgomery's white community that Parks was an outside agitator—a Communist or NAACP plant. According to King, "so persistent and persuasive" was the idea among Montgomery whites that Parks was an NAACP plant that "it convinced many reporters from all across the country."[59] Many white Montgomerians cast King as a middle-class leader "only looking out for himself," who wasn't actually concerned about working-class Black people. They portrayed the boycott as the work of ministers who were getting money from it and asserted that ordinary Black people were just too scared to oppose it, and that they certainly would not have come up with it or been able to maintain the protest themselves. King was also suspected of being a Communist sympathizer. By June 1956, the Alabama NAACP had been outlawed in the state as a "foreign organization." Whites who sympathized with the boycott were publicly attacked; librarian Juliette Morgan was targeted for her positive letter to the *Montgomery Advertiser* on the boycott and ultimately forced to resign from her job.[58]

At critical junctures, the city attempted to treat the MIA and the White Citizens' Council as two interest groups with competing claims that required balancing, rejecting the frame of morality or rights that King tried to bring to the meetings. When King protested the presence of a White Citizens' Council member in the negotiating sessions, he was criticized for introducing mistrust into the meeting. White members of the negotiating committee also accused King of dominating the discussion and having "preconceived ideas" himself.[59] He was treated as inflexible and unreasonable to deflect the MIA's position and allow city leaders to feel balanced and acting in good faith.

The city fought back in multiple ways. The police repeatedly harassed and ticketed car-pool drivers. They regarded the boycott as confrontational, annoying, and a threat that needed to be dealt with. In doing so,

they criminalized its leaders. Three months in, when ticketing and harassment hadn't broken the back of the protest, the city dredged up an old
anti-boycott law and indicted King and eighty-nine other boycott leaders
(including Parks and Nixon).

One of the great myths of the boycott stems from two well-known photos of Parks: her #7053 mugshot and a photo of her being fingerprinted,
wrongly attributed to the arrest on December 1, 1955. There was nothing
to suggest that December evening that her arrest was newsworthy or destined to change history—and if a mugshot was taken, it's not been found.
These two photos were taken during that second arrest, on February 22,
1956. Parks and Nixon did not wait to be arrested. Upon learning of the
indictments, and with crowds of people outside, they went to the police
station and presented themselves: "Are you looking for me? I am here."

The city's indictment strategy backfired tremendously. The community's resolve strengthened after the arrests; they had "committed the sin
of being tired of segregation . . . and [had] the moral courage to sit up and
express our tiredness," as King put it the night after the arrests, and they
were not going to be deterred.[62] The MIA's demands grew to full desegregation of the bus. And it was the city's move to indict these eighty-nine
boycott leaders (more than the boycott itself) that garnered national media attention and prompted the *New York Times* and *Washington Post* to
begin seriously covering the Montgomery protest.[63]

The tenth lesson is the value of multiple strategies of resistance. After months
of boycott, with the city engaging in numerous tactics to break it, young
lawyer Fred Gray, with the assistance of community activists, decided to
file a proactive federal case, *Browder v. Gayle*, challenging Montgomery's
bus segregation. Nixon had worried that the state would just tie up Parks's
case, like it had a decade earlier with Viola White. Gray had hoped to get
a minister or another man to be a plaintiff, but no one was willing, so the
four plaintiffs were Aurelia Browder, Susie McDonald, Claudette Colvin,
and Mary Louise Smith. Colvin and Smith took risks in choosing to be
part of the case that most adults were unwilling to be part of. (Colvin was
eight months pregnant.) A fifth woman, Jeanetta Reese, was named on the
case but pulled out the next day because both she and her husband were
threatened with physical violence. Parks was *not* on the case because Gray
didn't want to risk having it thrown out on a technicality, since Parks's

case was already in state court. In addition, Parks's long history with the NAACP might have been a liability, as opposition to the organization mounted in Alabama.

In June 1956, in a surprise decision, two judges in a three-judge panel of the US District Court for the Middle District of Alabama declared Montgomery's bus segregation unconstitutional. Six months later, the US Supreme Court upheld that decision, and on December 20, 1956, after a 382-day boycott, Montgomery's buses were desegregated and Black people could sit wherever they liked.

The success of the Montgomery bus boycott was accomplished through a combination of tactics: years of spadework to lay a foundation for the movement to emerge; Rosa Parks's willingness to pursue her case in state court; the yearlong consumer boycott and corresponding car-pool effort built by local people and their grassroots organization; the federal legal case *Browder v. Gayle*, with four women plaintiffs; a tremendous amount of fund-raising; and a campaign to get the word across the country about what was happening. All were necessary to build momentum, power, and community capacity to gain the national attention that led to decisive change in Montgomery.

A History for a Better World

CONSIDERING A FULLER history of the bus boycott moves us from the romanticized notion of Rosa Parks as a candle lighting the darkness to an appreciation of the persistence and long-term organizing that building and sustaining such a movement entails. "Choosing to do uncomfortable things," Equal Justice Initiative founder Bryan Stevenson explained, is foundational to understanding how it happened and what it takes to do it again. This moves us beyond a few key individuals to understanding the power of collective, sustained action. Movements are made by groups of people, not by singular people, no matter how remarkable.

Just as in the civil rights movement, our own contemporary struggles are long, hard, and painstaking. Just as Rosa Parks was not the first woman to resist on the bus, Michael Brown and Eric Garner were not the first people killed by police. An accumulation of injustice brings people to the breaking point; once that breaking point was reached—once Michael Brown's body had lain on the pavement for hours, once yet another woman had been arrested on the bus—there was no turning back. Many were angry, and that anger transformed into resolve. But that no-turning-back shift was disruptive. It often meant breaking the law and norms of propriety. It was not unified—civil rights activists often stepped out ahead of their family and neighbors, at times facing criticism as they did. And from Montgomery to Ferguson, the people who made those movements were diverse—poor as well as middle class, teenagers and parents and community elders, longtime activists and new freedom fighters—all people who were able to "do the uncomfortable."

The movement was leader-full, and even those civil rights heroes we recognize today were reviled in their day and made to feel crazy. Today's lamentation—that we need another King—misses the fact that we have many Kings and Parkses; we just do not necessarily recognize them. "Be more like King," commentators tell protesters today. Be careful what you wish for, this history reminds: disruption; civil disobedience; an analysis that interweaves race, poverty, and US war making; steadfast moral witness; and a willingness to call out liberals for their inaction is what it actually means to "be like King," and many follow in his footsteps.

The burnout Rosa Parks and her comrades experienced in the years before the boycott, as they unsuccessfully pressed for change, is familiar. The fact that it took months before the Montgomery bus boycott garnered substantive media coverage, and the way it was dismissed and demonized, resemble the ways movements are treated today—as do the serious class divisions activists encountered, which prior to December 1955 had made them grow pessimistic about the possibility of unified action. The story of the Montgomery bus boycott shows the capacity of a community to build structures and use existing ties to sustain a yearlong boycott. Here again, the story parallels the interplay of existing ties and new structures being built by movements like Black Lives Matter, the Dream Defenders, United We Dream, #Not1More, Moral Mondays, #NoDAPL, the Fight for $15, and the new Poor People's Campaign. So too does the wariness of national organizations toward more confrontational tactics and their unwillingness to commit needed resources. The varieties of white resistance the civil rights movement encountered also resonate today. The willingness to deflect and exceptionalize the problem—by describing it as a problem of "bad apple bus drivers," or asserting that movement activists are no better than their opposition, or arresting movement leaders to thwart the movement; or constantly asking for proof of the systemic nature of the problem—have ample contemporary parallels.

Fundamentally, the work of social change is work, and its challenge to the status quo is alarming to many in society. Many of the fears and critiques of movements such as Black Lives Matter are replicas of the fears and critiques of the civil rights movement. Just as activists of the civil rights movement did, activists today are asking us to see the legitimacy of their anger at systemic racial injustice and the need for massive societal transformation and public accountability. Such outrage and disruption makes society uneasy today, as it did sixty years ago. Like many activists today, civil rights activists were accused of being reckless, unreasonable, and inflexible, out for their own gain, and un-American. They insisted desegregation was a matter of policy and law, not just an affair of the heart. And they did take a freeway.

Similarly, older people cautioned younger people that they were not doing it the right way (while other elders delighted in the new militancy). So too, the myriad ways political officials, citizens, and law enforcement responded by dismissing and thwarting demands for racial justice; the silences of many who might see the injustice but felt powerless to challenge it; and the use of theories of cultural deficiency to explain and excuse present-day disparities—all were evident a half century ago as well as today.

In answer to those who claim young people protesting across the country against mass incarceration, police violence, deportation, school inequality, rising Islamophobia, global injustice, and environmental racism are nothing like the activists of storied days of the civil rights movement, our historically informed answer must be, they are. Too often, our memorials and fables of the movement stand in the way of such reckoning, hijacking the movement for nationalistic purposes, engaging us in easy celebration, and demanding little from us. "Now the crucial paradox which confronts us here," James Baldwin observed a half century ago, "is that the whole process of education occurs within a social framework and is designed to perpetuate the aims of society. … As one begins to become conscious one begins to examine the society in which he is being educated."[1]

What a fuller history shows is that there was nothing clear or destined about the civil rights movement. "It was hard to keep going when all our efforts seemed in vain," as Parks explained.[2] Over and over, they tried to find justice—and over and over there was no justice. They couldn't find lawyers to represent people. People became scared and refused to provide testimony. And when they did stand up, the cases went nowhere. Killers and rapists went free. Men were executed. Parks and her comrades filed affidavit after affidavit with the Justice Department, but it looked the other way. People were killed or assaulted for their activism. Given the political climate, most Black people in Alabama saw the NAACP as a futile undertaking; few individuals possessed the stamina, bravery, and vision required for active participation. There was "almost no way," Parks said, to see any discernible progress.[3] But her small crew kept at it, growing more tired and more bitter but plugging along because, as she put it, "someone had to do something" to show their dissatisfaction with the treatment they experienced. It is this courage of perseverance—the courage of raising an issue when people do not want to acknowledge it, and when the costs of raising one's voice are so high and so depleting—that gives us our heroes and heroines.

This is not the fable in which courage is inevitably rewarded, cases inevitably won, injustice inevitably vanquished. What the history of the civil rights movement shows us, what the Montgomery bus boycott shows us, is that when change does happen, it is often because people labored for decades and sometimes generations in the wilderness. These activists were slurred and ignored, slammed and surveilled, and ignored again. They kept going when all their efforts seemed in vain. In witnessing their persevering courage, other people found their own. They used tactics that had been used before and forged new ones, combining economic disruption, painstaking organizing, outside support, internal fund-raising, and proactive legal strategizing, and drew on religious faith, labor organizing, community networks, love, and anger. Their goal was much more than a bus seat—it was about access to jobs and criminal justice, educational justice, equitable city services, and full citizenship rights. And people around the nation watched, learned, and were inspired, taking up new paths in their own struggles. And still the movement was not over and there was more work to be done. This history is far more terrible than the fable shows us— but so much more beautiful as well.

Many of these movements never fully realized their vision of a just and equitable society. Amidst glorious triumphs and substantive change, it is not a history of happy endings but one that challenges where we are now in this country. By expanding our understanding of who the courageous were, it suggests who will lead us today: welfare moms, high school students, and church ladies, rural and urban, women and men, teenagers through octogenarians, Brooklyn to Birmingham to the Bay Area. Enlarging our imagination of what is possible, this fuller history demonstrates what is necessary: combining disruption, ongoing protests, study groups, legal strategies and civil disobedience; creating community institutions and national webs of solidarity; mentoring activists new to the struggle and learning from each other.

Speaking from the Lorraine Motel in Memphis on the forty-ninth anniversary of King's assassination, the Reverend William Barber proclaimed the need to "stop basking in our commemorations and visiting the tombs of the prophets." Calling for a new Poor People's Campaign, he insisted, "We have to pick up their burden and recommit ourselves to the task of justice." This more beautiful and terrible history provides a way to see our past and future anew. It shows us the persevering power and immense vision people summoned. And then it still required more courage, and still it requires our courage. A more sober account of racial injustice in the United States, this history demands our political imagination and action, a history for a better world.

Acknowledgments

WHILE I WAS FINISHING THIS BOOK, the 102nd anniversary of the Armenian Genocide came and went. The United States still refuses to recognize it, in unconscionable deference to Turkish proclivities and in complete denial of the historical record. Growing up Greek-Armenian in my politically active family made the importance of the histories we tell and those we deny potent and visceral. It made the parallel ways the United States does this about its own history of systemic racial inequality, violence, genocide, and centuries of Black struggle—and the national fables we tell about ourselves—more urgent to understand and expose.

Many friends and colleagues talked with me about the themes in this book, and its bigger ideas of justice and history. They have helped me make sense of the wild and lovely journey since my Rosa Parks biography came out and thought with me about the histories we get versus the histories we need. I am so grateful for Ujju Aggarwal, Chitra Aiyar, Alan Aja, Caroline Arnold, Juan Battle, Maricia Battle, Jennifer Bernstein, Mary Frances Berry, Stefan Bradley, Thomas Bradshaw, Naomi Braine, Kris Burrell, Tahir Butt, Adrienne Cannon, Brenda Cardenas, Julie Cooper, Matthew Countryman, Amalia Cuadra, Paisley Currah, Emily Drabinski, Sally Eberhardt, Jason Egenberg, Trey Ellis, Angela LeBlanc Ernest, Ken Estey, Henry Louis Gates, Dayo Gore, Aram Goudsouzian, Karen Gould, Richard Greenwald, Josh Guild, Sarah Haley, Roderick Harrison, Melissa Harris-Perry, LaShawn Harris, Carl Hart, Faisal Hashmi, Pam Horowitz, Erika Huggins, Hasan Jeffries, Amy Schmidt Jones, Peniel Joseph, Ira Katznelson, Robin Kelley, David Lucander, Melissa Madzel, Tom Martinez, Margaret McAleer, Deborah Menkart, Steven Millner, Khalil Muhammad, Naomi Murakawa, Jessica Murray, Alondra Nelson, Georgette Norman, Robert Reid Pharr, Boots Riley, Robert Scott, Simone Sebastian, Irene Sosa, Mark Speltz, Aviva Stahl, David Stein, Kelly Stupple, Celina Su, Keeanga-Yamahtta Taylor, Lynnell Thomas, Mark Ungar, Erik Wallenberg, Raphael

Warnock, Angela Sadler Williamson, Komozi Woodard, Jasmin Young, and Gary Younge.

Bennett Ashley, Say Burgin, Prudence Cumberbatch, Matthew Delmont, Joseph Entin, Arnold Franklin, Tarek Ismail, Arun Kundnani, Alejandra Marchevsky, Karen Miller, Mary Phillips, Annelise Orleck, Brian Purnell, and Clarence Taylor all read chapters and offered crucial feedback, ongoing conversation, support, and inspiration, renewing my spirit and conviction that this history was needed for the present. This book couldn't have happened without them. Adina Back's work—including her unpublished manuscript and the two chapters on Baker and Mallory—were invaluable. Erik Wallenberg did a wonderful job with the index.

I am deeply grateful to Carl Wendell Hines Jr. for allowing me to use his beautiful poem, to LeRoy Henderson for his incredible photographs, which grace the cover of this book and my other work, and to Amos Paul Kennedy Jr., whose magnificent Rosa Parks prints have adorned my walls and inspired me for years. Thanks also go to Brooklyn College and my colleagues in the Political Science Department and especially Barbara Haugstatter; to the Mellon Seminar on Public Engagement and Collaborative Research at the Center for the Humanities at the CUNY Graduate Center, particularly Kendra Sullivan, Jessica Murray, and Louise Lenihan; and to the Schomburg Center for Research in Black Culture, particularly Khalil Muhammad, Komozi Woodard, Deirdre Holland, and Aisha Becker-Burrowes, for their support of my work and abiding belief in the essential role this history must play in our present. I am grateful to the National Endowment for the Humanities for awarding Komozi Woodard and myself the opportunity to run a faculty seminar on the Jim Crow North, and to the wonderful and supportive community of faculty who came together in the summer of 2015 for "Rethinking Black Freedom Studies in the Jim Crow North."

I am lucky to know many people who carry forward the struggle for social justice. Their work shaped the arc of this book and provided a constant reminder of why this history is needed for our present: Sally Eberhardt, Pardiss Kebriaei, Aviva Stahl, Faisal Hashmi, Arun Kundnani, Tarek Ismail, Amna Akbar, Laura Rovner, Bill Quigley, Abi Hassan, Vikki Law, Bryan Stevenson, Reverend William Barber, Roz Pelles, Yara Allen, Pam Horowitz, Gloria Richardson, Ericka Huggins, Seth Wessler, Justin

Mazzola, Naz Ahmad, Ramzi Kassem, Diala Shamas, Saadia Toor, the late General Baker, Chitra Aiyar, Ujju Aggarwal, Purvi Shah, Shane Kadidal, Naomi Schiller, Joseph Entin, Alan Aja, Jocelyn Wills, Irene Sosa, Karen Miller, Say Burgin, Komozi Woodard, Alejandra Marchevsky, Dayo Gore, and Gareth Peirce.

I am deeply grateful to Beacon Press and the ways they interweave the urgency of the written word with a commitment to justice—particularly Helene Atwan, Tom Hallock, Pam MacColl, Marcy Barnes, Susan Lumenello, Peggy Field, Alyssa Hassan, Molly Velázquez-Brown, Perpetual Charles, Nicholas DiSabatino, and Rachael Marks. My editor, Gayatri Patnaik, is equal parts cherished friend, committed comrade, and thorough editor—a wonderful trifecta. I am lucky to have worked with them for more than a decade now.

My students at Brooklyn College have informed this book immeasurably, continually reminding me of the stakes of this fuller history for where we are today in this country. There is nothing in these dark days that gives me more hope than going to class and watching the critical engagement, resolve, and generosity that my students embody and the ways they understand knowledge as crucial to a better world. I am particularly grateful for Sarah Aly, Rabia Ahsin, Dominick Braswell, Ethan Barnett, and Terron Davis, who provided key assistance and insight.

I am blessed by the love and sustenance of family, chosen and kin. Alejandra Marchevsky, Emilio Elias Marchevsky, Jason Elias, Arnold Franklin, Komozi Woodard, Brenda Cardenas, Stephanie Melnick, Karen Miller, Prudence Cumberbatch, Marwa Amer, Susan Artinian, Julie Causton, Gretchen Lopez, Gabriela Lopez, George Theoharis, Liz Theoharis, Chris Caruso, Sam Theoharis, Ella Theoharis, Sophia Theoharis Caruso, and Luke Theoharis Caruso have sustained me and make all things possible. I count myself lucky every day to have siblings like George and Liz; their huge hearts, abiding good cheer, and steadfast voices for justice show me the way forward and make the journey so much better.

And finally, this book is dedicated to my parents, Nancy and Athan Theoharis, whose commitment to justice kindness, and truth-telling informs every page—and to my teacher and lifelong freedom fighter, Julian Bond, who died while I was writing this book and who insisted that this history shows us the way forward to a better world.

Notes

PREFACE

1. Gary Younge, "Eduardo Galeano: 'My Greatest Fear Is That We Are All Suffering from Amnesia,'" *Guardian*, July 23, 2013.

2. James Baldwin, "A Talk to Teachers," originally published in the *Saturday Review*, December 21, 1963.

3. Sam Wineburg and Chauncey Monte-Sano, "'Famous Americans': The Changing Pantheon of American Heroes," *Journal of American History* 94 (Spring 2008): 1190.

4. Sheldon Appleton, "Martin Luther King in Life . . . and Memory," *Public Perspective* (February/March 1995): 12.

5. G. Russell Seay Jr., "A Prophet with Honor?," in *The Domestication of Martin Luther King Jr.: Clarence B. Jones, Right-Wing Conservatism, and the Manipulation of the King Legacy*, ed. Lewis Baldwin and Rufus Burrow Jr. (Eugene, OR: Cascade Books, 2013), 244–47.

6. Civil rights tourism has flourished, often in the South right alongside of Confederate and Civil War tourism. At least fifteen museums have opened since 1990 commemorating civil rights activism. "Introduction" and Glenn Eskew, "New Ideology of Tolerance," in *The Civil Rights Movement in American Memory*, ed. Renee Romano and Leigh Raiford (Athens: University of Georgia Press, 2008).

7. See Ian Haney Lopez's *Dog Whistle Politics: How Coded Racial Appeals Have Reinvented Racism and Wrecked the Middle Class* (New York: Oxford University Press, 2014) for differences and overlap between postracial and color-blind ideologies.

8. James Oliver Horton, "Slavery in American History: An Uncomfortable National Dialogue," in *Slavery and Public History: The Tough Stuff of American History*, ed. James Oliver Horton and Lois E. Horton (Chapel Hill: University of North Carolina Press, 2008), 37.

9. Michel-Rolph Trouillot, *Silencing the Past: Power and the Production of History* (Boston: Beacon Press, 1995), 116.

10. Ibid., 2.

11. Ibid., 152.

12. For instance, in recent debates about Confederate statue removal, there's finally been discussion of how many of these statues were erected during the civil rights movement as resistance to Black freedom movements. See "Whose Heritage: Public Symbols of the Confederacy," Southern Poverty Law Center, April 21, 2016.

13. Here I refer to both the transatlantic slave trade, and Native American genocide and settler colonialism.

14. Eskew, "New Ideology of Tolerance," 29.

15. When asked at the 2008 Democratic National Convention where King would be if he were present, Obama answered honestly—that King would likely be outside the convention center protesting.

16. "Obama, Clinton Speeches in Selma, Alabama," *CNN Late Edition with Wolf Blitzer*, transcripts, March 4, 2007.

17. White House, "Remarks by the President at the 50th Anniversary of the Selma to Montgomery Marches," news release, March 7, 2015.

18. The set included *Stride Toward Freedom* (1958), *The Measure of a Man* (1959), *Strength to Love* (1963), *Why We Can't Wait* (1964), and *Where Do We Go from Here: Chaos or Community?* (1967).

19. Michelle Alexander brought this framing to national use in *The New Jim Crow: Mass Incarceration in the Era of Colorblindness* (New York: New Press, 2010).

20. Barbara Reynolds, "I Was a Civil Rights Activist in the 1960s. But It's Hard for Me to Get Behind Black Lives Matter," *Washington Post*, August 24, 2015.

21. Jennie Jarvie, "An Uneasy Standoff Between Police and Protesters as Black Lives Matter Returns to the Streets," *Los Angeles Times*, July 9, 2016.

22. See Cedric J. Robinson, *Forgeries of Memory and Meaning: Blacks and the Regimes of Race in American Theater and Film before World War II* (Chapel Hill: University of North Carolina Press, 2007).

23. Charles Mills, *The Racial Contract* (Ithaca, NY: Cornell University Press, 1998), 18–19. Emphasis in original.

24. Donald A. Yerxa, "Postwar: An Interview with Tony Judt," *Historically Speaking* 7 (January/February 2006), http://www.bu.edu/historic/hs/judt.html.

25. The first African American honored was a Washington, DC, policeman shot in the line of duty. Indeed, the only two nonpolitical officials before Parks who had lain in honor were policemen. Martin Luther King Jr. was not granted such an honor; J. Edgar Hoover was.

26. Cornel West has similarly referred to the "Santa Clausification" of Martin Luther King Jr. See "Stop the 'Santa Claus-ification' of Martin Luther King, Pleads Dr. Cornel West," Rollingout.com, January 18, 2010.

27. Eric Foner, *Forever Free: The Story of Emancipation and Reconstruction* (New York: Alfred A. Knopf, 2006), xxv.

28. Nathan Huggins, "The Deforming Mirror of Truth: Slavery and the Master Narrative of American History," *Radical History Review* 49 (Winter 1991).

29. This fits with a larger trend in civil rights historiography on the politics of memory. From Organization of American Historians president Jacquelyn Dowd Hall's much-cited article "'The Long Civil Rights Movement and the Political Uses of the Past," *Journal of American History* 91, no. 4 (March 2005), to Romano and Raiford's *The Civil Rights Movement in American Memory*, scholars have examined the growing ascendancy of the civil rights movement in American memory. They have analyzed civil rights legacies and Barack Obama's presidency, including Thomas Sugrue's *Not Even Past: Barack Obama and the Burden of Race* (Princeton, NJ: Princeton University Press, 2010), Peniel Joseph's *Dark Days, Bright Nights: From Black Power to Barack Obama* (New York: BasicCivitas, 2010), and Fredrick Harris's *The Price of the Ticket: Barack Obama and the Rise and Decline of Black Politics* (New York: Oxford University Press, 2012).

30. See Eric Foner's masterwork, *Reconstruction: America's Unfinished Revolution*, updated ed. (New York: Harper Perennial, 2014); David Blight, *Race and Reunion: The Civil War in American Memory* (Cambridge, MA: Harvard University Press, 2001); and Steven Hahn, *A Nation Under Our Feet: Black Political Struggles in the Rural South from Slavery to the Great Migration* (Cambridge, MA: Harvard University Press, 2005) for critiques of the ways the story of Reconstruction came to be remembered and told.

31. W. E. B. Du Bois, *Black Reconstruction in America* (1935; New York: Free Press, 1998), 714.

32. Jeanne Theoharis, *The Rebellious Life of Mrs. Rosa Parks* (Boston: Beacon Press, 2013); Matthew Delmont and Jeanne Theoharis, "Rethinking Boston's Busing Crisis," Special Issue Introduction, *Journal of Urban History* 43 no. 2 (March 2017); Jeanne Theoharis, "Accidental Matriarchs and Beautiful Helpmates: Gender and the Memorialization of the Civil Rights Movement," in *Local Studies, a National Movement*, ed. Emilye Crosby (Athens: University of Georgia Press, 2011); Jeanne Theoharis "'W-A-L-K-O-U-T!': High School Students and the Development of Black Power in Los Angeles, 1967-1969," in *Neighborhood Rebels: Local Black Power Activism*, ed. Peniel Joseph (New York: Palgrave Macmillan, 2010); Jeanne Theoharis, "Hidden in Plain Sight: Southern Exceptionalism and the Civil Rights Movement Outside of the South," in *The Myth of Southern Exceptionalism*,

ed. Matthew Lassiter and Joe Crespino (New York: Oxford University Press, 2009); Jeanne Theoharis, "'Alabama on Avalon': Rethinking the Watts Uprising and the Character of Black Protest in Los Angeles," in *The Black Power Movement: Rethinking the Civil Rights–Black Power Era*, ed. Peniel Joseph (New York: Routledge, 2006).

33. On the structures of racial inequity built in the twentieth century: Ira Katznelson, *When Affirmative Action Was White: An Untold History of Racial Inequality in Twentieth-Century America* (New York: W. W. Norton, 2005); Thomas Sugrue, *Sweet Land of Liberty: The Forgotten Struggle for Civil Rights in the North* (New York: Random House, 2008); and Craig Wilder, *A Covenant with Color: Race and Social Power in Brooklyn* (New York: Columbia University Press, 2001). On the Student Nonviolent Coordinating Committee (SNCC) and the Southern struggle: John Dittmer, *Local People: The Struggle for Civil Rights in Mississippi* (Champaign-Urbana: University of Illinois Press, 1995); Charles Payne, *I've Got the Light of Freedom: The Organizing Tradition and the Mississippi Freedom Struggle* (Berkeley: University of California Press, 1995); Akinyele Umoja, *We Will Shoot Back: Armed Resistance in the Mississippi Freedom Movement* (New York: New York University Press, 2014), Hasan Jeffries, *Bloody Lowndes: Civil Rights and Black Power in Alabama's Black Belt* (New York: New York University Press, 2009); Wesley Hogan, *Many Minds, One Heart: SNCC's Dream for a New America* (Chapel Hill: University of North Carolina Press, 2007); Emilye Crosby, *A Little Taste of Freedom: The Black Freedom Struggle in Claiborne County, Mississippi* (Chapel Hill: University of North Carolina Press, 2005); Emilye Crosby, ed., *Civil Rights History from the Ground Up: Local Struggles, a National Movement* (Athens: University of Georgia Press, 2011); Faith Holsaert et al., *Hands on the Freedom Plow: Personal Accounts by Women in SNCC* (Champaign-Urbana: University of Illinois Press, 2010); Chana Kai Lee, *For Freedom's Sake: The Life of Fannie Lou Hamer* (Champaign-Urbana: University of Illinois Press, 1999); Barbara Ransby, *Ella Baker and the Black Freedom Movement: A Radical Democratic Vision* (Chapel Hill: University of North Carolina Press, 2003); and Katherine Charron, *Freedom's Teacher: The Life of Septima Clark* (Chapel Hill: University of North Carolina Press, 2009). On the Black freedom movement outside the South: Jeanne Theoharis and Komozi Woodward, eds., *Freedom North: Black Freedom Struggles Outside the South, 1940–1980* (New York: Palgrave Macmillan, 2003), and *Groundwork: Local Black Freedom Movements in America* (New York: New York University Press, 2005); Clarence Taylor, *Civil Rights in New York City* (New York: Fordham University Press, 2011); Lassiter and Crespino, eds., *The Myth of Southern Exceptionalism*; Martha Biondi, *To Stand and Fight: The Struggle for Civil Rights in Postwar New York City* (Cambridge, MA: Harvard University Press, 2003); Heather Thompson, *Whose Detroit? Politics, Labor and Race in a Modern American City* (Ithaca, NY: Cornell University Press, 2004); Robert O. Self, *American Babylon: Race and the Struggle for Postwar Oakland* (Princeton, NJ: Princeton University Press, 2003); Josh Sides, *L.A. City Limits: African American Los Angeles from the Great Depression to the Present* (Berkeley: University of California Press, 2003); Matthew Countryman, *Up South: Civil Rights and Black Power in Philadelphia* (Philadelphia: University of Pennsylvania Press, 2006); Angela Dillard, *Faith in the City: Preaching Radical Social Change in Detroit* (Ann Arbor: University of Michigan Press, 2007); Suzanne Smith, *Dancing in the Street: Motown and the Cultural Politics of Detroit* (Cambridge, MA: Harvard University Press, 1999); Matthew F. Delmont, *Why Busing Failed: Race, Media, and the National Resistance to School Desegregation* (Berkeley: University of California Press, 2016); Mark Speltz, *North of Dixie: Civil Rights Photography Beyond the South* (Los Angeles: J. Paul Getty Museum, 2016). On Black radicalism and Black Power: Dayo Gore, *Radicalism at the Crossroads: African American Women Activists in the Cold War* (New York: New York University Press, 2011); Joseph, ed., *The Black Power Movement*; Joseph, ed., *Neighborhood Rebels*; Rhonda Williams, *Concrete Demands: The Search for Black Power in the 20th Century* (New York: Routledge, 2015); Donna Murch, *Living for the City: Migration, Education, and the Rise of the Black Panther Party in Oakland, California* (Chapel Hill: University of North Carolina Press, 2010); Robyn Spencer, *The Revolution Has Come: Black Power, Gender, and the Black Panther Party in Oakland* (Durham, NC: Duke University Press, 2016); Jakobi Williams, *From the Bullet to the Ballot: The Illinois Chapter of the Black Panther Party and Racial Coalition Politics in Chicago* (Chapel Hill: University of North Carolina Press, 2013); Brian Purnell, *Fighting Jim Crow in the County of Kings: The Congress of Racial*

Equality in Brooklyn (Lexington: University Press of Kentucky, 2013). On welfare rights and antipoverty organizing: Rhonda Y. Williams, *The Politics of Public Housing: Black Women's Struggles Against Urban Inequality* (New York: Oxford University Press, 2003); Premilla Nadasen, *Welfare Warriors: The Welfare Rights Movement in the United States* (New York: Routledge, 2004); Annelise Orleck, *Storming Caesar's Palace: How Black Mothers Fought Their Own War on Poverty* (Boston: Beacon Press, 2005); Felicia Kornbluh, *The Battle for Welfare Rights: Politics and Poverty in Modern America* (Philadelphia: University of Pennsylvania Press, 2007); Lisa Levenstein, *A Movement Without Marches: African American Women and the Politics of Poverty in Postwar Philadelphia* (Chapel Hill: University of North Carolina Press, 2009).

34. As historian Tracy K'Meyer observes, "For a generation historians have been writing a different story of the Black freedom struggle, one that downplays charismatic leadership, illuminates divisions within the Black community and emphasizes the long, hard, mundane work of organizing that actually brought about change. So why hasn't this new story affected not only the broader politics [or] . . . even many historians and scholars' ideas about how to achieve racial justice?" Tracy K'Meyer, "The Stories We Tell," *Journal of Civil and Human Rights* (Spring/Summer 2016).

35. "It's not your grandfather's civil rights movement" is also being used by some activists to differentiate the patriarchal notions of leadership at play in some parts of the civil rights movement from the more leader-full BLM movement with Black queer women at the center. See "Not Your Grandfather's Black Freedom Movement: An Interview with BYP100's Charlene Carruthers," *In These Times*, February 8, 2016.

INTRODUCTION: THE POLITICAL USES AND MISUSES OF CIVIL RIGHTS HISTORY AND MEMORIALIZATION IN THE PRESENT

1. Appleton, "Martin Luther King in Life . . . and Memory," 12.

2. As quoted in Seay, "A Prophet with Honor?," 242.

3. Ibid., 243–44.

4. Francis X. Clines, "Reagan's Doubts on Dr. King's Legacy Disclosed," *New York Times*, October 22, 1983.

5. As quoted in Eddie S. Glaude Jr., *Democracy in Black: How Race Still Enslaves the American Soul* (New York: Crown, 2016), 105.

6. Justin Gomer, "Race and Civil Rights Dramas in Hollywood," *Black Perspectives* (blog), March 24, 2017, http://www.aaihs.org/race-and-civil-rights-dramas-in-hollywood/.

7. Glaude, *Democracy in Black*, 109.

8. "Celebration of Martin Luther King Jr. Still Faces Pushback," *New York Times*, January 16, 2017.

9. Baldwin and Burrow, *The Domestication of Martin Luther King*, xix–xxi.

10. Ibid., xix.

11. In 1986, Congress passed Public Law 99–244, designating February 1986 as "National Black (Afro-American) History Month" and noting "the beginning of the sixtieth annual public and private salute to Black History as African American History Month," Law Library of Congress, July 31, 2015. By the 1930s, according to former Association for the Study of African American Life and History president Daryl Michael Scott, Woodson understood the dangers of the ways that the observance could commodify or trivialize Black history, warning of "the intellectual charlatans, black and white, popping up everywhere seeking to take advantage of the public interest in black history," "Origins of Black History Month," Association for the Study of African American Life and History, https://asalh.org/about-us/origins-of-black-history-month/.

12. Christopher Emdin, "For the Folks Who Killed Black History Month . . . and the Rest of Y'all Too," *Beacon Broadside* (blog), February 17, 2016.

13. President Bush in a 2010 interview: "I faced a lot of criticism as president . . . that I lied about Iraq's weapons of mass destruction or cut taxes to benefit the rich. But the suggestion that I was racist because of the response to Katrina represented an all-time low." "'George Bush Doesn't

Care about Black People': Reflections on Kanye West's Criticism 10 Years After," *Democracy Now!*, August 28, 2015.

14. Transcript of President Bush's remarks can be found at *CNN Live Today*, CNN.com, December 1, 2005.

15. "Full Text of Bush's NAACP Speech," *Denver Post*, July 20, 2006.

16. Joseph, *Dark Days, Bright Nights*, 211.

17. At his first inauguration, President Obama signed a program to Congressman John Lewis: "Because of you, John. Barack Obama."

18. Dianne Feinstein, "Opening Welcome Remarks at the 2009 Inauguration," January 20, 2009.

19. "Remarks by the President at the Martin Luther King Jr. Memorial Dedication," news release, October 16, 2011.

20. Philip Kennicott, "Revisiting King's Metaphor About a Nation's Debt," *Washington Post*, August 24, 2011.

21. A bust of Martin Luther King Jr., commissioned by Congress in 1982 and unveiled in 1986, appears in the Capitol Rotunda.

22. In contrast, in the Capitol Rotunda, a statue commemorating three suffragists—Lucretia Mott, Susan B. Anthony, and Elizabeth Cady Stanton—known now as "The Portrait Monument"— is rendered unfinished to denote the work ahead in the struggle for women's rights. A gift from the National Women's Party, the statue was commemorated in 1921 and promptly moved out of sight to the Capitol Crypt (and its feminist inscription "Woman, first denied a soul, then called mindless, now arisen, declared herself an entity to be reckoned" scraped off). James Brooke, "3 Suffragists (in Marble) to Move Up to the Capitol," *New York Times*, September 27, 1996.

23. The Justice Department explained: "As enacted in 1965, the first element in the formula was whether, on November 1, 1964, the state or a political subdivision of the state maintained a 'test or device' restricting the opportunity to register and vote . . . includ[ing] such requirements as the applicant being able to pass a literacy test, establish that he or she had good moral character, or have another registered voter vouch for his or her qualifications. The second element . . . [was if] less than 50 percent of persons of voting age were registered to vote on November 1, 1964, or that less than 50 percent of persons of voting age voted in the presidential election of November 1964. This resulted in the following states becoming, in their entirety, 'covered jurisdictions': Alabama, Alaska, Georgia, Louisiana, Mississippi, South Carolina, and Virginia. In addition, certain political subdivisions (usually counties) in four other states (Arizona, Hawaii, Idaho, and North Carolina) were covered. . . . In 1970, Congress . . . referenced November 1968 as the relevant date for the maintenance of a test or device and the levels of voter registration and electoral participation. This addition to the formula resulted in the partial coverage of ten states, including Alaska, Arizona, California, Connecticut, Idaho, Maine, Massachusetts, New Hampshire, New York, and Wyoming. Half of these states (Connecticut, Idaho, Maine, Massachusetts, and Wyoming) filed successful 'bailout' lawsuits. In 1975, the Act's special provisions . . . were broadened to address voting discrimination against members of 'language minority groups,' which were defined as persons who are American Indian, Asian American, Alaskan Natives or of Spanish heritage. . . . includ[ing] the practice of providing any election information, including ballots, only in English in states or political subdivisions where members of a single language minority constituted more than five percent of the citizens of voting age. This third prong of the coverage formula had the effect of covering Alaska, Arizona, and Texas in their entirety, and parts of California, Florida, Michigan, New York, North Carolina, and South Dakota." In 1982, and then again in 2006, it was renewed for twenty-five years, but the coverage formula was not changed.

24. Shelby County v. Holder, 570 US, http://www.supremecourt.gov/opinions/12pdf/12–96 _6k47.pdf.

25. Gary Younge, *The Speech: The Story Behind Dr. Martin Luther King Jr.'s Dream* (Chicago: Haymarket, 2013).

26. Eddie Glaude observes the speech framed racial matters "as a momentary stumble on our way to a more perfect union." Glaude, *Democracy in Black*, 156.

27. Department of Justice, *Investigation of the Ferguson Police Department*, report, March 4, 2015, 98.

28. The White House also tweeted it, saying, "Today is the 57th Anniversary of the day Rosa Parks refused to give up her seat. Pic: President Obama on Rosa Parks bus"—thus ensuring that everyone knew this was the Rosa Parks bus.

29. Juana Summers, "Hillary Clinton's Logo Accidentally Puts Rosa Parks in the Back of the Bus," *Mashable*, December 1, 2015.

30. Only four of the eighty that year went to Black people, and the vast majority over the years have gone to white people. The photo had been cropped because it also included rabid social conservative Anita Bryant, Joe DiMaggio, and Victor Borge. Christina Wilkie, "No, Donald Trump Did Not Win a Medal from the NAACP," *Huffington Post*, October 23, 2016.

31. Adam Shaw, "Sessions Well-Documented Praise of Rosa Parks Belies Racist Claim," *Fox News Politics*, November 18, 2016. Sessions had called for Parks to be awarded the Congressional Gold Medal in 1999 and attached an amendment to an appropriations bill that gave $1 million to Alabama for the Troy University Montgomery Campus Rosa Parks Library and Museum. This, many commentators alleged, demonstrated that Sessions was not a racist.

32. Snapchat also had filters for other women pioneers like Frida Kahlo and Marie Curie. Thanks to Olivia Pearson for alerting me to this.

33. Rosa Parks's actions are regularly compared with present-day acts of opposition. In 2000, country singer Larry Gatlin compared Katherine Harris (Florida's then secretary of state, who helped secure George W. Bush's election) to Rosa Parks. Rancher Cliven Bundy compared himself to Parks when he refused to pay the federal government grazing fees for using federal lands: "I am doing the same thing Rosa Parks did—I am standing up against bad laws which dehumanize us and destroy our freedom."

34. Ta-Nehisi Coates, "Fear of a Black President," *Atlantic*, September 2012.

35. Following public outcry upon George Zimmerman's acquittal in killing Trayvon Martin, President Obama weighed in on the understandability of Black anger and the fact of American progress: "It doesn't mean that racism is eliminated. But you know, when I talk to Malia and Sasha and I listen to their friends and I see them interact, they're better than we are . . . on these issues. And that's true in every community that I've visited all across the country."

36. David A. Graham, "Donald Trump's Narrative of the Life of Frederick Douglass," *Atlantic*, February 1, 2017.

37. Justin Gomer and Christopher Petrella, "Reagan Used MLK Day to Undermine Racial Justice," *Boston Review*, January 15, 2017.

38. Yamiche Alcindor, "In Trump's Feud with John Lewis, Blacks Perceive a Callous Rival," *New York Times*, January 15, 2017.

39. Ari Berman, "The GOP's Attack on Voting Rights Was the Most Under-Covered Story of 2016," *Nation*, November 9, 2016.

40. White House, "Remarks by the President at Howard University Commencement Ceremony," news release, May 7, 2016, https://www.whitehouse.gov/the-press-office/2016/05/07/remarks-president-howard-university-commencement-ceremony.

41. See Lee's *For Freedom's Sake*.

42. James Forman, Jr., *Locking Up Our Own: Crime and Punishment in Black America* (New York: Farrar, Straus and Giroux, 2017), 44. "Far from ignoring the issue of crime by blacks against other blacks, African American officials and their constituents have been consumed by it" (11).

43. Khalil Gibran Muhammad, "Power and Punishment: Two New Books About Race and Crime," *New York Times*, April 14, 2017.

44. Jabari Asim, "Did Cosby Cross the Line?," *Washington Post*, May 24, 2004.

45. "Dr. Bill Cosby Speaks at the 50th Anniversary Commemoration of the Brown v. Topeka Board of Education Supreme Court Decision," Eightcitiesmap.com, http://www.eightcitiesmap.com/transcript_bc.htm.

46. Harris, *Price of the Ticket*, 100–36.

47. Quoted in ibid., 131.

48. Thomas J. Sugrue, "Stories and Legends," *Nation*, June 7, 2010.

49. Charles Cobb, *This Nonviolent Stuff Will Get You Killed: How Guns Made the Civil Rights Movement Possible* (New York: Basic Books, 2014), 247.

50. Jacquelyn Dowd Hall, "The Long Civil Rights Movement," *Journal of American History* 91, no. 4 (March 2005): 1233–35.

51. Romano and Raiford, *The Civil Rights Movement in American Memory*; Renee Romano, *Racial Reckoning* (Cambridge, MA: Harvard University Press, 2014); Lassiter and Crespino, *The Myth of Southern Exceptionalism*; Joseph, *The Black Power Movement*; Clarence Lang, *Black America in the Shadow of the 1960s* (Ann Arbor: University of Michigan Press, 2015); Baldwin and Burrow, *The Domestication of Martin Luther King Jr.*; Herbert Kohl and Cynthia Stokes Brown, *She Would Not Be Moved: How We Tell the Story of Rosa Parks* (New York: New Press, 2007).

52. Reynolds, "I Was a Civil Rights Activist in the 1960s."

53. Ben Mathis-Lilley, "The Generational Divide Between Ferguson Protesters," *Slate*, October 13, 2014.

54. Brianna Ehley, "Huckabee: MLK Would Be 'Appalled' by Black Lives Matter Movement," *Politico*, August 19, 2010.

55. "Oprah Winfrey's Comments About Recent Protests and Ferguson Spark Controversy," *People*, January 1, 2005.

56. Lauren Victoria Burke, "Everyone Has So Much Grand Advice for #BlackLivesMatter, John Lewis Comments," *Politic365*, September 30, 2015.

57. Darren Sands, "Rep. John Lewis: Black Lives Matter Protestors Should Respect Everyone's Right to Be Heard," *BuzzFeed News*, October 30, 2015.

58. Jennie Jarvie, "Why the Gap Between Old and New Black Civil Rights Activists Is Widening," *Los Angeles Times*, July 28, 2016. According to the article, King biographer David Garrow supported older guard trepidation about Black Lives Matter: "'The vast majority of protesters don't have any specific agenda that they're arguing for.' . . . Nor, he added, do they seem to know much about civil rights history."

59. Isaac Singleton, "Dispatch from the Clock Tower," *University News*, St. Louis University, October 31, 2014.

60. Peggy McGlone, "'This Ain't Yo Mama's Civil Rights Movement' T-shirt from Ferguson Donated to Smithsonian Museum," *Washington Post*, March 1, 2016.

61. Megan Lasher, "Read the Full Transcript of Jesse Williams' Powerful Speech on Race at the BET Awards," *Time*, June 27, 2016.

62. Cambria Roth, "Harry Belafonte on Activism, Unrest, and the Importance of Making People Squirm," *Portside*, October 8, 2015.

63. I am grateful for the research of Terron Davis, who is beginning to document this across the country.

64. Vanessa Williams, "SNCC Defends Black Lives Matter Movement, Which Found a More Receptive Audience at the DNC," *Washington Post*, July 29, 2016.

65. Vann Newkirk II, "I'm a Black Lives Matter Activist. Here's What People Get Wrong About Black Lives Matter," *Vox*, December 8, 2015.

66. Parks speech, Box 18, Folder 9, Rosa Parks Collection (RPC), Library of Congress.

CHAPTER ONE: THE LONG MOVEMENT OUTSIDE THE SOUTH

1. Adina Back was one of my first colleague-friends who sought to integrate Northern struggles into our understanding of the era. Because of her untimely death, she did not complete her book, though her work "Exposing the 'Whole Segregation Myth': The Harlem Nine and New York City's School Desegregation Battles" appears in my coedited collection, *Freedom North*, and another chapter, "'Parent Power': Evelina Antonetty, the United Bronx Parents, and the War on Poverty," in

Annelise Orleck's *The War on Poverty: A New Grassroots History* (Athens: University of Georgia Press, 2011). This chapter draws on those chapters, her dissertation, our conversations, and draft chapters for the book she was working on, in particular an interview she did with Mae Mallory in 2000. Chapters in author's possession.

2. Martin Luther King Jr., "The Rising Tide of Racial Consciousness," address at the Golden Anniversary Conference of the National Urban League, September 6, 1960.

3. Fannie Lou Hamer, "The Special Plight and the Role of Black Women," in *Let Nobody Turn Us Around: An African American Anthology*, ed. Manning Marable and Leith Mullings (New York: Rowman & Littlefield, 2009).

4. There has been a raft of books and articles in the past fifteen years, including works by Komozi Woodard and myself, Clarence Taylor, Adina Back, Thomas Sugrue, Craig Wilder, Matthew Countryman, Brian Purnell, Patrick Jones, Martha Biondi, Khalil Muhammad, Nishani Frazier, Donna Murch, Josh Sides, Angela Dillard, Suzanne Smith, Rhonda Williams, Lisa Levenstein, Matthew Delmont, Karen Miller, Heather Thompson, Wendell Pritchett, Jack Dougherty, Shannon King, LaShawn Harris, Mark Speltz, and Kenneth Jolly.

5. See Matthew Lassiter's critique of the de facto/de jure binary "De Facto/De Jure: The Long Shadow of a National Myth" in Lassiter and Crespino, *The Myth of Southern Exceptionalism*. He writes, "The label of de facto segregation . . . is so wrapped in artificial binaries between South and North . . . that historians should discard it as an analytical and descriptive category and evaluate it instead as a cultural and political construct" (28).

6. See Clarence Taylor's important biography of Galamison, *Knocking at Our Own Door: Milton A. Galamison and the Struggle to Integrate New York City's Schools* (New York: Lexington Books, 2001).

7. Wilder, *A Covenant with Color*, 175–217.

8. Ibid. Thanks to Keeanga-Yamahtta Taylor for this citation in the 1938 Underwriters Manual: "If children are living in an area (otherwise favorable) are compelled to attend schools where a majority or a considerable number of the pupils represent a far lower level of society or an incompatible racial element, the neighborhood under consideration will prove far less stable and desirable than if this condition did not exist."

9. Jonna Perrillo, *Uncivil Rights: Teachers, Unions and Race in the Battle for School Equity* (Chicago: University of Chicago Press, 2012), 25.

10. Adina Back, "School Segregation: Naming a Northern Problem," unpublished chapter in author's possession.

11. See also Barbara Ransby, *Ella Baker & the Black Freedom Movement: A Radical Democratic Vision* (Chapel Hill: University of North Carolina Press, 2003), for more detailed discussion of Baker's work with the NAACP nationally and in New York City.

12. See Adina Back dissertation, "Exposing the 'Whole Segregation Myth,'" in *Freedom North*, and Adina Back, "School Segregation: Naming a Northern Problem," and "Taking School Segregation to the Courts," unpublished chapters in author's possession. See also Ransby's *Ella Baker*.

13. Preliminary statement of the Board of Education Resolution of Action, December 23, 1954, Board of Education Papers, as quoted in Back, "School Segregation: Naming a Northern Problem."

14. Ellen Cantarow and Susan Gushee, "Ella Baker: Organizing for Civil Rights," in *Moving the Mountain: Women Working for Social Change*, ed. Ellen Cantarow (New York: Feminist Press, 1980), 68.

15. As quoted in Back, "School Segregation: Naming a Northern Problem."

16. Abraham Lederman, "Pulse of the Public: Union Head Takes Issue with Supt. Jansen," *Amsterdam News*, July 3, 1954.

17. William Jansen, letter to the editor, *Amsterdam News*, November 23, 1954.

18. School leaders and local media referred to "problem schools" with large concentrations of Black students as "X" schools.

19. Paul Zuber, "The De-facto Segregation Hoax," *Liberator* 3, no. 8 (August 1963), as quoted in Purnell, *Fighting Jim Crow in the County of Kings*, 171.

20. Lassiter and Crespino, *The Myth of Southern Exceptionalism*, 27.

21. Researchers identified a predominantly "continental white school" as an elementary or junior high school where Black and Puerto Rican students constituted less than 10 percent of the total population, labeling these schools "Group Y." They characterized a predominantly Black and Puerto Rican elementary school as one in which the Black and Puerto Rican population was 90 percent of the student body, and a Black and Puerto Rican junior high school was one in which the Black and Puerto Rican student body was 85 percent or more of the student body, and labeled these schools "Group X."

22. *PEA Report*, 17, as cited by Back, "School Segregation: Naming a Northern Problem."

23. Ella Baker, interview by Sue Thrasher and Casey Hayden, April 19, 1977, interview 4007, Southern Oral History Program Collection, Wilson Library, University of North Carolina at Chapel Hill, 48–49. See also Joanne Grant, *Ella Baker: Freedom Bound* (New York: John Wiley & Sons, 1998), 96.

24. Edward Hausner, "Parents Picket City Hall Over Delay in Integration; Parents Demand Integration Here," *New York Times*, September 20, 1957.

25. Testimony by Mallory (speaker #38) from the PS #10 PTA at the Board of Education Commission on Integration Public Hearing, January 17, 1957, as quoted in Back, "School Segregation: Naming a Northern Problem."

26. As quoted in Adina Back, "Taking School Segregation to the Courts," unpublished chapter in author's possession. Back interviewed Mallory in 2000 for her book centering on the work of five pioneering Black and Puerto Rican New York activists: Ella Baker, Elaine Bibuld, Mae Mallory, Evelina Antonetty, and Antonia Pantoja.

27. Ibid.

28. "Letters from Prison," Monroe Defense Committee, circa 1962, quoted in Jeanette Merrill and Rosemary Neidenberg, "Mae Mallory: Unforgettable Freedom Fighter Promoted Self-Defense," *Workers World*, February 26, 2009.

29. Ibid.

30. Mae Mallory, interview by Malaika Lumumba, February 27, 1970, Ralph Bunche Oral History Collection, Moorland-Spingarn Research Center, Howard University, Washington, DC, as quoted in Back, "Taking School Segregation to the Courts."

31. See Adina Back "Exposing the Whole Segregation Myth," in *Freedom North*.

32. Back, "Taking School Segregation to the Courts."

33. Back, "Exposing the Whole Segregation Myth," 65.

34. Ibid., 80–81.

35. Ashley Farmer, "Mae Mallory: Forgotten Black Power Intellectual," *Black Perspectives* (blog), June 3, 2016, http://www.aaihs.org/mae-mallory-forgotten-black-power-intellectual/, and e-mail. FBI files in author's possession.

36. Quoted in Sugrue, *Sweet Land*, 193.

37. Joan Cook, "Paul B. Zuber Is Dead at Age 60: Fought Segregated Schools," *New York Times*, March 10, 1987.

38. Quoted in Sugrue, *Sweet Land*, 190.

39. Jennifer de Forest, "The 1958 Harlem School Boycott: Parental Activism and the Struggle for Educational Equity in New York City," *Urban Review* 40, no. 1 (March 2008), 37.

40. Quoted in Wilder, *A Covenant with Color*, 221.

41. Taylor, *Knocking at Our Own Door*.

42. Milton Galamison interview by Robert Penn Warren, June 17, 1964, Robert Penn Warren's Who Speaks for the Negro: An Archival Collection, Robert Penn Warren Center for the Humanities at Vanderbilt University, http://whospeaks.library.vanderbilt.edu/interview/milton-galamison.

43. Taylor, *Civil Rights in New York City*, 104.

44. Quoted in Back, "Exposing the Whole Segregation Myth," 71.

45. Ibid., 68.

46. See Delmont, *Why Busing Failed*, for further evidence and analysis.

47. Tahi Mottl, "Social Conflict and Social Movements: An Exploratory Study of the Black Community of Boston Attempting to Change the Boston Public Schools," PhD diss., Brandeis University, 1976, 147.

48. *New York Age*, February 9, 1952, quoted in Back, "Exposing the Whole Segregation Myth."

49. Clarence Taylor, *Reds at the Blackboard: Communism, Civil Rights, and the New York City Teachers Union* (New York: Columbia University Press, 2011).

50. Matthew Delmont, "Jim Crow Must Go," *Salon*, February 3, 2016.

51. Leonard Buder, "Board to Limit Boycott Penalty," *New York Times*, February 22, 1964.

52. Fred Powledge, "More Than 10,000 March in Protest on School Pairing," *New York Times*, March 13, 1964.

53. Delmont, *Why Busing Failed*, chapt. 1.

54. Ibid., 49–52.

55. Quoted in Delmont, *Why Busing Failed*, 50.

56. Matthew Delmont, "When Black Voters Exited Left," *Atlantic*, March 31, 2016.

57. Gary Orfield, *The Reconstruction of Southern Education: The Schools and the 1964 Civil Rights Act* (New York: Wiley, 1969), 151–207.

58. John Kucsera and Gary Orfield, *New York State's Extreme School Segregation: Inequality, Inaction, and a Damaged Future*, Civil Rights Project/Proyecto Derechos Civiles, March 26, 2014.

59. Renee Graham, "Yes, Boston You Are Racist," *Boston Globe*, March 29, 2017.

60. Ruth Batson interview, Civil Rights Documentation Project, Moorland Spingarn Research Center, Howard University, Washington, DC, 3.

61. Ruth Batson, "Statement to the Boston School Committee," in *The Eyes on the Prize Civil Rights Reader: Documents, Speeches, and Firsthand Accounts from the Black Freedom Struggle, 1954–1990*, ed. Clayborne Carson et al. (New York: Penguin, 1991), 598.

62. Ruth Hill, interview by Ellen Jackson, *Black Women's Oral History Project*, Schlesinger Library, Radcliffe Institute, Harvard University.

63. Alan Lupo, *Liberty's Chosen Home: The Politics of Violence in Boston* (Boston: Little, Brown, 1977), 142–43.

64. Ruth Batson, "Presentation on Mental Health and Desegregation," School Desegregation Conference, November 1, 1978, Box 1, Ruth Batson Papers, Schlesinger Library, Radcliffe Institute, Harvard University.

65. Mel King, *Chain of Change: Struggles for Black Community Development* (Boston: South End Press, 1981), 33.

66. Batson, "Statement to the Boston School Committee," 597–98.

67. Henry Hampton and Steve Fayer, *Voices of Freedom: An Oral History of the Civil Rights Movement from the 1950s through the 1980s* (New York: Bantam, 1991), 589.

68. J. Michael Ross and William M. Berg, *"I Respectfully Disagree with the Judge's Order": The Boston School Desegregation Controversy* (Washington, DC: University Press of America, 1981), 49.

69. Ruth Batson, *A Chronology of the Educational Movement in Boston*, manuscript in Ruth Batson's Papers 2001-M194, Box 1, Schlesinger Library, Radcliffe Institute, Harvard University; Hampton and Fayer, *Voices of Freedom*, 590–91.

70. Batson, *Chronology*, 48.

71. Ibid., 144.

72. Ibid., 116.

73. "Boston: 'I am a symbol of resistance'—Hicks," *New York Times*, November 5, 1967; Emmett Buell, *School Desegregation and Defended Neighborhoods* (Lexington, MA: Lexington Books, 1982), 64–65.

74. Batson, *Chronology*.

75. Ibid., addendum 221a.

76. Ibid., 222.

77. Gerald Gill, "Struggling Yet 'In Freedom's Birthplace': The Civil Rights Movement in Boston, 1955–1965," unpublished paper courtesy of Lyda Peters, 21.

78. See Tess Bundy, "'Revolutions Happen Through Young People!': The Black Student Movement in the Boston Public Schools, 1968–1971," *Journal of Urban History* 43, no. 2 (March 1, 2017).

79. Tatiana Cruz, "'We Took 'Em On': The Latino Movement for Justice, 1965–1980," *Journal of Urban History* 43, no. 2 (March 1, 2017).

80. Robert Dentler and Marvin Scott, *Schools on Trial: An Inside Account of the Boston Desegregation Case* (Cambridge, MA: ABT Books, 1981), 5.

81. Ibid., 5, 16, 28.

82. George Metcalf, *From Little Rock to Boston: The History of School Desegregation* (Westport, CT: Greenwood, 1983), 201.

83. "Southie Fights On," *Time*, September 23, 1974.

84. Garrity's meticulous decision ran 152 pages, withstood numerous appeals, and was given a bar association award the next year. Dentler and Scott, *Schools on Trial*, 4.

85. Ruth Batson, interview by author, January 16, 1991.

86. "Boston: Echoes of Little Rock," *Newsweek*, September 23, 1974.

87. King, *Chain of Change*, 163.

88. Gerald Ford, news conference transcript, October 9, 1974.

89. Buell, *School Desegregation and Defended Neighborhoods*, 16. White had made similar comments in a press release that came out before school started.

90. Ronald Formisano, *Boston Against Busing: Race, Class, and Ethnicity in the 1960s and 1970s* (Chapel Hill: University of North Carolina Press, 1991), xi.

91. Most of these earlier historical works on Boston sought to contextualize white resistance to "busing" as a class-based ethnic struggle and largely ignored Black and Latino organizing in the city. These include J. Anthony Lukas, *Common Ground* (New York: Alfred A. Knopf, 1985); Lupo, *Liberty's Chosen Home*; Metcalf, *From Little Rock to Boston*; and Formisano, *Boston Against Busing*.

92. "Of Thee I Read," *New York Times*, August 4, 2016.

93. San Antonio Independent School District v. Rodriguez, 411 U.S. 35 (1973).

94. Milliken v. Bradley, 418 U.S. 782 (1974).

95. Kucsera and Orfield, *New York State's Extreme School Segregation*.

96. Edwin Rios, "More than One in Three Black Students in the South Attend an Intensely Segregated School," *Mother Jones*, May 26, 2017.

97. "Top Ten Most Segregated Cities in the US," *Atlanta Black Star*, March 14, 2014.

CHAPTER TWO: REVISITING THE UPRISINGS OF THE 1960S AND THE LONG HISTORY OF INJUSTICE AND STRUGGLE THAT PRECEDED THEM

1. Robert Coles, "James Baldwin Back Home," *New York Times*, July 31, 1977.

2. Martin Luther King Jr., "Beyond the Los Angeles Riots: Next Stop: the North," *Saturday Review*, November 13, 1965, 33–35, 105.

3. Ibid.

4. King, "The Rising Tide of Racial Consciousness."

5. "Martin Luther King's Address to the Mass. State Legislature" *Bay State Banner*, January 20, 2014.

6. Chester Himes, *The Quality of Hurt: The Early Years* (New York: Paragon House, 1990), 74.

7. Marnesba Tackett, interview by Michael Balter, 1988, Oral History Program, University of California, Los Angeles, Department of Special Collections, 75.

8. Ibid., 80.

9. John Caughey, *To Kill a Child's Spirit* (Itasca, IL: Peacock Publishers, 1973), 15–16.

10. John and LaRee Caughey, *School Segregation on Our Doorstep: The Los Angeles Story* (Los Angeles: Quail Books, 1966), 10.

11. Gerald Horne, *Fire This Time: The Watts Uprising and the 1960s* (New York: Da Capo Press, 1995), 228.

12. "'Happy Slave' View in Textbooks Scored," *California Eagle*, November 15, 1962.

13. Tackett interview; "Greatest Freedom Rally Here Nets Heroes Over $75,000" *Los Angeles Sentinel*, May 30, 1963.

14. Tackett interview, 128-29.

15. Sides, *L.A. City Limits*, 163; Tackett interview, 106-7.

16. Caughey, *To Kill a Child's Spirit*, 16.

17. Report of the Ad Hoc Committee on Equal Education Opportunity, September 12, 1963, Box 164, John Caughey Papers, Department of Special Collections, UCLA.

18. "Los Angeles Choice: End Segregation or Face Mass Action," *California Eagle*, June 13, 1963.

19. "Baldwin Tells L.A. Bitter Facts on Bias," *California Eagle*, May 16, 1963.

20. "USC Dean Won't Let Farmer Speak" *California Eagle*, November 7, 1963.

21. Tackett interview.

22. "School Board Plan 'Gives Us Nothing'" *California Eagle*, December 5, 1963.

23. NAACP Branch Files, Reel 4.

24. "Muslim Accuses Officer," *Long Beach Independent*, May 5, 1962.

25. Manning Marable, *Malcolm X: A Life of Reinvention* (New York: Penguin, 2011).

26. According to Marable, "Malcolm told Mosque No. 7's Fruit of Islam that the time had come for retribution . . . and he began to recruit members for an assassination team to target LAPD officers. But the Messenger denied him. 'Brother, you don't go to war over a provocation.' . . . He ordered the entire FOI to stand down. Malcolm was stunned; he acquiesced, but with bitter disappointment." Marable, *Malcolm X*, 207-10.

27. Roy Wilkins to Claude Hudson, September 12, 1962, Papers of the NAACP, Selected Branch Files, Part 27, Series D: The West, 1956-1965, Reel 4.

28. Karl Evanzz, *The Judas Factor: The Plot to Kill Malcolm X* (New York: Basic Books, 1992).

29. Mandalit Del Barco, "Critics Decry Naming of LAPD Building for Ex-Chief," NPR, April 24, 2009.

30. "Yorty Calls Racial Situation Tense, Asks Federal Help," *Los Angeles Times*, 1962.

31. "NAACP Head Blasts Report on Brutality," *California Eagle*, January 9, 1964.

32. "Housing Foes Picket King, CRB Banquet," *California Eagle*, February 20, 1964.

33. "Hate Picket Thank God for Chief Parker," *California Eagle*, May 7, 1964.

34. Kurt Schuparra, *Triumph of the Right: The Rise of the California Conservative Movement* (Armonk, NY: M. E. Sharpe, 1998), 105.

35. King, "Beyond the Los Angeles Riots."

36. The Supreme Court declared the proposition unconstitutional in 1967.

37. Celes King, "Black Leadership in Los Angeles," interview by Bruce Tyler and Robin Kelley, 1988, Oral History Program, Department of Special Collections, University Library, University of California, Los Angeles.

38. Quintard Taylor, *In Search of the Racial Frontier: African Americans in the American West, 1528-1990* (New York: W. W. Norton, 1998), 300.

39. Kirse Granat May, *Golden State, Golden Youth: The California Image in Popular Culture, 1955-1966* (Chapel Hill: University of North Carolina Press, 2002), 160. Mayor Sam Yorty had also recently testified to the US Civil Rights Commission that "we have the best race relations in our city of any large city in the United States," Sides, *L.A City Limits*, 169.

40. Peniel Joseph, *Waiting 'Til the Midnight Hour: A Narrative History of Black Power in America* (New York: Henry Holt, 2006), 111.

41. Sides, *L.A. City Limits*, 175; Celes King, "Black Leadership in Los Angeles."

42. Horne, *Fire This Time*, 99.

43. T. M. Tomlinson and David O. Sears, *Los Angeles Riot Study: Negro Attitudes Toward the Riot*, Report MR-97 (UCLA Institute of Government and Public Affairs, 1967).

44. Alfred Ligon, interview by Ranford Hopkins, 1988, Oral History Program, Department of Special Collections, University Library, University of California, Los Angeles.

45. The interim Kerner Report's staff summary of 1,500 pages of data and testimony was ruled too controversial (historians Lerone Bennett and Benjamin Quarles worked on the project). When the White House got its hands on the draft, the budget was cut and most of the staff terminated. Mark Krasovic, *The Newark Frontier: Community Action in the Great Society* (Chicago: University of Chicago Press, 2016), 140–43.

46. "Detroiters Poised for Bias March," *Detroit News*, June 23, 1963.

47. David Brinkley, *Rosa Parks: A Life* (New York: Penguin, 2000), 67.

48. Rosa Parks, Civil Rights Documentation Project, Moorland-Spingarn Research Center, Howard University, Washington, DC, 26.

49. Sidney Fine, *Violence in the Model City: The Cavanagh Administration, Race Relations, and the Detroit Riot of 1967* (Ann Arbor: University of Michigan Press, 1989).

50. Smith, *Dancing in the Street*, 34–35.

51. Hampton, *Voices of Freedom*, 374.

52. General Baker, author interview, October 21, 2009.

53. Smith, *Dancing in the Street*, 37–40.

54. Ibid., 52; Grace Lee Boggs, *Living for Change: An Autobiography* (Minneapolis: University of Minnesota Press, 1998), 126.

55. Fine, *Violence in the Model City*, 106.

56. Angela D. Dillard, *Faith in the City: Preaching Radical Social Change in Detroit* (Ann Arbor: University of Michigan Press, 2007), 257; *Freedom Now! Newsletter*, Folder 2–8, Rosa Parks Papers, Walter P. Reuther Library, Wayne State University. Cleage would later change his name to Jaramogi Abebe Agyeman; Richard and Milton Henry would change their names to Imari and Gaidi Obadele.

57. Dillard, *Faith in the City*, 267.

58. Ibid., 252; Al Cleage, "Nuff to Make You Stop and Think," *Illustrated News*, July 22, 1963.

59. Dillard, *Faith in the City*, 267.

60. "Summary Statement," December 14-15, 1960, Box III: C65, Folder 5, NAACP Papers, Library of Congress.

61. "Police Gulf Grows" *Freedom Now!*, October 14, 1964.

62. May 15, 1963, flyer, http://projects.lib.wayne.edu/12thstreetdetroit/exhibits/show/beforeunrest/panel6.

63. Johnson, *Race and Remembrance*, 56.

64. Elaine Latzman Moon, *Untold Tales, Unsung Heroes: An Oral History of Detroit's African American Community, 1918-1967* (Detroit: Wayne State University Press, 1993), 381.

65. "Youths on the Street Hate, Blame Police," *Michigan Chronicle*, August 20, 1966.

66. Nancy Milio, *9226 Kercheval: The Store that Did Not Burn* (Ann Arbor: University of Michigan Press, 1971), 105.

67. Arthur L. Johnson, *Race and Remembrance: A Memoir* (Detroit: Wayne State University Press, 2008), 57.

68. In 1966, students walked out of Northern High School protesting the lack of college classes and qualified teachers and called for the removal of the principal and security officer.

69. Hampton, *Voices of Freedom*, 374.

70. Frank Joyce, "The 1967 Riot or Rebellion?," *Detroit Free Press*, July 23, 2016.

71. "Youths on the Street Hate, Blame Police."

72. Hampton, *Voices of Freedom*, 391.

73. Smith, *Dancing in the Street*, 197.

74. "The Administration of Justice in the Wake of the Detroit Civil Disorder of July 1967," *Michigan Law Review* 66, no. 7 (May 1968): 1549.

75. Say Burgin "'The Shame of Our Whole Judicial System': George Crockett Jr., the New Bethel Shoot-In and the Nation's Jim Crow Judiciary," in *The Strange Careers of the Jim Crow North*, ed. Brian Purnell and Jeanne Theoharis (New York: New York University Press, forthcoming).

76. As cited by George Crockett, "Recorder's Court and the 1967 Civil Disturbance," *Journal of Urban Law* 45 (Spring/Summer 1968): 841–47.

77. Ibid., 844, 847.

78. George Crockett, "The Role of a Black Judge," *Journal of Public Law* 20 (1971): 394.

79. Earl Selby and Miriam Selby, *Odyssey: Journey Through Black America* (New York: G. P. Putnam's Sons, 1971), 66.

80. Ibid.

81. As cited in Smith, *Dancing in the Street*, 197.

82. Martin Luther King, Jr., "The Role of the Behavioral Scientist in the Civil Rights Movement," address to the APA, September 1, 1967.

83. "Whatever Happened to Mrs. Rosa Parks," *Ebony*, August 1971.

84. John Hersey, *The Algiers Motel Incident* (New York: Hamilton, 1968), 350.

85. Martin Luther King Jr., "The Other America," speech, Grosse Pointe, Michigan, March 14, 1968, www.gphistorical.org/mlk/mlkspeech.

CHAPTER THREE: BEYOND THE REDNECK

1. Gary Young, "White History 101," *Nation*, February 21, 2007.

2. Thompson argues that "once Americans came to believe that the South finally had modernized, they had little desire to intervene any further on behalf of inmate rights anywhere." Heather Thompson, "Blinded by a Barbaric South," in Lassiter and Crespino, *The Myth of Southern Exceptionalism*, 76.

3. The assumption of working-class racism casts racism as a natural response to class anxiety—rather than one that is created, nourished, and reinforced.

4. Mary Dudziak, *Cold War Civil Rights: Race and the Image of American Democracy* (Princeton, NJ: Princeton University Press, 2000).

5. In interviews with Montgomery whites, white researchers sent by Fisk sociologist Preston Valien found widespread paranoia about the boycott but also awe at how Black people were pulling off this organized, months-long boycott. See the Preston and Bonita Valien Papers, Amistad Research Center, Tulane University.

6. See Thomas Sugrue, *The Origins of the Urban Crisis: Race and Inequality in Postwar Detroit* (Princeton, NJ: Princeton University Press, 2014); Purnell, *Fighting Jim Crow in the County of Kings*; Arnold Hirsch, *Making the Second Ghetto: Race and Housing in Chicago* (Chicago: University of Chicago Press, 1993); Becky Nicolaides, *My Blue Heaven: Life and Politics in the Working-Class Suburbs of Los Angeles* (Chicago: University of Chicago Press, 2002); Lisa McGirr, *Suburban Warriors: The Origins of the New American Right* (Princeton, NJ: Princeton University Press, 2001).

7. Payne, *I've Got the Light of Freedom*.

8. Tony Judt, "The Problem of Evil," *New York Review of Books*, February 14, 2008.

9. Ira Berlin makes a similar argument about Northern white disregard for Black rights furthering Southern slavery in the early 1800s in *The Long Emancipation: The Demise of Slavery in the United States* (Cambridge, MA: Harvard University Press, 2015).

10. Karen Miller, *Managing Inequality: Northern Racial Liberalism in Interwar Detroit* (New York: New York University Press, 2014).

11. Ibid., 4.

12. Martin Luther King, Jr., *Where Do We Go From Here: Chaos and Community?* (Boston: Beacon Press, 2010).

13. Carol Anderson, *White Rage* (New York: Bloomsbury, 2016), 3. See also Eduardo Bonilla-Silva, *Racism Without Racists: Color-Blind Racism and the Persistence of Racial Inequality* (Lanham, MD: Rowman & Littlefield, 2003).

14. In one article, Dearborn mayor Orville Hubbard boasted: "Negroes can't get in here. . . . These people are so anti-colored, much more than you in Alabama." David Goode, *Orvie, the Dictator of Dearborn* (Detroit: Wayne State University Press, 1989).

15. Delmont, *Why Busing Failed*, 54–76.

16. Ibid., 54.

17. Kevin Kruse, *White Flight: Atlanta and the Making of Modern Conservatism* (Princeton, NJ: Princeton University Press, 2005), 6. By the 1970s, according to historian Nancy MacLean, conservatives had largely abandoned a language of "massive resistance," "states' rights," and "anticommunism" for "color-blindness" and formal equality (against "special preferences")—seeing it as a way to attract more white working- and middle-class people and rehabilitate the appeal of conservatism. Nancy MacLean, *Freedom Is Not Enough: The Opening of the American Workplace* (Cambridge, MA: Harvard University Press, 2006).

18. In some ways, this idea for realignment began with a February 1963 article by the *National Review*'s editor William Rusher calling for the Republican Party's realignment by appealing to white Southerners disaffected with the Democratic Party and the civil rights movement. Jeet Heer, "How the Southern Strategy Made Donald Trump Possible," *New Republic*, February 18, 2016.

19. Rick Perlstein, "Exclusive: Lee Atwater's Infamous Interview on the Southern Strategy," *Nation*, November 13, 2012.

20. Nixon speechwriter Jeffrey Hart called it a "border state" strategy. Nixon's 1968 campaign ads included photos of urban riots in Northern cities.

21. Noliwe Rooks, *Cutting School: Privatization, Segregation, and the End of Public Education* (New York: New Press, 2017), 117.

22. As John Ehrlichman later told *Harper's* writer Dan Baum, "The Nixon campaign in 1968, and the Nixon White House after that, had two enemies: the antiwar left and black people. . . . We knew we couldn't make it illegal to be either against the war or black[s], but by getting the public to associate the hippies with marijuana and blacks with heroin, and then criminalizing both heavily, we could disrupt those communities. We could arrest their leaders, raid their homes, break up their meetings, and vilify them night after night on the evening news. Did we know we were lying about the drugs? Of course we did." Dan Baum, "Legalize It All," *Harper's* (April 2016).

23. Hampton, *Voices of Freedom*, 589.

24. Batson, *Chronology*, 134.

25. Purnell, *Fighting Jim Crow*, 154–55.

26. As Fredrick Harris shows in *The Price of the Ticket*, themes of personal responsibility that dominate President Obama's approach on Black issues marry two discursive traditions: the politics of respectability and the increasing turn in the social sciences to "cultural" explanations of race.

27. Alice O'Connor, *Poverty Knowledge: Social Science, Social Policy, and the Poor in Twentieth-Century US History* (Princeton, NJ: Princeton University Press, 2002).

28. St. Clair Drake and Horace Cayton, *Black Metropolis: A Study of Negro Life in a Northern City* (New York: Harcourt Brace, 1945). While Drake and Cayton made clear that limited job, housing, and educational opportunities for Black people in Chicago resulted from political decision and white behavior, the book's ethnography of Bronzeville still kept one eye trained on Black behavior. The original research for their study was framed around investigating juvenile delinquency, which undeniably affected the ways the ethnography proceeded. Henri Peretz, "The Making of *Black Metropolis*," *Annals of America Academy of Political and Social Science* 595 (September 2004).

29. E. Franklin Frazier, *The Negro Family in the United States* (New York: Dryden Press, 1948); Gunnar Myrdal, *An American Dilemma: The Negro Problem and American Democracy* (New York: Harper & Row, 1944).

30. Lee Rainwater, *Behind Ghetto Walls: Black Family Life in a Federal Slum* (New York: Aldine Transaction Publications, 1970); Ulf Hannerz, *Soulside: Inquiries into Ghetto Culture and Community* (New York: Columbia University Press, 1969); Eliot Lebow, *Tally's Corners: A Study of Negro Streetcorner Men* (New York: Little, Brown, 1967).

31. See Gaston Alonso, "Culture Trap," in *Our Schools Suck: Students Talk to a Segregated Nation on the Failures of Urban Education*, ed. Gaston Alonso, Noel Anderson, Celina Su, and Jeanne Theoharis (New York: New York University Press, 2009).

32. Oscar Lewis, *La Vida: A Puerto Rican Family in the Culture of Poverty, San Juan and New York* (New York: Random House, 1966). Lewis, who is credited with coining the term "culture of poverty," had stressed that structural forces produce self-defeating cultural practices, but it was the cultural part of his argument that gained public attention.

33. US Department of Labor Office of Policy Planning and Research, *The Negro Family: A Case for National Action* [often referred to as the Moynihan Report], March 1965.

34. King, "The Role of the Behavioral Scientist."

35. According to political scientist Naomi Murakawa, in her study of the liberal 1960s roots of contemporary mass incarceration, "liberals 'criminalized' the race problem often toward the end of compelling reform. . . . In this sense, liberal law-and-order agendas flowed from an underlying assumption of racism: racism was an individual whim, an irrationality and therefore racism could be corrected with 'state-building' . . . that is, the replacement of personalized power of government officials with codified, standardized and formalized authority." Thus mandatory minimums in sentencing were pushed partly as a way to get away from the bias of judges—to devastating result. Naomi Murakawa, *The First Civil Right: How Liberals Built Prison America* (New York: Oxford University Press, 2014), 9–11.

36. Robin D. G. Kelley, *Yo Mama's Disfunktional! Fighting the Culture Wars in Urban America* (Boston: Beacon Press, 1997); Alonso et al., *Our Schools Suck*.

37. These sorts of cultural approaches also dominated the Obama administration's initiative, My Brother's Keeper, which focused on cultural skills and mentoring for Black boys (rather than opening up job and educational opportunities and changing law enforcement strategies and assumptions).

38. As Coates observes: "The bearer of this unfortunate heritage [President Obama] feebly urging 'positive habits and behavior' while his country imprisons some ungodly number of black men may well be greeted with applause in some quarters. The black freedom struggle is not about raising a race of hyper-moral super-humans. It is about all people garnering the right to live like the normal humans they are." Ta-Nehisi Coates, "Black Pathology and the Closing of the American Mind," *Atlantic* (March 21, 2014). Obama steadfastly defended the appropriateness of these cultural framings in speeches geared toward Black people: "It's true that if I'm giving a commencement at Morehouse that I will have a conversation with young black men about taking responsibility as fathers that I probably will not have with the women of Barnard. And I make no apologies for that." "Obama Defends Respectability Politics Speeches Criticized by Black Progressives," *Slate*, May 12, 2015.

CHAPTER FOUR: THE MEDIA WAS OFTEN AN OBSTACLE TO THE STRUGGLE FOR RACIAL JUSTICE

1. Malcolm X, "At the Audubon," December 13, 1964, in *Malcolm X Speaks: Selected Speeches and Statements* (New York: Grove Press, 1965.).

2. "A Summer Carnival of Riot," editorial, *Los Angeles Times* August 13, 1965.

3. "Anarchy Must End," editorial, *Los Angeles Times*, August 14, 1965.

4. "A Time for Prayer," editorial, *Los Angeles Times*, August 15, 1965; "A City Demands the Answers," editorial, *Los Angeles Times*, August 17, 1965.

5. Theodore H. White, "Lessons of Los Angeles," *Los Angeles Times*, August 22, 1965.

6. "We Must Speak to Each Other," editorial, *Los Angeles Times*, August 29, 1965.

7. Ibid.

8. Christopher Strain, *Pure Fire: Self-Defense as Activism in the Civil Rights Era* (Athens: University of Georgia, 2005), 124.

9. W. Arthur Garrity, Papers on the Boston Schools Desegregation Case 1972–1977, University of Massachusetts, Boston.

10. Gene Roberts and Hank Klibanoff, *The Race Beat: The Press, the Civil Rights Struggle, and the Awakening of a Nation* (New York: Alfred A. Knopf, 2006), 407.

11. Not to mention that, for decades prior to 1955, they had ignored the deep injustice and those who sought to highlight it in the South.

12. Stokely Carmichael, "Black Power Address at UC Berkeley," October 29, 1966, available at *American Rhetoric*, www.americanrhetoric.com.

13. Delmont, *Why Busing Failed*; Mark Speltz, *North of Dixie: Civil Rights Photography Beyond the South* (Los Angeles: J. Paul Getty Museum, 2016).

14. Speltz, *North of Dixie*, 26.

15. In the avalanche of praise for *The Race Beat*, few reviewers seemed to notice the authors had not analyzed the ways the press covered the movement in Northern cities to reach their laudatory conclusions of the role of the media in the civil rights movement.

16. "How the Civil Rights Movement Was Covered in Birmingham," *All Things Considered*, NPR, June 18, 2013.

17. See "The Boycott's 'Success,'" editorial, *New York Times*, September 15, 1964.

18. A chief complaint of South Bostonians against the *Globe* was the fact that resistance was happening throughout the city, but they alone were pictured as the bad guys.

19. Christine Rossell's study of the *Boston Globe* during desegregation showed that its focus on antidesegregation whites and desegregation-related conflicts led the public to have an overinflated sense of the costs and problems associated with desegregation, and thus the public was more likely to oppose it. Robert Taylor, *Desegregation in Boston and Buffalo: The Influence of Local Leaders* (Albany: State University of New York Press, 1998), 85.

20. Robert Levey, "'Busing'—A Non-Word with Racial Emphasis," *Boston Globe*, June 6, 1965.

21. Robert Levey, "School Board—NAACP Parley Short, Unhappy," *Boston Globe*, August 16, 1963; Robert Levey, "School Report Stirs New Storm," *Boston Globe*, April 16, 1965; Anne Kirchheimer, "White Parents Shape Antibusing Campaign," *Boston Globe*, November 24, 1974.

22. Batson, *Chronology*, 264.

23. Robert Reinhold, "More Segregated than Ever," *New York Times*, September 30, 1973.

24. "A Balanced Ruling for Boston," *Boston Globe*, June 25, 1974.

25. "Racial imbalance" was the Northern term for segregation to describe schools with a student body that was more than 50 percent nonwhite; an all-white school was still considered a racially balanced school. The 1965 Massachusetts Racial Imbalance Act (which the Boston School Committee fought to repeal and then sought to delay in court) applied only to schools that were more than 50 percent nonwhite.

26. "Ready for School Opening," editorial, *Boston Globe*, September 6, 1974; "A Fine Beginning," editorial, *Boston Globe*, September 13, 1974. The paper ultimately did use the term "desegregation" in its news coverage but provided little historical context.

27. "Opposition to Busing Led by Publicity-Shy ROAR," *Boston Globe*, September 27, 1974.

28. Jon Hillson, *The Battle of Boston* (New York: Pathfinder Press, 1977), 89.

29. See Delmont, *Why Busing Failed*, for a longer exposition of this phenomenon.

30. Two prodesegregation marches at the end of 1974 drew a combined 14,500 people, and a 40,000-person march for desegregation and peace took place in Boston in 1975—yet captured far less attention. For more, see Jeanne Theoharis, "'I'd Rather Go to School in the South': How Boston's School Desegregation Complicates the Civil Rights Paradigm," in Theoharis and Woodard, *Freedom North*, 139.

31. Ibid.

32. Benjamin Fine, "Northern Cities Confront the Problem of De Facto Segregation," *New York Times*, February 10, 1957.

33. Ibid.

34. "And in New York Schools," editorial, *New York Times*, September 4, 1963.

35. Benjamin Fine, "Negro Sues City on School Zoning," *New York Times*, July 18, 1957.

36. Robert H. Tertet, "City School Integration," *New York Times*, October 22, 1963.

37. "Calm Rights Leader: Milton Arthur Galamison," *New York Times*, December 17, 1963; "Boycotting a 600 Level School," editorial, *New York Times*, January 21, 1965; "The School Boycott Spreads," editorial, *New York Times*, February 11, 1965; Leonard Buder, "New Men for the Board and Some Surprises," *New York Times*, July 21, 1968; "Brooklyn Sit-In Bars 2nd Hearing by School Board," *New York Times*, December 21, 1966.

38. "Now Schools," editorial, *New York Times*, September 8, 1963.

39. "A Boycott Solves Nothing," editorial, *New York Times*, January 31, 1964; "No More School Boycotts," editorial, *New York Times*, February 3, 1964. Similar accusations of violence occurred over the summer, when Brooklyn CORE began to make plans for a disruptive stall-in around opening day of the World's Fair. See Purnell, *Fighting Jim Crow*, 257–72.

40. "A Boycott Solves Nothing," editorial, *New York Times*, January 31, 1964.

41. "The School Boycott," editorial, *New York Times*, February 4, 1964.

42. Ibid.

43. McCandlish Phillips, "Many Clergymen and Educators Say Boycott Dramatized Negro's Aspirations," *New York Times*, February 4, 1964.

44. Fred Powledge, "More Than 10,000 March in Protest of School Pairing," *New York Times*, March 13, 1964.

45. "Now Schools," *New York Times*.

46. "The Boycott's 'Success,'" editorial *New York Times*, September 15, 1964.

47. "Birmingham Shut Schools Scheduled for Integration," *New York Times*, September 5, 1963; "Standing Up to Wallace" *New York Times*, September 7, 1963.

48. Brian Purnell, "Drive Awhile for Freedom: Brooklyn CORE's 1964 Stall-In and Public Discourse on Protest Violence," in Theoharis and Woodard, *Groundwork*, 53.

49. "This Helps Civil Rights?," editorial, *New York Times*, April 11, 1964.

50. Purnell, *Fighting Jim Crow in the County of Kings*, 257–59; Wilder, *A Covenant with Color*, 236.

51. Joseph Tirella, "A Gun to the Heart of the City?," *Slate*, April 22, 2014.

52. Wilder, *Covenant with Color*, 238.

53. Johnson, *Race and Remembrance*, 57.

54. Dan Aldridge, interview by Detroit Historical Society, June 22, 2016, http://detroit1967 .detroithistorical.org/items/show/357.

55. All as quoted in Horne, *Fire This Time*, 325.

56. Ibid.

57. Hampton, *Voices of Freedom*, 470.

58. Maya Angelou, *A Song Flung Up to Heaven* (New York: Virago, 2002), 82–83.

59. Thomas Pynchon, "A Journey into the Mind of Watts," *New York Times Magazine*, June 6, 1966.

60. Jack Jones, "The View from Watts Today: Parents and Children Hunger for Knowledge," *Los Angeles Times*, July 20, 1967.

61. Peter Levy, "The Media and H. Rap Brown: Friend or Foe of Jim Crow," in Purnell and Theoharis, *The Strange Careers of the Jim Crow North*.

62. "Walkout: The True Story of the Historic 1968 Chicano Student Walkout in East LA," *Democracy Now* (March 29, 2006).

63. Sugrue, *Sweet Land*, 300.

64. As quoted in Speltz, *North of Dixie*, 86.

65. Spencer, *The Revolution Has Come*, 72.

66. James Dao, "40 Years Later Civil Rights Makes Page One," *New York Times*, July 13, 2004.

67. Kate Taylor, "Race and Class Collide in a Plan for Two Brooklyn Schools," *New York Times*, September 22, 2015.

68. Ujju Aggarwal and Donna Nevel, "Building Justice: School Segregation in NYC Schools Is No Accident," *City Limits*, October 24, 2016.

69. "Harlem Schools Are Left to Fail as Those Not Far Away Thrive," *New York Times,* January 24, 2017.

70. Farah Stockman, "Still Deciding What Busing Gained and What It Cost," *Boston Globe,* June 21, 2014.

71. Meghan Irons, Shelley Murphy, and Jenna Russell, "History Rolled In on a Yellow School Bus," *Boston Globe,* September 6, 2014.

72. Farah Stockman, "Did Busing Slow Boston's Desegregation?," *Boston Globe,* August 9, 2015.

73. Farah Stockman published a lengthy story in 2015 in the *Globe* about Ruth Batson—without any corrective or admission about how the *Globe* had backgrounded Batson's work for decades—and framed it as a battle between two women, Batson and Hicks. Farah Stockman, "How a Standoff over Schools Changed the Country," *Boston Globe,* December 20, 2015.

74. Doug Smith, "Stunned by the Watts Riots, the L.A. Times Struggled to Make Sense of the Violence," *Los Angeles Times,* August 12, 2015.

75. Martin Luther King Jr., *Where Do We Go from Here: Chaos or Community?* (1967; Boston: Beacon Press, 2010), 5.

CHAPTER FIVE: BEYOND A BUS SEAT

1. Theoharis, *The Rebellious Life of Mrs. Rosa Parks,* 70.

2. Ruth Hill, *Black Women's Oral History Project from the Schlesinger Library* (Westport, CT: Mechler, 1991), 117.

3. Handwritten notes from Highlander, Folder 2-18, Rosa Parks Papers, Walter Reuther Library, Wayne State University, Detroit.

4. Ella Baker, "Bigger Than a Hamburger," April 1960, downloaded at http://hutchinscenter.fas .harvard.edu/sites/all/files/Bigger%20than%20a%20Hamburger%20-%20Ella%20Baker.pdf.

5. Hogan, *Many Minds, One Heart*; Jeffries, *Bloody Lowndes*; Payne, *I've Got the Light of Freedom.*

6. Derek Seidman, "The History of the SNCC Research Department," *Eyes on the Ties,* May 2, 2017, https://news.littlesis.org/2017/05/02/the-hidden-history-of-the-sncc-research-department/.

7. Charlie Cobb, *This Nonviolent Stuff Will Get You Killed: How Guns Made the Civil Rights Movement Possible* (New York: Basic, 2014), 4.

8. "Full Transcript: President Obama's Speech on the 50th Anniversary of the March on Washington," *Washington Post,* August 28, 2013.

9. Payne, *I've Got the Light of Freedom,* xiii.

10. Aisha Harris, "How True Is The Butler?," *Slate,* August 15, 2013.

11. See Williams, *Concrete Demands.*

12. The *New York Times* called *The Butler* "a brilliantly truthful film on a subject that is usually shrouded in wishful thinking, mythmongering and outright denial." A. O. Scott, "Black Man, White House, and History," *New York Times,* August 15, 2013.

13. Will Jones, "The Forgotten Radical History of the March on Washington," *Dissent* (Spring 2013).

14. Robin D. G. Kelley, *Freedom Dreams: The Black Radical Imagination* (Boston: Beacon Press, 2002).

15. See Danielle McGuire's *At the Dark End of the Street: Black Women, Rape, and Resistance—A New History of the Civil Rights Movement from Rosa Parks to the Rise of Black Power* (New York: Alfred A. Knopf, 2010).

16. Phillip Hoose, *Claudette Colvin: Twice Toward Justice* (New York: Farrar, Straus & Giroux, 2009), 23–24.

17. "Jazz Drummer Dies in Electric Chair," *Jet,* April 10, 1958.

18. Transcript of a statement King made at a prayer pilgrimage following Reeves's execution can be found here: http://okra.stanford.edu/transcription/document_images/Vol04Scans/396_6 -Apr-1958_Statement%20Delivered%20-%20Jeremiah%20Reeves.pdf.

19. Mamie Till-Mobley says that Parks told her this when they met in 1989. Mamie Till-Mobley and Christopher Benson, *Death of Innocence: The Story of the Hate Crime That Changed America* (New York: Random House, 2003), 257.

20. Box 18, Folder 10, RPC.

21. Troy Jackson, *Becoming King* (Lexington: University of Kentucky Press, 2008).

22. Martin Luther King, Jr., "I Have a Dream," August 28, 1963, full text available at *American Rhetoric*.

23. Jones, "Forgotten Radical History."

24. Gwendolyn Zoharah Simmons," From Little Memphis Girl to Mississippi Amazon," in *Hands on the Freedom Plow*; Jeffries, *Bloody Lowndes*.

25. Amy Nathan Wright, "The 1968 Poor People's Campaign, Marks, Mississippi, and the Mule Train," in Crosby, *Civil Rights History from the Ground Up*, 110–11.

26. Thomas Jackson, *From Civil Rights to Human Rights: Martin Luther King, Jr., and the Struggle for Economic Rights* (Philadelphia: University of Pennsylvania Press, 2007), 343.

27. These included the steering committee composed of key Native American, Latino, and poor white leaders including Hank Adams, Robert Fulcher, Corky Gonzalez, Reis Tijerina, Grace Mora Newman, Peggy Terry, Gerena Valentin, and Tillie Walker. Others in attendance included John Lewis, Carl Braden, Myles Horton, Appalachian Volunteers from Kentucky, welfare rights activists, California farmworkers, organized tenants, and the American Friends Service Committee.

28. Michael K. Honey, *Going Down Jericho Road: The Memphis Strike, Martin Luther King's Last Campaign* (New York: W. W. Norton, 2007), 186.

29. Wright, "The 1968 Poor People's Campaign," 110.

30. Ibid., 128.

31. Roland Freeman, *The Mule Train: A Journey of Hope Remembered* (Nashville: Rutledge Hill Press, 1998), 109.

32. John Kelley, "Before Occupy There Was Resurrection City," *Washington Post*, December 2, 2011.

33. Wright, "The 1968 Poor People's Campaign," 131–34.

34. As quoted in ibid., 137.

35. Dorothy Roberts, *Killing the Black Body: Race, Reproduction, and the Meaning of Liberty* (New York: Vintage, 1988), 207.

36. Mary Poole, *The Segregated Origins of Social Security: African Americans and the Welfare State* (Chapel Hill: University of North Carolina Press, 2006).

37. Jill Quadagno, *The Color of Welfare: How Racism Undermined the War on Poverty* (New York: Oxford University Press, 1994), 19–24; ibid.

38. Spencer, *The Revolution Has Come*.

39. Johnnie Tillmon, "Welfare Is a Women's Issue," *Ms.*, 1972.

40. Premilla Nadasen "'We Do Whatever Becomes Necessary': Johnnie Tillmon, Welfare Rights and Black Power," in *Want to Start a Revolution?: Radical Women in the Black Freedom Struggle*, ed. Dayo Gore, Jeanne Theoharis, and Komozi Woodard (New York: New York University Press, 2009).

41. Alejandra Marchevsky, "Forging a Black-Brown Movement: Chicana and Black Women Organizing for Welfare Rights," in *Chicana Movidas: New Narratives of Women's Activism and Feminism in the Movimiento Era*, ed. Maylei Blackwell, Maria Cotera, and Dionne Espinosa (Austin: University of Texas Press, forthcoming).

42. Catherine Jermany, interview by Premilla Nadasen, October 11, 2003, quoted in Marchevsky, "Forging a Black-Brown Movement."

43. "Watts Lame, Blind, Poor Protest Cut in Medical Care," *Jet*, October 26, 1967, 16.

44. Quoted in Marchevsky, "Forging a Black-Brown Movement."

45. Ibid.

46. CWRO broke with NWRO when the NWRO rejected Escalante's proposal to include Spanish-language services among its key demands.

47. Nadasen, "'We Do Whatever Becomes Necessary,'" 324.

48. Michael Katz, *In the Shadow of the Poorhouse: A Social History of Welfare in America* (New York: Basic Books, 1996), 275–76. With origins in a World War II surplus food subsidy program, food stamps commenced as an early 1960s pilot program, became nationwide with the Food Stamp Act of 1964, and expanded in 1977.

49. See Orleck, *Storming Caesar's Palace*; Nadasen, *Welfare Warriors*; Kornbluh, *The Battle for Welfare Rights*; Levenstein, *A Movement without Marches*; Alejandra Marchevsky and Jeanne Theoharis, *Not Working: Latina Immigrants, Low-Wage Jobs and the Failure of Welfare Reform* (New York: New York University Press, 2006).

50. Martin Luther King Jr., "Remaining Awake Through a Great Revolution," in *A Knock at Midnight* (New York: Warner Books, 1998).

51. Laura Visser-Maessen, *Robert Parris Moses: A Life in Civil Rights and Leadership at the Grassroots* (Chapel Hill: University of North Carolina Press, 2016), 282.

52. Lorraine Hansberry, unpublished letter to the editor, *New York Times*, April 23, 1964, in *To Be Young, Gifted and Black: Lorraine Hansberry in Her Own Words* (New York: Signet, 1970), 51–52. Thanks to Balthazar Becker for bringing this letter to my attention.

53. See Gore, *Radicalism at the Crossroads*; Carol Anderson, *Eyes off the Prize: The United Nations and the African American Struggle for Human Rights, 1944–1955* (New York: Cambridge University Press, 2003); Penny Von Eschen, *Race Against Empire: Black Americans and Anticolonialism, 1937–1957* (Ithaca, NY: Cornell University Press, 1997); Kimberley Phillips, *War! What Is It Good For? Black Freedom Struggles and the U.S. Military from World War II to Iraq* (Chapel Hill: University of North Carolina Press, 2012); Kevin Gaines, *American Africans in Ghana: Black Expatriates and the Civil Rights Era* (Chapel Hill: University of North Carolina Press, 2008).

54. Fannie Lou Hamer, "What Have We to Hail?," speech delivered in Kentucky, summer 1968, in *The Speeches of Fannie Lou Hamer* (Jackson: University of Mississippi Press, 2011).

55. Stephen Carter, "The Beauty of Julian Bond's Voice," *Chicago Tribune*, August 17, 2015.

56. Julian Bond's "Vietnam: An Antiwar Comic" (1967) can be downloaded here: http://www2 .iath.virginia.edu/sixties/HTML_docs/Exhibits/Bond/Bond_comic_page_01.html.

57. Pamela Pennock, *The Rise of the Arab American Left: Activists, Allies, and Their Fight Against Imperialism and Racism, 1960s–1980s* (Chapel Hill: University of North Carolina Press, 2017), 84–86.

58. "Dr. King's Error," editorial, *New York Times*, April 7, 1967; "N.A.A.C.P. Decries Stand of Martin Luther King," *New York Times*, April 11, 1967.

59. Martin Luther King Jr., "Beyond Vietnam—A Time to Break Silence," speech, Riverside Church, New York City, April, 1967.

60. Roxanne Brown, "Mother of the Movement: Nation Honors Rosa Parks with Birthday Observance," *Ebony*, February 1988.

61. Box 19, Folder "General 1956–1964, 1972–1990," RPC.

62. Riptide Communications, "Diverse Coalition of Americans Speak Out Against War as Solution to Terrorism," press release, September 17, 2001, printed in *Yes! Magazine*.

CHAPTER SIX: THE GREAT MAN VIEW OF HISTORY, PART I

1. Quoted in Augustus Hawkins, "Inside Government: The Agonies of Social Change," *Los Angeles Sentinel*, March 21, 1968.

2. Angela Davis, International Women's Day speech, London's Southbank Centre, March 8, 2017. Video found here: https://www.facebook.com/AFROPUNK/videos/10154505324126623/.

3. Barbara Johns (1935–1961) Jim Crow Stories, *The Rise and Fall of Jim Crow*, PBS.

4. Bob Smith, *They Closed Their Schools: Prince Edward County, Virginia, 1951–1964* (Greensboro: University of North Carolina Press, 1965), 27–35.

5. Ibid.

6. Ibid, 48.

7. Taylor Branch, *Parting the Waters: America in the King Years, 1954–63* (New York: Simon and Schuster, 1988), 48.

8. As quoted in Willy S. Leventhal, ed., *The Children Coming On: A Retrospective of the Montgomery Bus Boycott and the Oral Histories of Boycott Participants* (New York: Black Belt Press, 1998), 156–58.

9. Hoose, *Claudette Colvin*, 88.

10. As quoted in Hogan, *Many Minds, One Heart*, 32.

11. Workshop with Rosa Parks, Septima Clark, and others, May 27, 1960, Highlander UC 515A, tape 202, part 1, Highlander Papers, State Historical Society of Wisconsin.

12. See Branch, *Parting the Waters*; Jackson, *From Civil Rights to Human Rights*.

13. Judith Kafka, *The History of "Zero Tolerance" in American Public Schools* (New York: Palgrave, 2011).

14. Jefferson High School had recently been transferred, with the rest of the Black high schools, from the southern conference to the eastern conference, which included these East LA schools, so the schools were having regular contact through athletics, and the students likely knew each other.

15. Ernesto Chavez, *"¡Mi Raza Primero!": Nationalism, Identity and Insurgency in the Chicano Movement in Los Angeles, 1966–1978* (Berkeley: University of California Press, 2002), 45.

16. Ian Haney Lopez, *Racism on Trial: The Chicano Fight for Justice* (Cambridge, MA: Harvard University Press, 2003), 20.

17. F. Arturo Rosales, *Chicano! The History of the Mexican American Civil Rights Movement* (Houston: Arte Publico Press, 1997), 190.

18. "Student Disorders Erupt at 4 High Schools; Policeman Hurt," *Los Angeles Times*, March 7, 1968. By the early 1930s, most Black students in the city attended Jefferson or Jordan High School; Jefferson did not become all-Black until after World War II.

19. Lawrence Bible, author interview, June 12, 2006.

20. Chavez, *"¡Mi Raza Primera!,"* 47.

21. Bible interview.

22. Bible interview.

23. Bible continued to encounter these assumptions when he attended UCLA; because he'd attended all-Black Jefferson, which was considered a bad school, they "put you in a category."

24. Bob Lucas, "Black Boycott Victor," *Los Angeles Sentinel*, March 14, 1968.

25. Paul Houston, "3 Negro Officials Take Over at Jefferson High," *Los Angeles Times*, March 14, 1968.

26. Robert Long Mauller, "An Analysis of the Conflicts and the Community Relationships in Eight Secondary Schools of the Los Angeles Unified School District, 1967–1969," PhD diss., University of California, Los Angeles, 1976, 111. The meeting was adjourned before anyone from the East LA schools got to address the board.

27. Jack McCurdy, "1,000 Walk Out in School Boycott," *Los Angeles Times*, March 9, 1968.

28. Bob Lucas, "'Black' Boycott Victory," *Los Angeles Sentinel*, March 14, 1968.

29. Bible interview.

30. The footage was discovered decades later, during the making of the documentary series *Chicano*—it had been saved by the news stations but never shown.

31. The decision not to indict members of local Black groups, like the Black Congress, the US Organization, or the United Parents Council, who were supporting Black student protesters, on conspiracy charges similar to those of their Chicano counterparts might have stemmed from the recent assassination of Martin Luther King on April 4. Black community leaders maintained order in the wake of King's assassination—but officials still feared potential trouble.

32. Dial Torgenerson, "Negro Strike Forces 2-School Shutdown," *Los Angeles Times*, March 11, 1969.

33. Bundy, "Revolutions Happen Through Young People!"

34. "Walkout: The True Story of the Historic 1968 Chicano Student Walkout in East L.A.," *Democracy Now!*

CHAPTER SEVEN: THE GREAT MAN VIEW OF HISTORY, PART II

1. Described as an "unassuming seamstress" who undertook a "small act of defiance" in Maria Newman, "Thousands Pay Final Respects to Rosa Parks in Detroit," *New York Times*, November 2, 2005; an "accidental matriarch" in Michael Janofsky, "Thousands Gather at the Capitol to Remember a Hero," *New York Times*, October 31, 2005; as "quiet" and "humble" in "Parks Remembered for Her Courage, Humility," CNN.com, October 20, 2005; as "humble" in Carlos Osorio, Associated Press, "Thousands Attend Rosa Parks funeral in Detroit," *USA Today*, November 2, 2005; and as "quiet" in Peter Slevin, "A Quiet Woman's Resonant Farewell," *Washington Post*, November 2, 2005.

2. Described as the "matriarch of the movement" in "Coretta Scott King Dies," CNN.com, January 31, 2006, and in Shaila Dewan and Elisabeth Bumiller, "At Mrs. King's Funeral, a Mix of Elegy and Politics," *New York Times*, February 8, 2006; as having "grace and serenity" in Associated Press, "Coretta Scott King Dead at 78," MSNBC.com, January 31, 2006; as an "avid proselytizer for his vision" in Peter Applebome, "Coretta Scott King, 78, Widow of Dr. Martin Luther King Jr., Dies," *New York Times*, January 31, 2006; as having "poise, grace and enduring dignity" in Larry Copeland, "'Queen of Black America' Coretta Scott King Dies at 78," *USA Today*, January 31, 2006; as the "closest thing possible to African-American royalty" in Ernie Suggs, "Coretta Scott King 1927–2006," *Atlanta Journal-Constitution*, January 31, 2006.

3. Dewan and Bumiller, "At Mrs. King's Funeral, a Mix of Elegy and Politics."

4. When MSNBC published my piece on women and the March on Washington around the event's fiftieth anniversary, it cut the section on the important roles women, including Anna Arnold Hedgeman, had played in the march's organization and made it just about the sexism.

5. Erin McCann, "Coretta Scott King's 1986 Statement to the Senate About Jeff Sessions," *New York Times*, February 8, 2017.

6. Jordain Carney, "Sanders, Dems Read Coretta Scott King's Letter After Warren Silenced," *Hill*, February 8, 2017.

7. Warren read the letter live on Facebook. It was watched by more than two million people, and news outlets covered it assiduously.

8. Barbara Reynolds, "The Biggest Problem with 'Selma' Has Nothing to Do with LBJ or the Oscars," *Washington Post*, January 19, 2015.

9. Coretta Scott King, "Address to Antioch Reunion," *Antiochian*, June 25, 2004, www.antioch-college.edu/Antiochian/archive/Antiochian_2004fall/reunion/king/.

10. Ibid.

11. "Carson's Next Volume of MLK Work: 10/98; In King's Own Words: New Book Explores Courtship, Marriage," *Stanford Report*, October 28, 1998, http://news.stanford.edu/news/1998/october28/mlkcarson1028.html.

12. James Baldwin, "The Dangerous Road Before Martin Luther King," *Collected Essays* (New York: Library of America, 1998), 649–50.

13. Jacqueline Trescott, "The New Coretta Scott King: Emerging from the Legacy," *Washington Post*, January 15, 1978.

14. "The World of Coretta King: A Word with Trina Grillo," *New Lady*, January 1966.

15. Barbara Reynolds, "Coretta Scott King, Martin Luther King's Other Half," *Washington Post*, October 21, 2011, https://www.washingtonpost.com/blogs/therootdc/post/coretta-scott-king-martin-luther-kings-other-half/2011/10/20/gIQA2t853L_blog.html.

16. As quoted in Hoose, *Claudette Colvin*, 80.

17. Derrick Jackson, "The King Who Led on World Peace," *Boston Globe*, February 1, 2006.

18. Barbara Reynolds, "The Real Coretta Scott King," *Washington Post*, February 4, 2006.

19. Coretta Scott King, *My Life with Martin Luther King Jr.* (New York: Henry Holt, 1993), 272–73.

20. Ibid., 4.

21. Grillo, *New Lady*, 37.

22. Taylor Branch, *At Canaan's Edge: America in the King Years, 1965–68* (New York: Simon & Schuster, 2006).

23. Jackson, *From Civil Rights to Human Rights*, 313.

24. Stewart Burns, *To the Mountaintop: Martin Luther King Jr.'s Sacred Mission to Save America, 1955–1968* (New York: Harper, 2003), 321.

25. Honey, *Going Down Jericho Road*, 454.

26. Quoted in Vicki Crawford, "Coretta Scott King and the Struggle for Civil and Human Rights: An Enduring Legacy," *Journal of African American History* 92, no. 1 (Winter 2007): 113.

27. Honey, *Going Down Jericho Road*, 453–54.

28. Ibid., 454.

29. Martha Burk, "Black Women Make History Too: An Interview on Coretta Scott King," *Huffington Post*, February 12, 2012.

30. Coretta Scott King, "How Many Men Must Die?," *Life*, April 19, 1968.

31. Coretta Scott King, "10 Commandments on Vietnam," April 27, 1968, available at http://www.americanrhetoric.com/speeches/corettascottkingvietnamcommandments.htm.

32. Ibid.

33. Freeman, *The Mule Train*, 23.

34. Ibid., 109.

35. Barbara Reynolds, "I Am Acting in the Name of Martin Luther King," *Chicago Tribune*, January 11, 1976.

36. Jackson, *From Civil Rights to Human Rights*, 358.

37. Ibid., 358.

38. Coretta Scott King, *My Life, My Love, My Legacy* (New York: Henry Holt., 2017), 189.

39. Reynolds, "I Am Acting in the Name of Martin Luther King."

40. David Stein, "'This Nation Has Never Honestly Dealt with the Question of a Peacetime Economy': Coretta Scott King and the Struggle for a Nonviolent Economy in the 1970s," *Souls*, 18, no. 1 (2016).

41. Charlayne Hunter, "Panel of 100 Asks Full Employment," *New York Times*, June 15, 1974.

42. Stein, "'This Nation Has Not Honestly Dealt with the Question of a Peacetime Economy'"; David Stein, "Why Coretta Scott King Fought for a Job Guarantee," *Boston Review*, May 17, 2017.

43. Coretta Scott King spoke out against war on January 16, 2003, declaring: "True homeland security should be about protection of liberties." A partial transcript can be found at www.blink.org.uk/pdescription.asp?key=1549&grp=27.

44. Mubarik Dahir, "Mrs. King's Legacy of Love," *AlterNet*, February 2, 2006. In 1998, she stated, "Homophobia is like racism and anti-Semitism and other forms of bigotry," *Chicago Defender*, April 1, 1998. In 2003, King spoke at the Creating Change Conference, and, in 2004, linked the struggle for gay marriage to the civil rights struggle. "Coretta Scott King Gives Support to Gay Marriage," *USA Today*, March 24, 2004.

45. Dyana Berger, "Coretta Scott King Dies at 78," *Washington Blade*, February 3, 2006.

46. Ibid.; "Anti-Gay Church to Picket King's Funeral," *Washington Blade*, February 3, 2006.

47. "The World of Coretta King," 34. Scott King sent Rosa Parks a copy of the article with an inscription reading: "To Mrs. Rosa Parks with love, respect and deep admiration Coretta Scott King."

48. Jennifer Scanlon, *Until There Is Justice: The Life of Anna Arnold Hedgeman* (New York: Oxford University Press, 2016), 157–58.

49. Ibid., 158–62.

50. Ibid., 161–62.

51. Dorothy Height, "We Wanted the Voice of a Woman to Be Heard," in *Sisters in the Struggle: African American Women in the Civil Rights–Black Power Movement*, ed. Bettye Collier-Thomas and V.P. Franklin (New York: New York University Press, 2001), 86.

52. Lynne Olson, *Freedom's Daughters: The Unsung Heroines of the Civil Rights Movement from 1830 to 1970* (New York: Simon and Schuster, 2001), 288.

53. Pauli Murray, *Song in a Weary Throat: An American Pilgrimage* (New York: Harper and Row, 1987), 353.

54. Brittney Cooper, "Black, Queer, Feminist, Erased from History: Meet the Most Important Legal Scholar You've Likely Never Heard Of," *Salon*, February 18, 2015.

55. Pauli Murray, *Song in a Weary Throat*, 109.

56. William Powell Jones, *The March on Washington: Jobs, Freedom, and the Forgotten History of Civil Rights* (New York: W. W. Norton, 2013), 175.

57. Ibid., 176.

58. Despite pleas from women journalists to join the protest, Randolph and King addressed the gender-segregated National Press Club, which didn't admit women as members until 1971. Everette Dennis and Robert W. Snyder, eds., *Covering Congress* (New York: Transaction Press, 1998), 137.

59. Bayard Rustin Papers, Harvard University.

60. Jones, *March on Washington*, 175.

61. King, *My Life, My Love, My Legacy*, 114–15.

62. King, *My Life with Martin*, 237.

63. Peter Levy, "Gloria Richardson and the Civil Rights Movement in Cambridge, Maryland," in Theoharis and Woodard, *Groundwork*, 107.

64. Ibid., 108.

64. Nash was listening to the event on the radio and was surprised to hear her name called. Younge, *The Speech*, 86.

66. King, *My Life, My Love, My Legacy*, 115.

67. Charles Euchner, *Nobody Turn Me Around: A People's History of the 1963 March on Washington* (Boston: Beacon Press, 2010), 158.

68. Decades later, Julian Bond reported coming into a hotel suite where Rosa Parks and Daisy Bates were ordering room service and "talking about people they knew in the NAACP and how awful these men were. . . . A women's view, so inside but not really inside. Talking about the guys (John Morsell, Wilkins's right-hand man) and how mean they were. . . . I thought Daisy Bates and Rosa Parks had very different personalities, and it was interesting that they agreed on them." Julian Bond, author interview, November 15, 2010.

69. Davis Houck and David Dixon, *Women and the Civil Rights Movement, 1954–1965* (Jackson: University of Mississippi Press, 2009), x.

70. "Civil Rights Pioneer Gloria Richardson, 91, on How Women Were Silenced at the March on Washington," *Democracy Now*, August 27, 2013.

71. Jennifer Scanlon, "Where Were the Women in the March on Washington," *New Republic*, March 16, 2016.

72. "Civil Rights Pioneer Gloria Richardson," *Democracy Now*.

73. Gloria Richardson, "The Energy of the People Passing Through Me," in *Hands on the Freedom Plow*, 288.

74. Anna Arnold Hedgeman, *The Trumpet Sounds: A Memoir of Negro Leadership* (New York: Holt, Rinehart and Winston, 1964), 189.

75. Krissah Thompson, "Women—Nearly Left Off March on Washington Program—Speaking Up Now," *Washington Post*, August 22, 2013.

76. *Democracy Now* was one of the only news outlets to provide a fuller story of women at the MOW. Gloria Richardson, *Democracy Now*, August 27, 2013.

CHAPTER EIGHT: EXTREMISTS, TROUBLEMAKERS, AND NATIONAL SECURITY THREATS

1. Gary Younge, "Everybody Loves Mandela," *Nation*, June 19, 2013.

2. Box 18, Folders 9 and 10, Rosa Parks Collection, Library of Congress.

3. Box 18, Folder 10, RPC.

4. Box 18, Folder 9, RPC.

5. Box 18, Folder 10, RPC.

6. Box 18, Folder 9, RPC.

7. Box 18, Folder 10, and Box 19, Folder 2, RPC.

8. Box 18, Folder 11; Box 18, Folder 10, RPC.

9. Selby and Selby, *Odyssey*, 66.

10. Box 18, Folder 9, RPC

11. Box 28, Folder 1, RPC.

12. See Simmons, "From Little Memphis Girl to Mississippi Amazon"; Septima Clark with Cynthia Stokes Brown, *Ready from Within: Septima Clark and the Civil Rights Movement* (Navarro, CA: Wild Trees Press, 1986); Charron, *Freedom's Teacher*; and Endesha Ida Mae Holland, *From the Mississippi Delta: A Memoir* (New York: Simon & Schuster, 1998).

13. Septima Clark, *Ready from Within*, 36–37.

14. Ibid., 37.

15. Ibid., 39.

16. Simmons, "From Little Memphis Girl," in *Hands on the Freedom Plow*, 14–19.

17. Holland, *From the Mississippi Delta*.

18. Sarah van Gelder, "Rev. Sekou on Today's Civil Rights Leaders," *Yes!*, July 22, 2015.

19. Baldwin and Burrow, *The Domestication of Martin Luther King*, 2–10.

20. Data from the Roper Center for Public Research, quoted in Elahe Izadi, "Black Lives Matter and America's Long History of Resisting Civil Rights Protest," *Washington Post*, April 19, 2016.

21. Fred Powledge, "Polls Show Whites in City Resent Civil Rights Protest," *New York Times*, September 21, 1964. This poll took place after a growing civil rights movement in the city, the February 1964 school boycott, and the white counterprotest by Parents and Taxpayers.

22. Izadi, "Black Lives Matter and America's Long History of Resisting Civil Rights Protest."

23. Appleton, "Martin Luther King in Life . . . and Memory."

24. Tom Greenwood, "Grosse Pointe Recalls King's Emotional Visit in 1968," *Detroit News*, March 14, 1968.

25. King, "The Other America."

26. Jimmy Carter, "Remarks by Former US President Jimmy Carter at Coretta Scott King Funeral," February 7, 2006, https://www.cartercenter.org/news/documents/doc2295.html. In these remarks, he implicitly drew parallels to post-9/11 eavesdropping.

27. Younge, *The Speech*.

28. Speltz, *North of Dixie*, 117.

29. Kenneth O'Reilly, *Racial Matters: The FBI's Secret File on Black America, 1960–1972* (New York: Free Press, 1991), 130.

30. Ransby, *Ella Baker*, 403

31. Dittmer, *Local People*, 291.

32. As cited in ibid., 292.

33. Ibid., 292–93.

34. Ibid., 293.

35. O'Reilly, *Racial Matters*, 280.

36. FBI, Special Agent in Charge, Mobile, AL, "Teletype to Director, FBI: Racial Situation, Montgomery, Alabama," September 8, 1956.

37. See the powerful documentary *Home of the Brave*.

38. King, *My Life, My Love, My Legacy*, 159.

39. "FBI Spied on Coretta Scott King, Files Showed," *Los Angeles Times*, August 31, 2007.

40. Ibid.

41. Karl Evanzz, *The Messenger: The Rise and Fall of Elijah Muhammad* (New York: Pantheon, 1999).

42. Marable, *Malcolm X*, 95, 277–78.

43. Zaheer Ali, "What Really Happened to Malcolm X," CNN, February 17, 2015.

44. Ward Churchill and Jim Vander Wall, *The COINTELPRO Papers: Documents from the FBI's Secret Wars Against Dissent in the United States* (Boston: South End Press, 2002).

45. Betty Medsger, *The Burglary: The Discovery of J. Edgar Hoover's Secret FBI* (New York: Alfred A. Knopf, 2014), 26.

46. Ibid., 228.

47. Ibid., 231.

48. Ibid., 231.

49. Ibid., 173.

50. Betty Medsger, "In 1971 Muhammad Ali Helped Undermine the FBI's Illegal Spying on Americans," *The Intercept*, June 6, 2016.

51. Victor Mather, "FBI Monitored Muhammad Ali Connections to the Nation of Islam," *New York Times*, December 15, 2016.

52. Mike Marqusee, *Redemption Song: Muhammad Ali and the Spirit of the Sixties* (New York: Verso, 1999).

53. Su'ad Abdul Khabeer, response to Amna Akbar and Jeanne Theoharis, "Islam on Trial," *Boston Review*, February 27, 2017.

54. Akbar and Theoharis, "Islam on Trial"; Jeanne Theoharis, "My Student, the Terrorist," *Chronicle Review* (April 3, 2011); Human Rights Watch, *Illusion of Justice*, report, July 21, 2014.

55. Trevor Aaronson, "The Informants," *Mother Jones*, September/October 2011; Aviva Stahl, "NYPD Undercover Converted to Islam to Spy on Muslim Students," *Gothamist*, October 29, 2015.

56. George Joseph, "NYPD Officers Accessed Black Lives Matters Activists' Texts, Documents Show," *Guardian*, April 4, 2017; Alleen Brown, Will Parrish, and Alice Speri, "Leaked Documents Reveal Security Firms Counterterrorism Tactics at Standing Rock to 'Defeat Pipeline Insurgencies,'" *The Intercept*, May 27, 2017; Color of Change and CCR v. Department of Homeland Security and Federal Bureau of Investigation, federal lawsuit filed October 20, 2016: Jana Winter and Sharon Weinberger, "The FBI's New U.S. Terrorist Threat: 'Black Identity Extremists,'" *Foreign Policy* (October 6, 2017).

57. Del Quentin Wilber, "Aspiring Agents Learn from Mistakes of FBI's Shameful Investigation of Martin Luther King, Jr.," *Los Angeles Times*, August 11, 2016.

CHAPTER NINE: LEARNING TO PLAY ON LOCKED PIANOS

1. Vincent Harding, "King for the 21st Century Calls Us to Walk with Jesus," speech, Goshen College, January 21, 2005.

2. Leventhal, *The Children Coming On*, 13.

3. McGuire, *At the Dark End of the Street*, 3–39.

4. Extensive correspondence found in Box II: C4, Folder 2, and Box II: C390, Folder 4, NAACP Papers, Library of Congress.

5. Box 4, Folder 13, RPC.

6. Rosa Parks with Jim Haskins, *My Story* (New York: Puffin Books, 1992), 102.

7. Ibid., 99.

8. Rosa Parks, interview by Steven Millner, in *The Walking City: The Montgomery Bus Boycott, 1955–1956*, ed. David Garrow (New York: Carlson, 1989), 556–57.

9. Box 4, Folder 1, Preston and Bonita Valien Papers, Amistad Research Center, Tulane University. The Preston and Bonita Valien Papers at Tulane's Amistad Research Center provide a remarkable, real-time account of the Montgomery bus boycott. Preston Valien, a professor at Fisk University, sent an interracial team of graduate researchers to Montgomery a month into the boycott, and they were on hand to record the unfolding movement and white reaction to it.

10. Hoose, *Twice Toward Justice*, 53.

11. Ibid., 129–30.

12. Marisa Chappell, Jenny Hutchinson, and Brian Ward, "'Dress modestly as if you were going to church': Respectability, Class and Gender in the Montgomery Bus Boycott and Early Civil Rights Movement," in *Gender in the Civil Rights Movement*, ed. Peter J. Ling and Sharon Monteith (New York: Routledge, 1999); Gary Younge, "She Would Not Be Moved," *Guardian*, December 15, 2000.

13. "Local NAACP Rolls Up Big Membership," *Los Angeles Sentinel*, April 12, 1956.

14. Clark, *Ready from Within*, 33–34.

15. "Keep On Fighting Says Mrs. Parks," *Baltimore Afro-American*, May 24, 1958.

16. Box 18, Folder 10, RPC.

17. Emily Rovetch, ed., *Like It Is: Arthur E. Thomas Interviews Leaders on Black America* (New York: E. P. Dutton, 1981), 50.

18. Parks, *My Story*, 129.

19. Ibid., 134.

20. Patrick L. Cooney, "Martin Luther King and Vernon Johns," in Cooney, *The Life and Times of the Prophet Vernon Johns*, Vernon Johns Society website, http://www.vernonjohns.org.

21. Jo Ann Robinson, interview by Steven Millner, in Garrow, *The Walking City*, 570.

22. Jo Ann Robinson, *The Montgomery Bus Boycott and the Women Who Started It: The Memoir of Jo Ann Robinson* (Knoxville: University of Tennessee Press, 1987), 45.

23. Rosa Parks, interview by Millner, in Garrow, *The Walking City*, 563.

24. See Boxes 2–4, Valien Papers.

25. Donnie Williams with Wayne Greenshaw, *The Thunder of Angels: The Montgomery Bus Boycott and the People Who Broke the Back of Jim Crow* (Chicago: Lawrence Hill, 2006), 60.

26. Vernon Jarrett, "The Forgotten Heroes of the Montgomery Bus Boycott" series, *Chicago Tribune*, December 1975.

27. Martin Luther King Jr., *Stride Toward Freedom* (1959; Boston: Beacon Press, 2010), 22–23.

28. Davis Houck and David Dixon, *Women and the Civil Rights Movement, 1954–1965* (Jackson: University of Mississippi Press, 2009), 83.

29. King, *My Life with Martin*, 115.

30. L. C. Fortenberry, "The Sentinel Queries Rosa Parks," *Los Angeles Sentinel*, August 17, 1958; Rosa Parks, interview by Academy of Achievement, June 2, 1995.

31. Box 18, Folder 9, RPC.

32. Jarrett, "Forgotten Heroes."

33. B. J. Simms, interview by Millner, in Garrow, *The Walking City*, 584.

34. Box 15, Folder 5, RPC.

35. Robinson, *Montgomery Bus Boycott*, 37.

36. Mary Stanton, *Journey Toward Justice: Juliette Hampton Morgan and the Montgomery Bus Boycott* (Athens: University of Georgia Press, 2006); interview with Juliette Morgan, Box 3, Folder 15, Valien Papers.

37. Box 4, Folder 3, Valien Papers.

38. Simms, interview by Millner, in Garrow, *The Walking City,*, 580.

39. Box 4, Folder 2, Valien Papers.

40. "The 2-Edged Sword," editorial, *Montgomery Advertiser*, December 13, 1955; Box 3, Folder 15, Valien Papers.

41. Box 3, Folder 14, Valien Papers.

42. Sarah Coleman, interview, Box 4, Folder 3, Valien Papers.

43. Carolyn Light, *Stand Your Ground: America's Love Affair with Lethal Self-Defense* (Boston: Beacon Press, 2017), 114.

44. "Reminiscences," Black Women's Oral History Project, Schlesinger Library, Radcliffe College, Cambridge, MA, 255; Parks interview, Rosa Parks File, Box 2 File 7, George Metcalf Papers, Schomburg Center for Research on Black Culture of the New York Public Library, New York, NY.

45. Box 18, Folder 9, RPC.

46. Box 24, Folders 16 and 17, RPC.

47. Ransby, *Ella Baker*, 165–67; "16,000 Rally in New York," *Pittsburgh Courier*, June 2, 1956.

48. Clark, *Ready from Within*, 16–17.

49. Rosa Parks, Myles Horton, and E. D. Nixon, radio interview by Studs Terkel, Box 14, Folder 4, Myles Horton Papers, State Historical Society of Wisconsin.

50. Aldon Morris, *The Origins of the Civil Rights Movement: Black Communities Organizing for Change* (New York: Free Press, 1986), 149.

49. Clark, *Ready from Within*, 34.

50. Box 22, Folder 22, Highlander Papers.

51. Leventhal, *The Children Coming On*, 45–46.

52. Parks, Horton, and Nixon, Terkel interview, June 8, 1973, Myles Horton Papers.

53. As quoted in J. Mills Thornton, *Dividing Lines: Municipal Politics and the Struggle for Civil Rights in Montgomery, Birmingham, and Selma* (Tuscaloosa: University of Alabama Press, 2002), 57.

54. Box 4, Folder 3, Valien Papers.

55. Box 4, Folder 1, Valien Papers.

56. Box 18, Folder 10, RPC.

57. King, *Stride Toward Freedom*, 31.

58. Anne Braden to Virginia Durr, April 19, 1958, Box 2, Folder 3, Virginia Durr Papers, Schlesinger Library, Radcliffe Institute, Harvard University.

59. Branch, *Parting the Waters*, 148–49.

60. "Alabama Negroes Rally in Church," article, Box VI, C53, Folder 10, NAACP Papers, Library of Congress.

61. "'Crime Wave' in Alabama," editorial, *New York Times*, February 24, 1956.

AFTERWORD

1. Baldwin, "A Talk to Teachers."

2. Parks, *My Story*, 99.

3. Parks, Civil Rights Documentation Project, 16–17.

Index